stimulus → *respond*

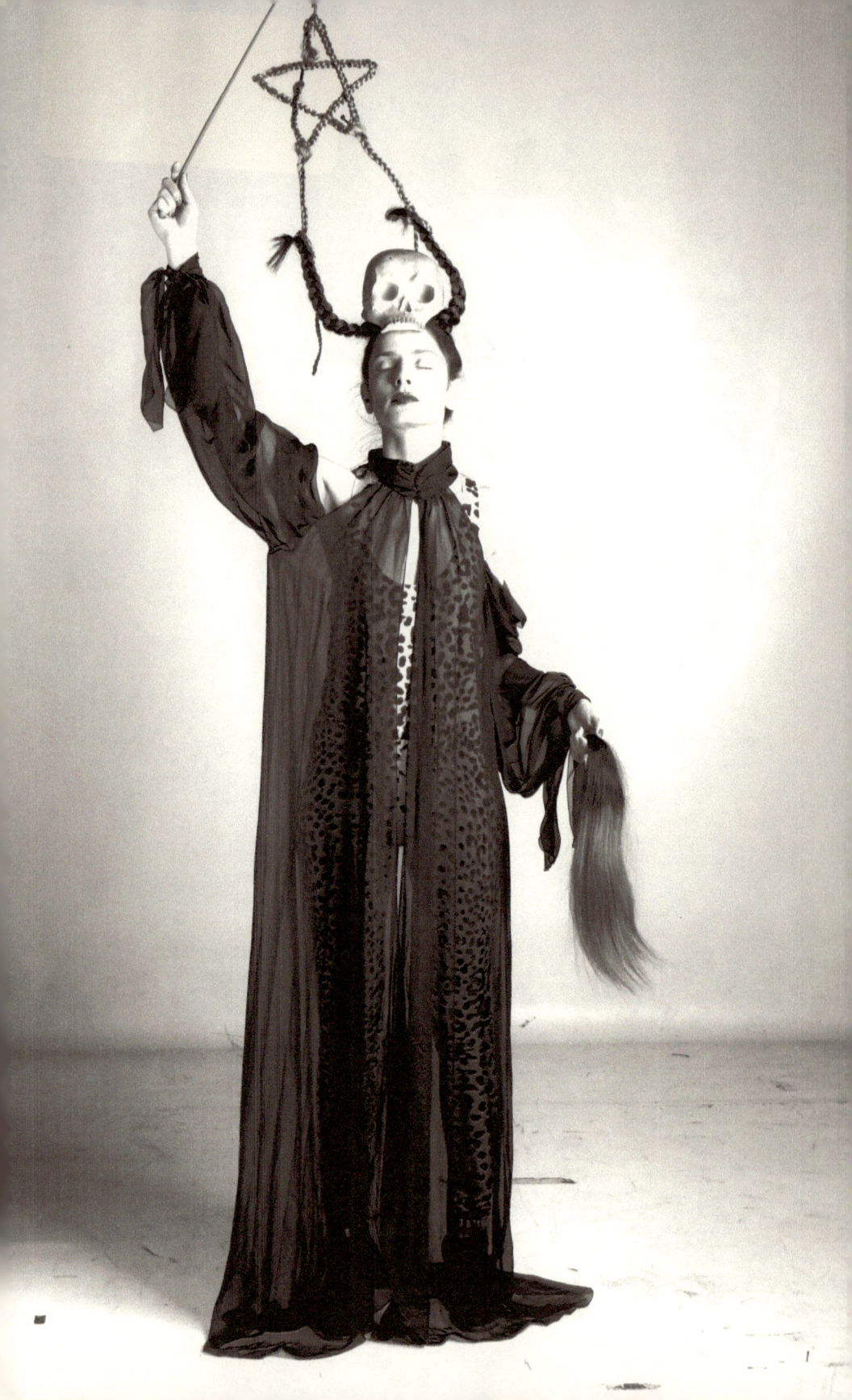

HAND PICKED

stimulus → *respond*

EDITED BY
JACK BOULTON

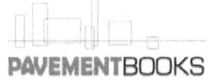

PAVEMENTBOOKS

Pavement Books
London, UK
www.pavementbooks.com

Hand Picked Stimulus Respond

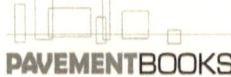
PAVEMENTBOOKS

CONTENTS

image *Stelios Kallinikou*   ii
editors 2004-2014   ix
foreword *Sharmaine Lovegrove*   xi
acknowledgements   xv

Introduction   1
Jack Boulton
Illustration by *Simon Foxall*

Post-Structure   5
Edith Bergfors

On Paper   18
JD Taylor

Klaxons Silenced   25
Robert Glowacki

Untitled   33
Geraldine Monk

The Politics of Cats   37
John Hutnyk
Illustrations by *Evripidis Sabatis*

Dogue   43
Miki Barlok

This is Privilege   52
Scott Thurston

Rituals – Voices   56
Martin L. Davies

Dead Birds   61
Michael Taussig
Illustrations by *Atalya Laufer*

Space Attack   65
Johannes Gierlinger

Masterpiece – *Précis of a Work Unwritten*   74
Rob Ward

The Ministry of Defense *(A Work in Progress)*   81
Danny Hoffman

The Papers Want to Know   99
Yannis Tsitsovits

Torrence & Friends   102
Steve Gronert Ellerhoff

Untitled   107
Steve Willey

Line Breaks Iconography
     109
Phil Sawdon

RAW   115
Harris Kyprianou

Spectacular Transports   123
John Hutnyk
Illustration by *Estella Mare*

'No Asians Please' –
Same-Sex Sexuality and Ethnic
Minorities in Belgium   129
Wim Peumans

Many Ways of Leaving   141
Christina Lovin

Untitled   143
Francis Kruk

Damn Romance   145
Robert Glowacki

Seven Drawn Days   152
Phil Sawdon

Renato   161
Justino Esteves

Why I Don't Eat Beef   173
Christina Lovin

The End is Nigh   175
Alan Dunn

Fragile Youth   191
Harris Kyprianou

Vehicles   199
Yannis Tsitsovits

Images on pages 35, 121 and 201
Simon Foxall

EDITORS 2004-2014

Jack Boulton (Co-founder)
Sharmaine Lovegrove (Co-founder)
Ben Parry (Art)
Alan Dunn (Art)
Andreas Koumas (Fashion)
Rose Cooper-Thorne (Architecture)
Matthew Holroyd (Fashion)
Phil Sawdon (Literature)
Marsha Meskimmon (Literature)
Hannah Yelin (Music)
Christopher Thomas (Art)
Christos Kyriakides (Fashion)
Jeremy Allen (Music)
Jonna Dagliden (Features)
Ellen Sampson (Art)
Georgina Colby (Poetry)
Harriet Fuest (Music)
Yannis Tsitsovits (Art)
Amin Samman (Music)
William Alderwick (Music)
Tara Blake-Wilson (Literature)
Theresa Mikuriya (Photography)
Mary Byrnes (Poetry)
Melina Nicolaide (Fashion)
Mark Kanak (Poetry)
Louie Stowell (Poetry)

FOREWORD

Sharmaine Lovegrove
Co-Founder

DURING MY EARLY TWENTIES, I often thought of London as being like a city version of Gaudí's Sagrada Família. Someone had once had a grand vision and began to realise it, but it was destined to remain incomplete for generations to come. Now everyone has an opinion of it, and the city is a cacophony of styles assembled through different times.

When it started to dawn on me that the golden years of the previous generation would never be enjoyed by me and my peers, I began to wonder why we weren't rallying against the messages of consumerism and aspiration that were being pumped around us. The reality was that these things had nothing to do with the life many of us wanted to lead, or indeed the reality we inhabited at that time.

It was frustrating for me that I always fell somewhere between two camps for printed matter: an older, intellectually confident literary crowd schooled in *The London Review of Books* or *Granta*, and a younger 'lite' crowd of *Dazed and Confused* or the brilliant but now defunct *Sleazenation*. Yes, I wanted to be informed of interesting (and beautiful) developments in international fashion, but I also wanted to understand the thoughts and ideas of my generation from a global perspective.

It was 2000, and as we marvelled at the efficiency of our Hotmail accounts it was clear the internet was here to stay. Living aboard neighbouring houseboats on the Thames, between Chelsea and Vauxhall Bridges, Jack and myself would drink tea on the mooring and question the society that we were living in and how, at the age of 20, we already felt marginalised within it despite having only been allowed to vote once.

Alongside our studies in Politics and Anthropology at different University of London colleges, we read radical theorists such as Guy Debord, philosophers like Walter Benjamin and feminist thought from Luce Irigaray and beyond. We strived to better understand existentialism, utilitarianism, painting and photography. Although even writing it today sounds clichéd, we were trying to make sense of the world.

A few years later, in 2003, Jack and I were again neighbours, this time on solid ground but with only flimsy self-made walls dividing us in a warehouse in London Fields. Although we had completed our studies and were settling into our careers, Jack in research and myself in publishing, those well-thumbed books had travelled with us. The passages that we'd underlined and the notes we'd made were as compelling to us as ever before. I clearly remember the huge desire to make something compelling, thought provoking, and stylish – a magazine was always the medium we would use to communicate this.

Stimulus Respond was created. The name came from our insistence that the magazine be literally stimulating, and a powerful response to the societal position we occupied. We adopted the term urban anthropology to define our interest in urban environments, the endless flux of city spaces. Above all, the magazine was to be a study of our generation. For the articles, we hoped to attract writers that would inspire, and each call for submission was like a call to arms.

There was an urgency in what we wanted to achieve. Thinking back, our corner of east London was changing so fast, and I believe it was important for us to create something that felt real and tangible. A magazine that would reach out to writers and readers and provoke questions.

The themed issues allowed ideas to be brought together coherently. Without this framework, I am not sure we could have handled the sheer volume of ideas and the diverse range of writing we found in our inbox. I fondly recall the submissions coming in for the first issues: we had sent a call and the response came, via this burgeoning technology that I didn't really understand but Jack was almost fluent in. Writers from all over the globe submitted their stories and thoughts, they asked questions and responded to our theme in forms and contexts we had not envisaged.

The passion that stemmed from the *Stimulus* community was contagious and we now had a feeling of responsibility for carrying what we felt was an important message. We were reading, writing, editing and discussing. It was everything we'd wanted and it was coming from us rather than being imposed on us.

Looking at the magazine today, I feel a glow of achievement. When we initially devised the idea, Jack and I were young and feisty and in many ways naïve. From the rough edges, fuzzy details and zero budget of the beginning, it has evolved into a sleek and tuned body of work that still provokes and inquires. The result is a testimony to the *Stimulus* contributors and readers: people who, like us, just wanted to read something different yet utterly special.

ACKNOWLEDGEMENTS

For the push to start this volume

John Hutnyk

For encouragement along the way
*My parents, Phil Sawdon, Alan Dunn, Steven Van Wolputte,
Georgina Colby, Sophie Fuggle, Wim Peumans, Rose Cooper-Thorne*

And of course, the contributors and editors who have made *Stimulus Respond*
the magazine that it is, and will be.

Thank you.

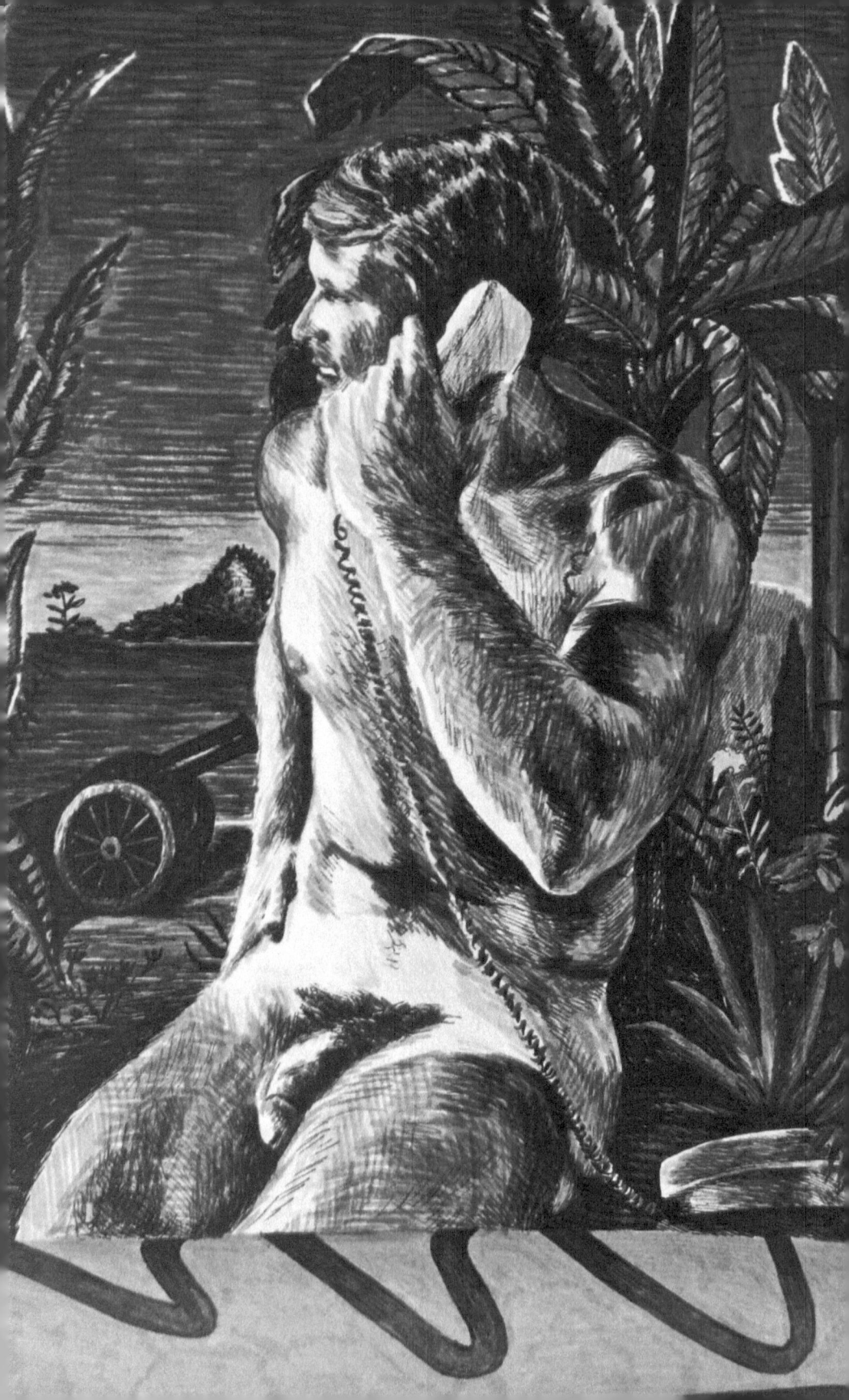

INTRODUCTION

Jack Boulton
Editor in Chief
Illustrations by *Simon Foxall*

AS I WRITE, IT IS ALMOST ten years to the day that Sharmaine and I first had the idea for *Stimulus Respond*. It has come a long way since those early times. It is perhaps poetic (or, simply, disorganisation) that many of the early issues no longer exist, lost in the digital ether as websites were lost or changed, or hidden on a CD-R in a long-forgotten box. But despite its online format, Stimulus was always a magazine more than a website, and magazines are by nature ephemeral; only as good as the last issue. It was pleasing to go back and find that so much of the content still 'works' outside of the context of its original publication, and that whilst, originally, each feature was tied to the theme of a particular issue, the pieces in this book still 'stand up', some of them ten years after they were originally composed.

The pieces presented here then, rather than being representative of how the magazine has developed over the years, are perhaps more indicative of the way the magazine is now. The volume is, fittingly, eclectic in its approach. Whilst each issue of *Stimulus* is given a theme, and there are section editors, there are no set criteria for the way that topic has to be explored; it is very much up to what contributions people send in. The sections themselves have changed over time as new people become involved. One of the benefits

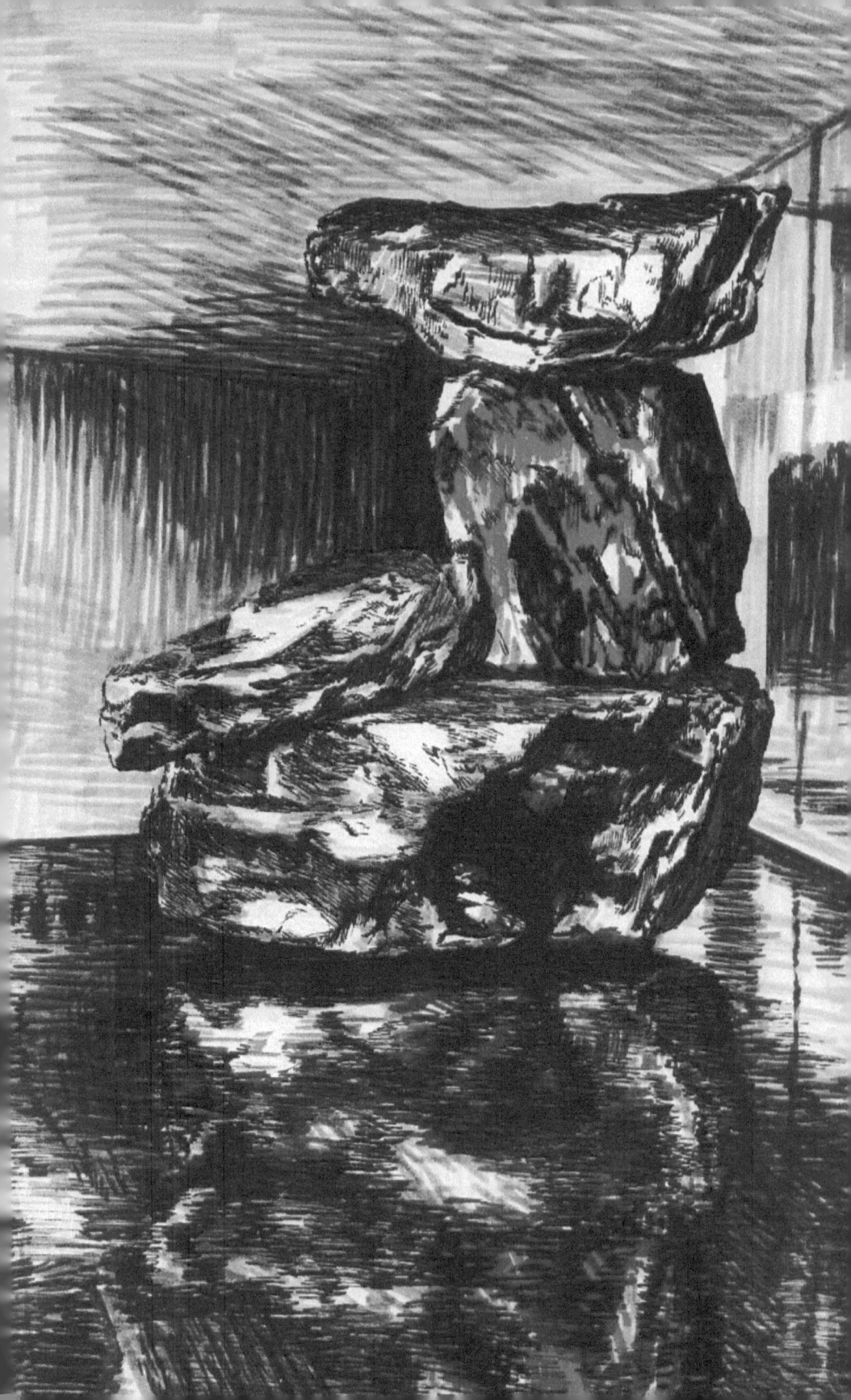

of this is that the journal never feels prescriptive – it is what it is. Some issues are short (issue four, *Work*, I remember being particularly slight), whilst others are over two hundred pages. Thankfully, most veer towards the latter – a measure, somewhat, of the contributors' and readers' involvement in, and enthusiasm for, the magazine.

What follows is a combination of many different disciplines – art, literature, fashion, architecture, to name just four – unified under a common umbrella of anthropology. Perhaps I run the risk here of having to make a statement about what anthropology is – I will eschew that quandary for now, simply saying it is the study of culture. The forms these explorations take are, however, manifold. Therefore whilst the 'classic' form of the anthropological study is, of course, the scientific paper, or the monograph, there is no reason for them to take this form other than being a generally accepted, and culturally facilitated, form of knowledge dissemination. Being anthropological, and yet also cross-disciplinary, this book is something of an experiment; from one perspective, a random volume of articles from ten years of *Stimulus Respond*, and from another, a diverse collection of genres that combine to give a reflection on many aspects of contemporary life.

The cover illustration, by David Richter, Associate Professor at the Department of Mathematics of Western Michigan University, is a representation of Mathieu group M_{24}, a hyperbolic space in which seven numbered triangles form irregular polyhedrons which repeat themselves to infinity. To each of these triangles has been assigned one of the seven related colours of Aristotle – seven basic colours analogous to seven music concords. Each polyhedron therefore represents a complete colour space – working as a metaphor for previous *Stimulus* issues. I did say we were cross-disciplinary.

Enjoy the book.

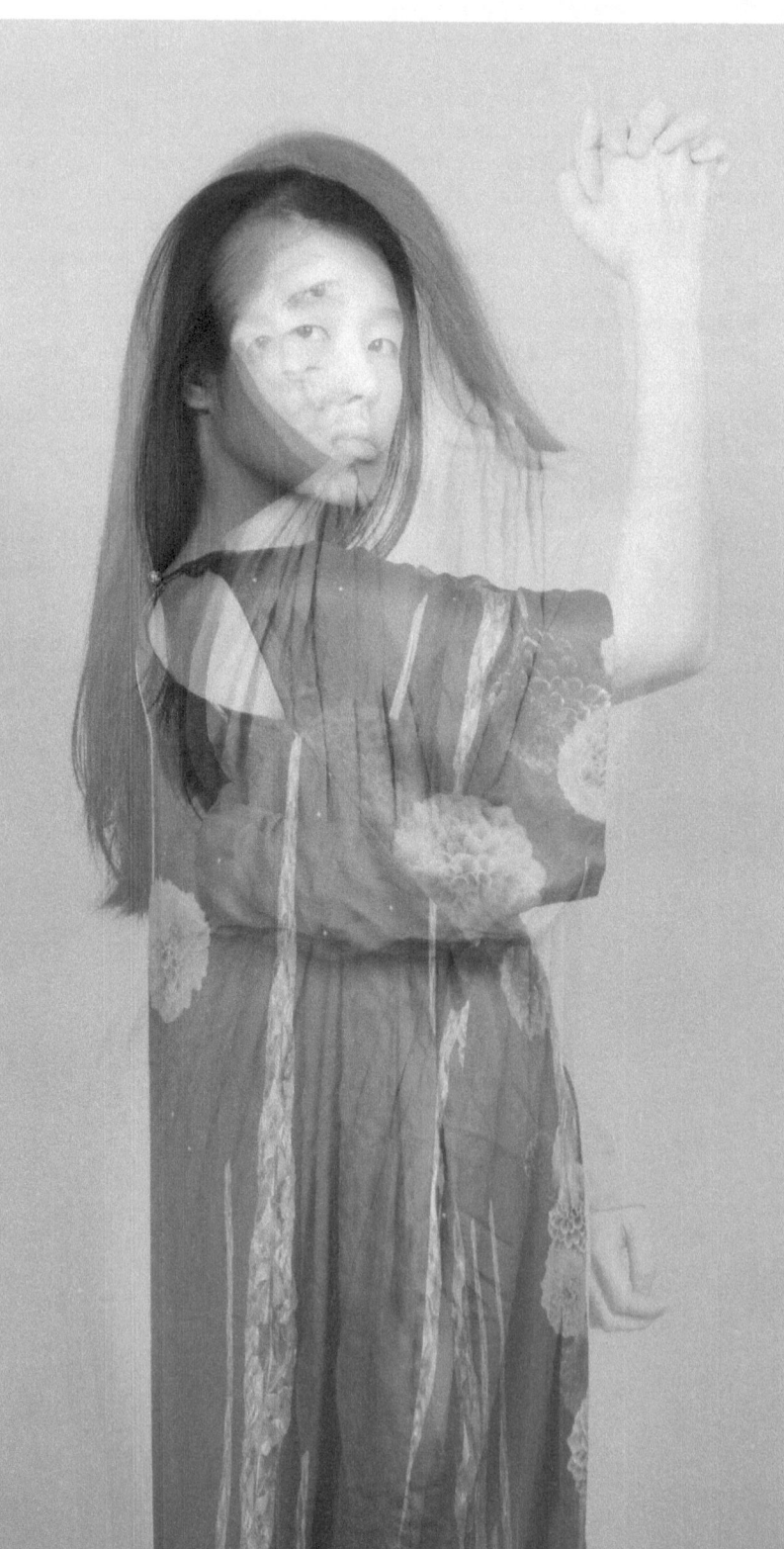

POST-STRUCTURE

Photography by *Edith Bergfors*
Fashion by *Matthew Holroyd*
Hair and Grooming by *Noriko Takayama, Yuhi Kim*
Set Design by *Emily Pugh*
Make-up by *Natsumi Narita*
Set Design Assistants *Emma DeClercq* and *Owen Raffety Gonzalez*
Models *Ally, Imogen, Ying* and *Maya*

Previous: Dress by Sabrina Dehoff
Below: Shirt by Weekday; skirt by Ikou Tschüss
Opposite: Dress Gemma Slack, earrings stylist's own

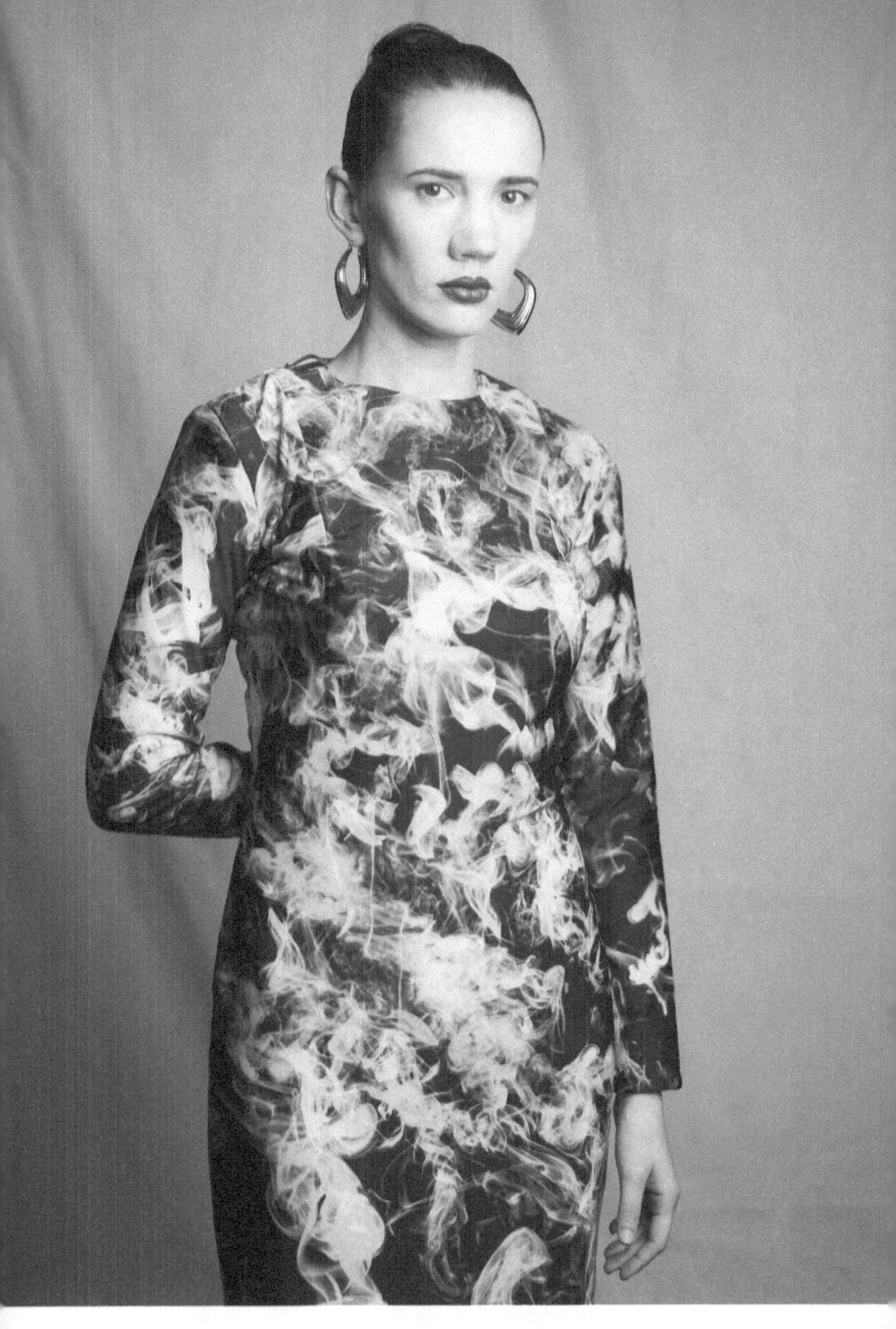

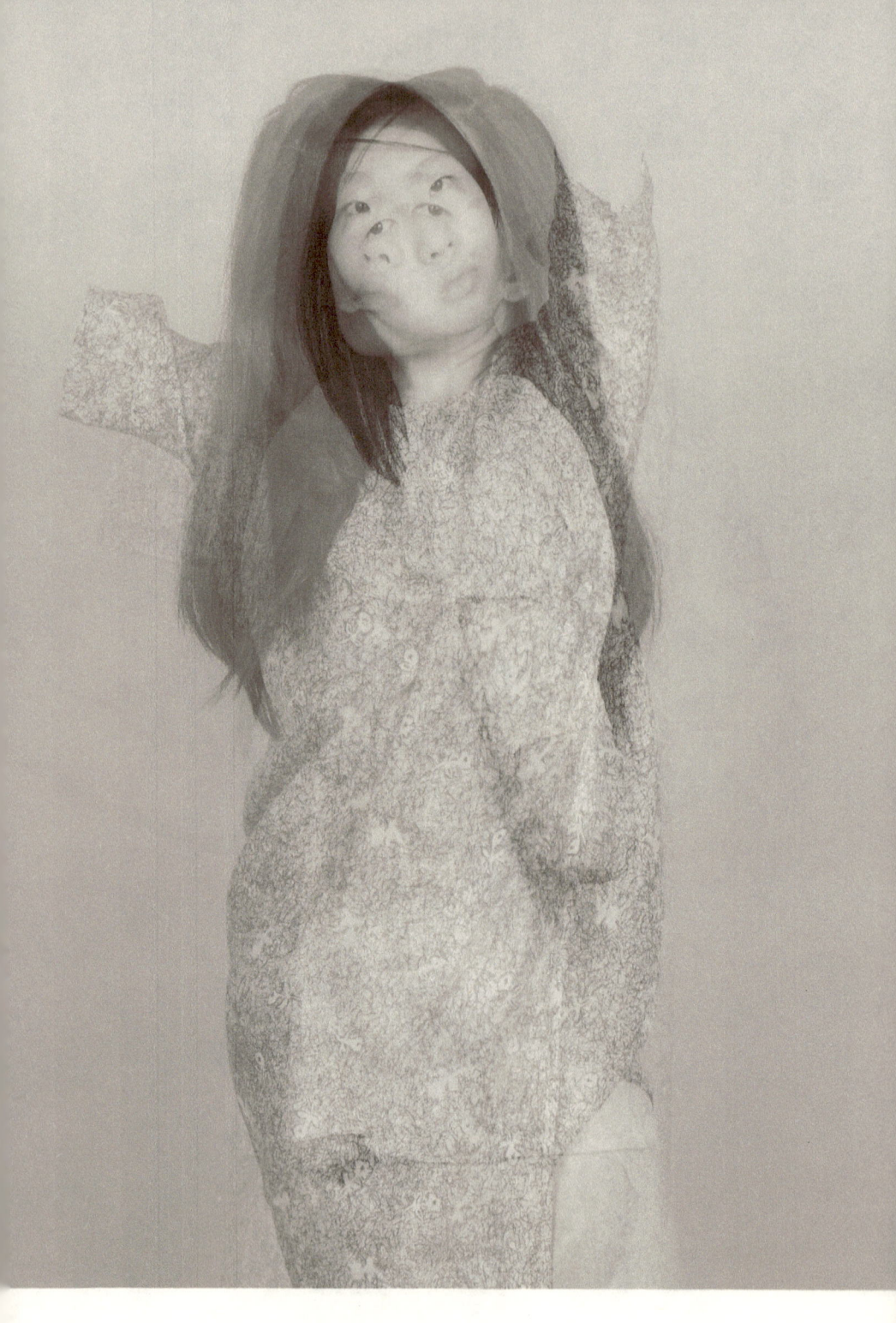

Above: Dress by Minä Perhonen
Opposite: Body Bora Aksu, skirt Paul & Joe, earrings stylist's own

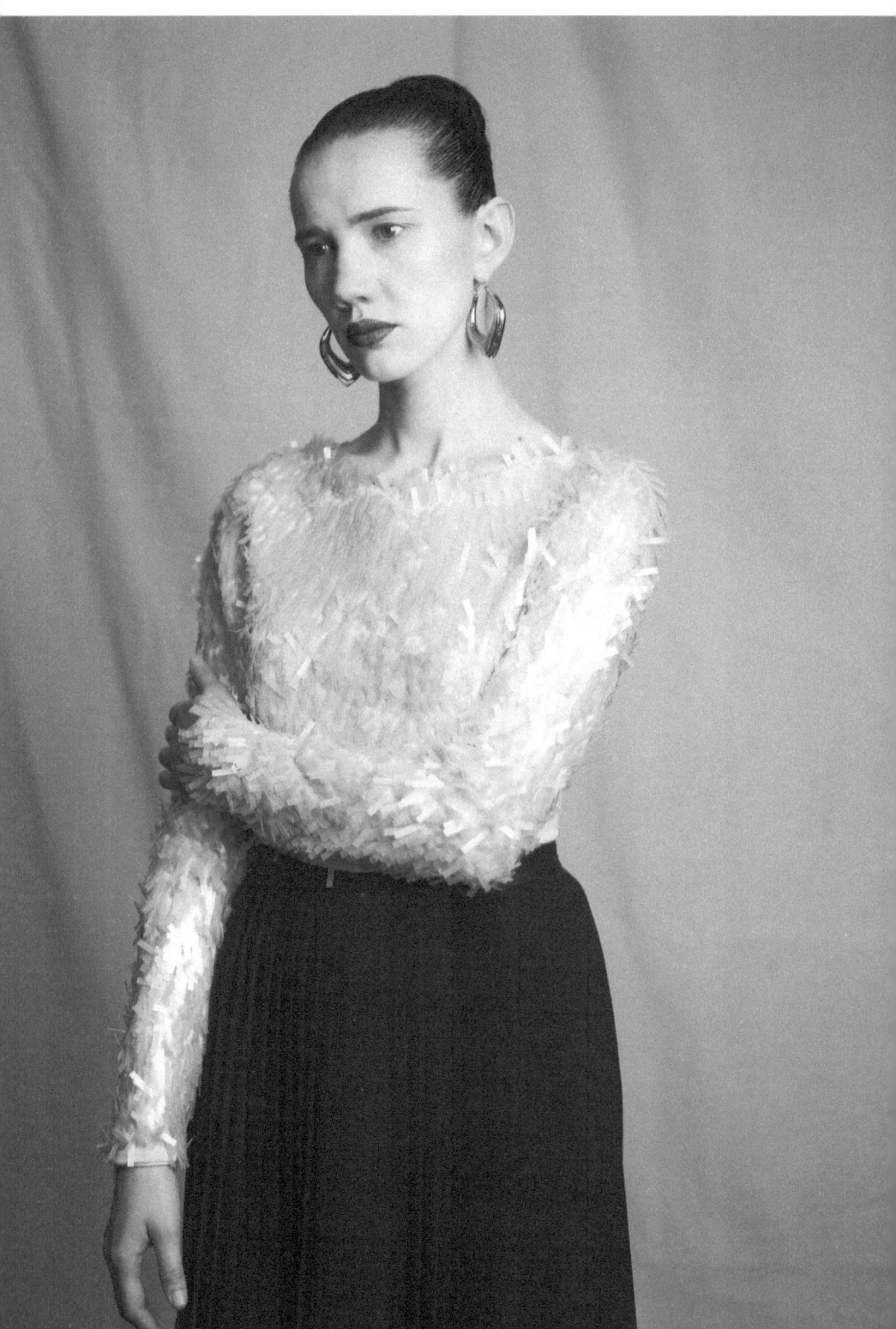

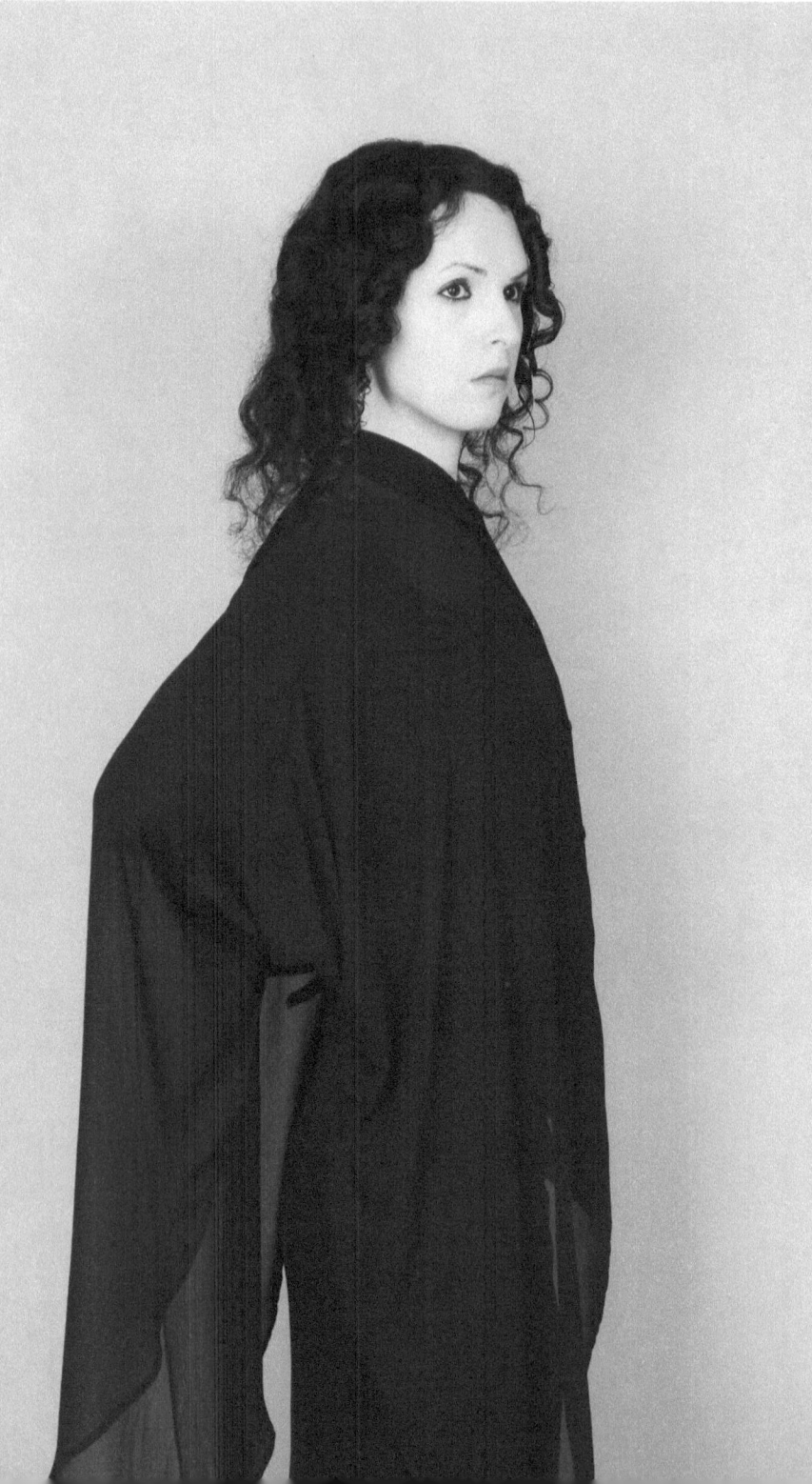

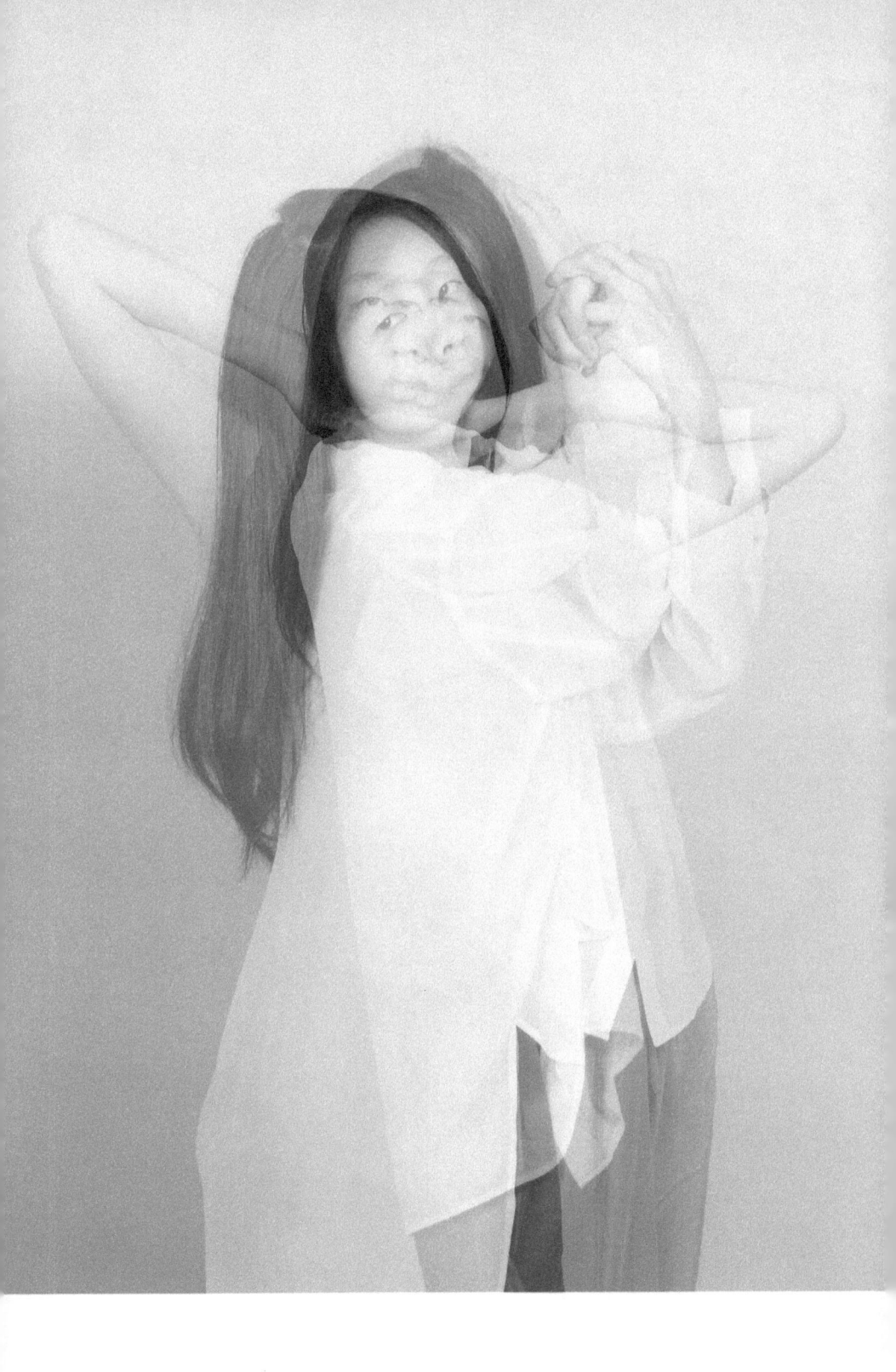

Dress by Ann Demeulemeester, earrings stylist's own

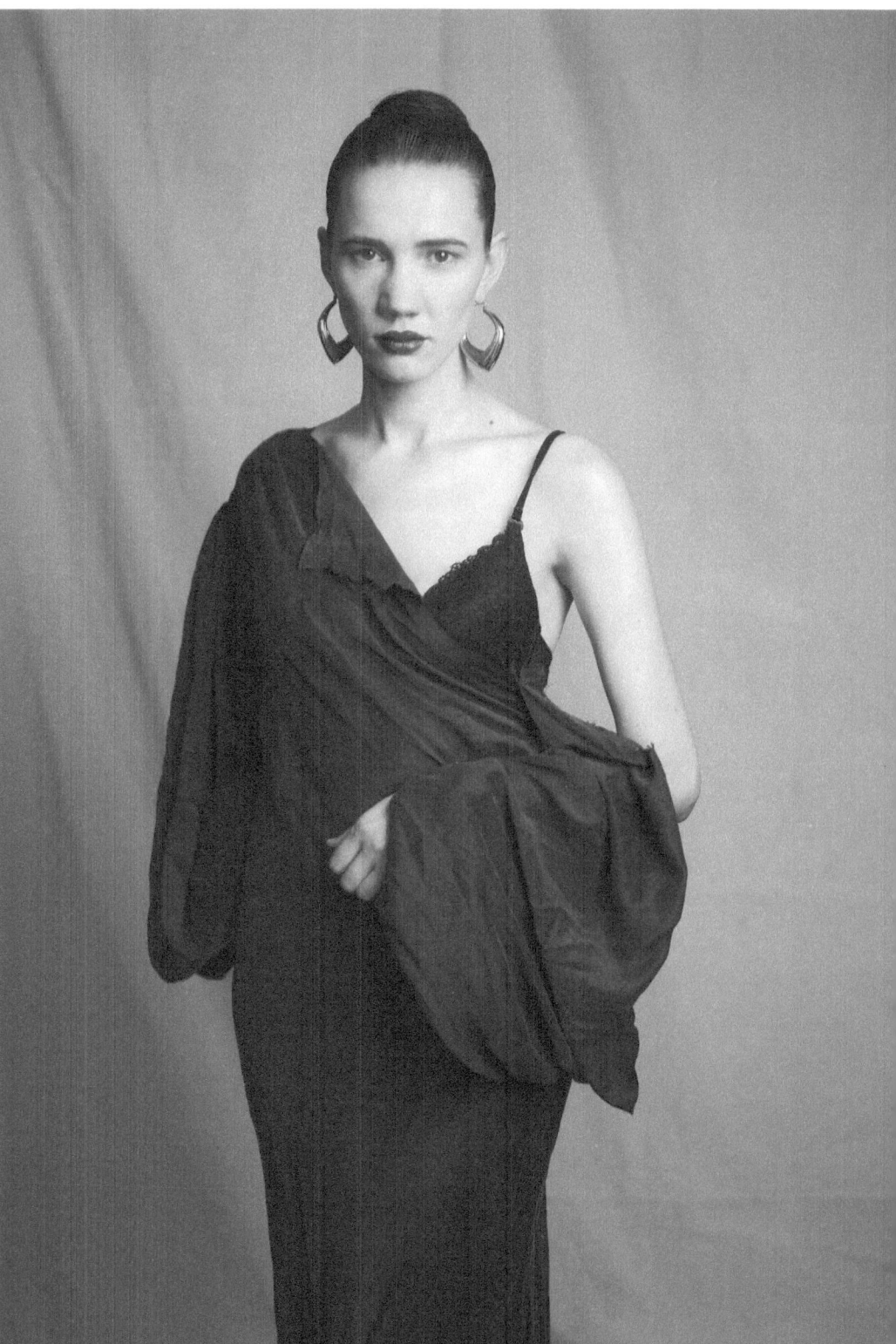

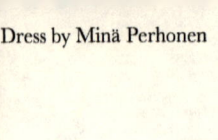Dress by Minä Perhonen

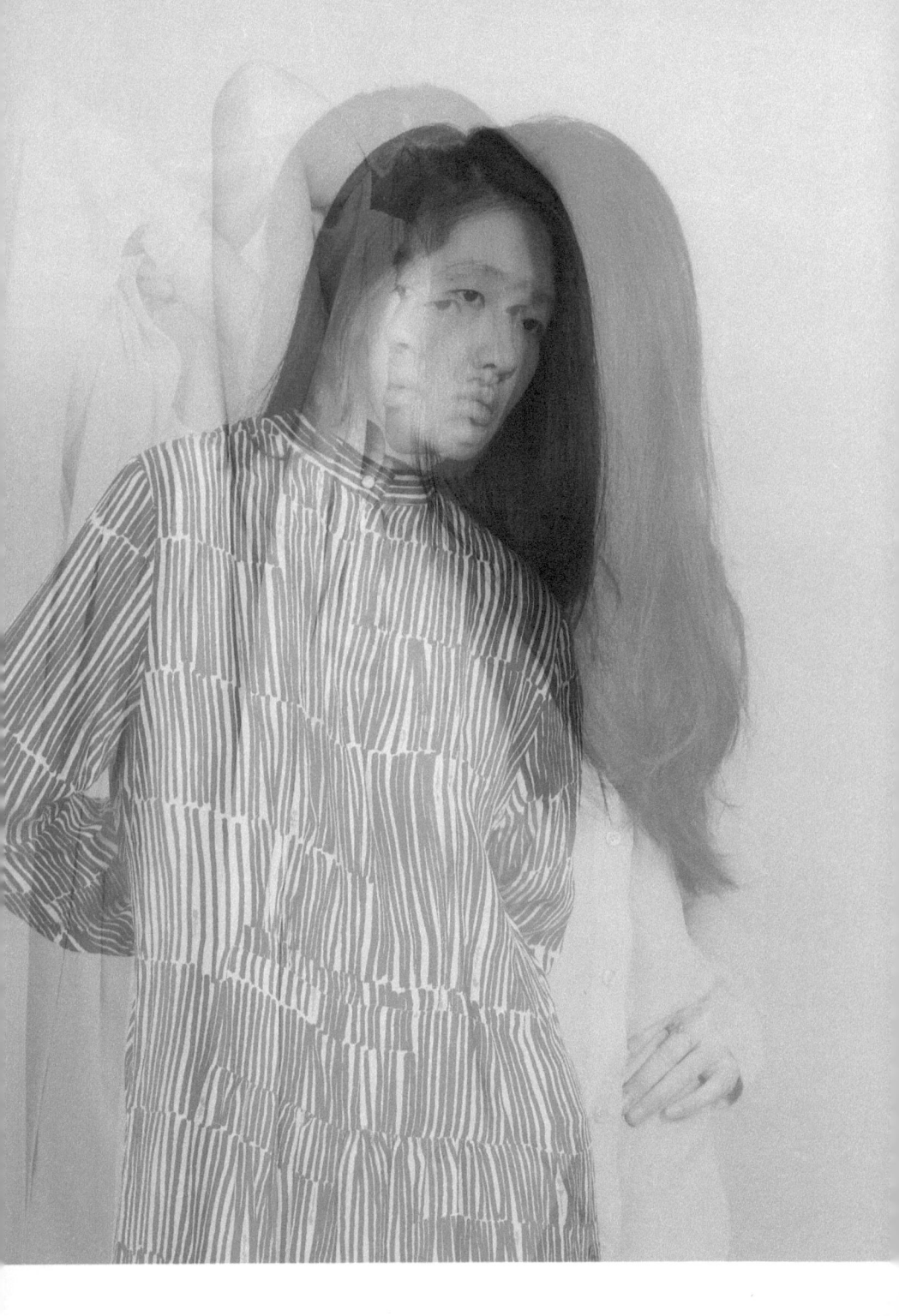

ON PAPER

JD Taylor

"THE MOON WHO SIMULTANEOUSLY SEES US BOTH": these words, dislocated from context or history, were found on just one of so many pages from books pasted on the walls and doors of the decaying suburb streets. From a distance, they made the surfaces they were pasted on look almost reflective, like liquid surfaces, so small and close together were these pages, that perhaps behind them one might enter some other world. On second thought, it may well have just been another advertising device or cynical art student's masquerade. In any case, the irony was lost on the cracked and creased-up streets of this suburb, where populations laid-off from life cooped together in mediocre housing to stare in isolation, silently, at the vast redundancy of most modern life through the borders of a smartphone screen.

The library was long ago relocated to the basement of the town hall, an archaic and derelict building which one might find on a paper map, but certainly not on any digitised device. Its use had expired, its demolition deferred due to local council budget efficiencies enforcement. Paper had no use – expensive, liable to tear, disintegrate, err in its multiplicity. Digitised information offered the security of coming from one company, it could be copied and shared across other digitised devices, it demanded less attention. One could always switch to a game or social website in between reading information, unlike a book, which always stood tyrannical, demanding devotion and faithful interest.

A Librarian had come to occupy the basement of this town hall for some years now. His name and background were not known. It was also possibly true that he could not even read the books which he attentively cared for, and compiled in increasingly complex interdisciplinary systems that mocked the block-headedness of earlier cataloguers. He feared the power of these books, which had once through mere words sent heretics to their deaths and sent others into madness or brave, ludicrous adventures across continents, morality, the heart, soul, and other nouns which the Librarian strived to understand but which no-one of the age could teach. Such nouns could, if exposed and liberated from the repressive confines of their hardback borders, intensify and enrich the imaginations and intellects of the sickly-looking residents of the nearby high-rises and the crumbling Victorian terraces. The Librarian sat for hours each day staring at words and phrases that he could pick out in the shape-shifting pages, in the hope that, like learning how to shoot or drive an armoured vehicle, or locate the enemy's position in flat, deserted hillscapes and barren farmland, through careful and close study the correct intelligence required to command the situation would arise intuitively. He had become an expert in the sacred geometries of Persian Islamic art, in the haunted and mordant scenes of Goya, Caravaggio, Breughel and others, but his real interest was in harnessing the power of the unknown word for some good. At night, interrupted occasionally by the occasional fox or drunken reveller, he would temporarily desert the library to paste these pages onto disused shop shutters, broken payphone booths, parked cars, bollards and walls. The effect was manic, inspired, and utterly disregarded by the local residents.

Back in the night, beneath the moon, the Entrepreneur marvelled at what "the sadness of a God", from a ripped page pasted on the back of a supermarket delivery van, might possibly signify. A sadness of unknowable depths, or melancholia in contemplating the squandered gifts of those creatures once lovingly manufactured. It was possible that the basis of social well-being and harmony had always been charity, justice, reason, tolerance, cooperation and humility – ideals already suggested in the religious prophets. Envisioning the health of such societies, these prophets used the only persuasive means at their disposal to persuade reluctant and ignorant masses to follow their rule, using their imaginations to conjure wrathful and benevolent Gods to provoke fear and superstition. Each era's prophets were forced to recourse to catastrophic visions of differing sorts to call for such simple, easily forgotten ideals.

The Entrepreneur had no interest in ideals, unless they could be translated into another currency. This perhaps was the one ideal of his digitised era. He had seen the pages pasted all 'round the suburban outer rings of the city, with incomprehensible words and diagrams on paper, of all things, that useless and environmentally-unsustainable material still used, sometimes, to mop up wounds in hospitals. Words he could understand, usually no more than three hundred or so alongside flashing images and interactive links. But pages and pages of just words were much harder to concentrate on. Poverty, vanity and vainglory will often co-conspire in a man's mind and present absurd, outlandish conceptions, like that within these pages might be found some forgotten technology or concept that had not been translated into digitisation, which might now curry great favour in the economy.

It was by chance while sleeping in his car that the Entrepreneur was interrupted by the Librarian pasting some large pages from a history book, countless small horses and flamboyant soldiers' uniforms, on the side of his car. It had been easy from thereon to persuade the Librarian to allow the Entrepreneur to visit the damp and dusty museum in the derelict old school where he lived and worked. The nameless Entrepreneur gasped at the sheer density of textbooks, many of which could not have previously belonged to the small rooms but must've been brought to the safekeeping of the librarian. Mould suffused the air, and alongside the scarcity of light and use of candles, gave an atmosphere that one was not entering down a small flight of stairs but into a grotto deep beneath the earth. After a couple of visits, where both sat beneath the claustrophobic artillery of two strangers' shared silence, the Entrepreneur's comings and goings were no longer pre-arranged but became regular, until he too found it most convenient to also sleep in the library, in order to carry out his research into these magical books by day.

The Librarian often fell into a kind of fogged silence, and was the kind of man who always felt sorry for something he hadn't done. It felt like the entire world might be blaming him for some truly awful crime which he had no memory of committing, yet the fact that everyone blamed him for it meant it was probably true, or that he deserved punishment anyway. As a child, he had often owned up to the pranks and misbehaviour of his peers, and yet hated this heavy responsibility. The pages meant more to him than just words. Their thick paper suggested an intimacy and understanding with the body that he had rarely experienced before, a new kind of beauty, utterly alien to all the transient sexual encounters when he'd been off-duty, which would be found in writing upon and mapping each other's skin. The disappearance of paper explained the disappearances too of physicality and of the need and use of materials and physical labour. Digitisation had made redundant almost anything, with an individual's value determined only economically, and in their passive consumption of digital goods. The books suggested a return to the body and to an embodied skin where history was unwritten and unstable, and therefore organically and spiritually charged with a very violent active potential, if it could be unlocked. These wandering reveries for the Librarian often drifted on such great journeys that their origin, end and all else were soon forgotten.

The Entrepreneur observed these very long silences like following the movement of a bird across the skies, and convinced him further of the Librarian's great wisdom and magic which soon he would be able to exploit. Frequently, the Librarian would stare into a corner, no longer concentrating on his books, as if conversing with the dead. Such small observations, and the information he could extract from the books, all co-conspired in the Entrepreneur's mind to suggest that luck and divine election were about to bestow upon him some expensive new truth for market. The Librarian did in fact have an assistant of sorts, the Woman, who would visit irregularly to clean the library and sell sandwiches and drinks. Her cleaning rarely extended beyond dusting and rearranging the piles of plucked-out pages on the great issue desk where the Librarian and Entrepreneur sat silently in study, usually with their backs to each other. Although the Librarian seemed to have no sexual proclivities beyond his ascetic attachment to paste and paper, the Entrepreneur increasingly found his eye wandering to this mousy-haired woman who was perhaps in her late twenties. She became increasingly beautiful and erotic to behold, until his mind could no longer focus on experimental combustion technologies from the Encyclopaedia Britannica. Her poverty, coarse manners and illfitting leopard-print overcoat all turned him on even more. One afternoon, when the Librarian was out carrying out 'experiments', something he had been recently preoccupied with, the Entrepreneur made his move. She was busy pulling out pages with diagrams in one of the library antechambers piled with books, in what might once have been the disabled toilet. The Entrepreneur explained that he believed he had finally discovered the great technology for which both he and the Librarian had been striving, and that if she wished to see it, she would need to undress. Their long and silent acquaintance had rendered their relations like that of a wife and husband, and she wearily responded to his command. Agog in amazement at how easily she removed her clothes, he quickly climbed out of his jumpsuit and began running his mouth across her body. "Won't you need the book" she replied monotonously. "Of course, how silly to forget", and after a polite though lacklustre mutual masturbation, their bodies alight like new matter, he placed the nearest book he could grab on her back, Hegel's *Science of Logic*, and as she rested her elbows and chest against an outstretched baby-changing board, he entered her from behind and began chanting random words that came into his head about God, morality, the devil, hell, terrorism, and the other nouns which the Librarian had told him about.

The brownfield flat landscapes were not his enemy. Within the communities of rubble, fenced off military installations now disused, Pentecostal churches in former factories, randomly dispersed blocks of high-rise social housing, the Librarian found the tools needed for his experiment: diesel, extracted from numerous parked cars; flint, and matches from a store; carbon monoxide, extracted carefully over time from a rewired engine; a small piece of silver, from melting down his wife's wedding ring; pages and pages of paper, taken from the canonical works of the world's major religions; rain water collected in old mop buckets he'd laid out some time ago, greyish-green, beauteously suffused with life living, in potential, and long dead; and finally, numerous different substances and extracts the Librarian had also cultivated and discovered which could not possibly be translated into terms familiar to contemporary understanding. In his journeys across the estates and waste-lands south of the city, he would often bump into similar souls searching through waste with metal detectors, dogs, or fishing rods, each silently pre-occupied with the profound transience of existence, chewing on chips and chocolate, the cans of strong cider and lager left behind where they had once sat before.

In one of his few words to the Research Assistant who had moved into the library with him, he remarked at the increasing number of copycat page-pasting occurring across the city. The necessity of tattoo text and de-sign for individual self-expression also suggested a repressed desire for sensu-ous expression through the word. Yet there was a danger too that someone else would stumble first on the elemental combination of words that would transform history, rewrite wrongs, including all his wrongs. He had spent too much of his life as a runner-up, good effort, see you next year. Not this time. He hurried back to the Library to complete the final stages of the Transfor-mation.

In the midst of their tarrying in that claustrophobic antechamber of textbooks, the Woman's foot had accidentally knocked over a pile of books into a wooden panel which collapsed, revealing a small secret room. The pair detached themselves, and the Entrepreneur snaked his head into the small room, no larger than six foot by six foot, which contained a desk full of papers, strange diagrams, and a fridge, which on further inspection was full of glass jars containing little pieces of dirt and material. Clearly the Librarian had been learning to write himself with a pen, based on the scribbles beneath the lines of a children's illustrated school book. As they gaped at each other, the Librarian trampled in across the spilt books.

Now dressed, the Librarian, the Entrepreneur and the Woman stood in the pot-holed car park adjacent to the library, beneath the Moon and the buddleia bursting through the bricks of the abandoned upper part of the town hall. The lower part of the building was entirely plastered with torn pages, some from the Quran, the Bible, and various chemistry textbooks, clearly in-dicating to the very occasional traffic that this was some significant site. After spending some time arranging carefully a pile of objects into a large plastic bucket, the Librarian poured over diesel and began uttering the words, with a prophet's phosphorescent haloed irises. Truly the goods of life would be found inward. Life is an infinite process of combustion and expenditure, of burning and destroying matter, and transforming that energy into enterprises wild, or vain, or poetic, or committed only to the further destruction of life and the burden of living. The only tragedy is running out of time.

The Entrepreneur had been secretly filming all this on his smartphone, which he had pretended to have abandoned as a condition of using the library. The number of online followers of 'Papierism' and its various social media presences was just over the seven-figure mark as the Librarian continued uttering his incomprehensible but fear-inspiring words. Papierist actions had been erupting across the cities, alongside great fires that burnt not just pages but plastics, combustible fabrics and chemicals, in a great rejection of digitised abstraction, and usually accompanied by exuberant expressions of physicality, like bare-knuckle boxing or violent orgies, always performed by amateurs, based on the video responses the Entrepreneur had found time to watch through. The Librarian's insane passions had accurately translated into the marketable actions of a contemporary prophet. As the Librarian began pouring the diesel over his faded-blue sports tracksuit and finally onto his balding thick black hair, the Entrepreneur could clearly see that his actions were entirely co-aligning with his predictions, for once.

In defiance of time, the body must be reclaimed against the forces of death, labour and digitisation. Life is beautiful. Beauty alone is indestructible and eternal, returning life to death and bringing to death future life. Only inwardly, in the private architectures of the soul, will each person find something to cling to against the rapid enticements and sufferings of life deceived and negligent of its beauty. And so with these words, the Librarian flicked a match against the box and, in a moment that seemed so quick it registered as little more than a still image, a frozen second the Entrepreneur was later forced to revisit and relive again and again and again, the Librarian dropped the match into the bucket and, not quite so simply, disappeared thereafter.

Opposite page, coat by Unconditional, trousers by Ann
Demeulemeester, shoes by Balenciaga. This page, shirt by Junya
Watanabe for Comme Des Garcons, trousers by Ann Demeulemeester,
shoes by Balenciaga.

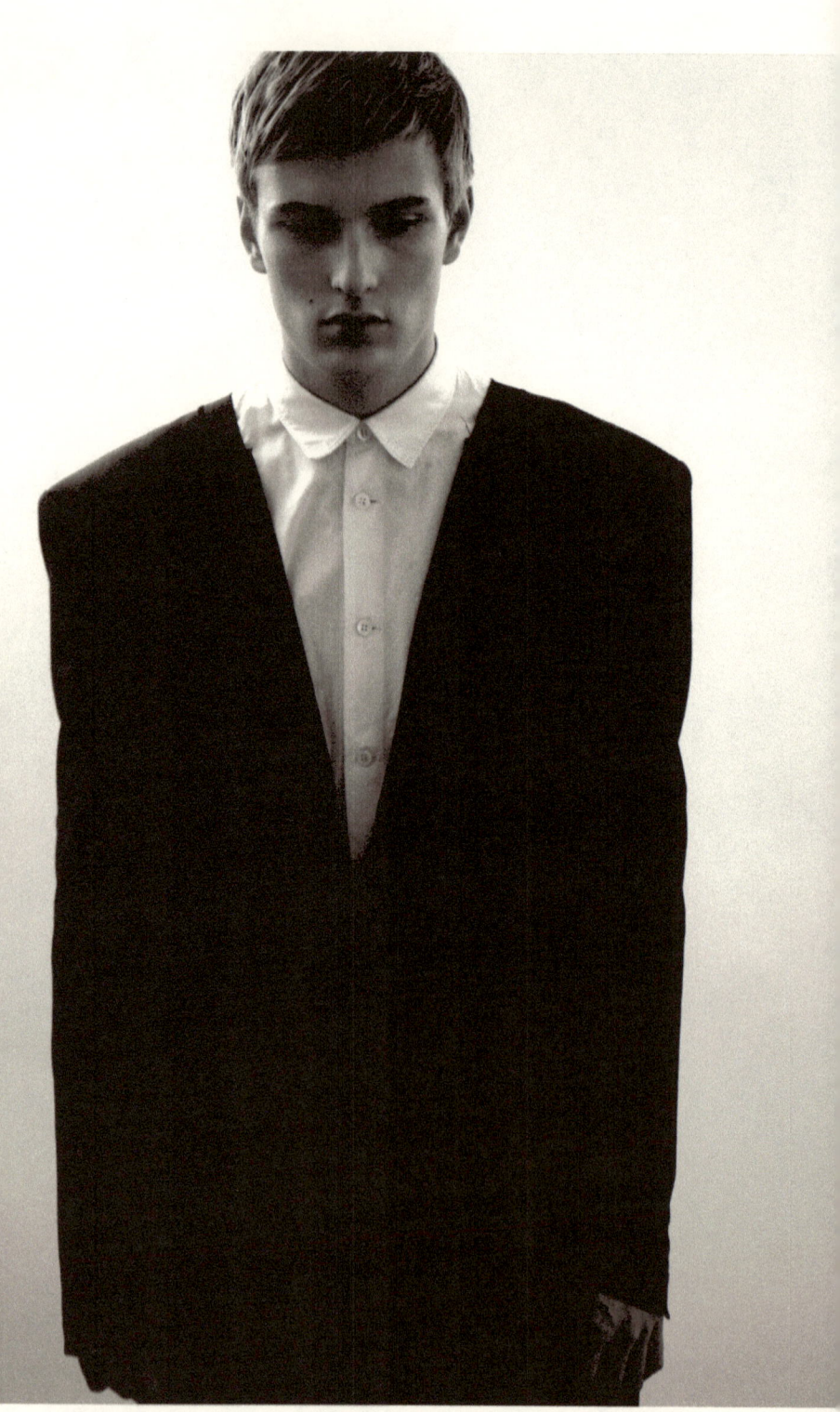

KLAXONS SILENCED

photographer/Robert Glowacki
fashion editor/Christos Kyriakides
make-up artist/Ken Nakano using Estee Lauder
hair stylist/Hisae
model/Anders @ Storm

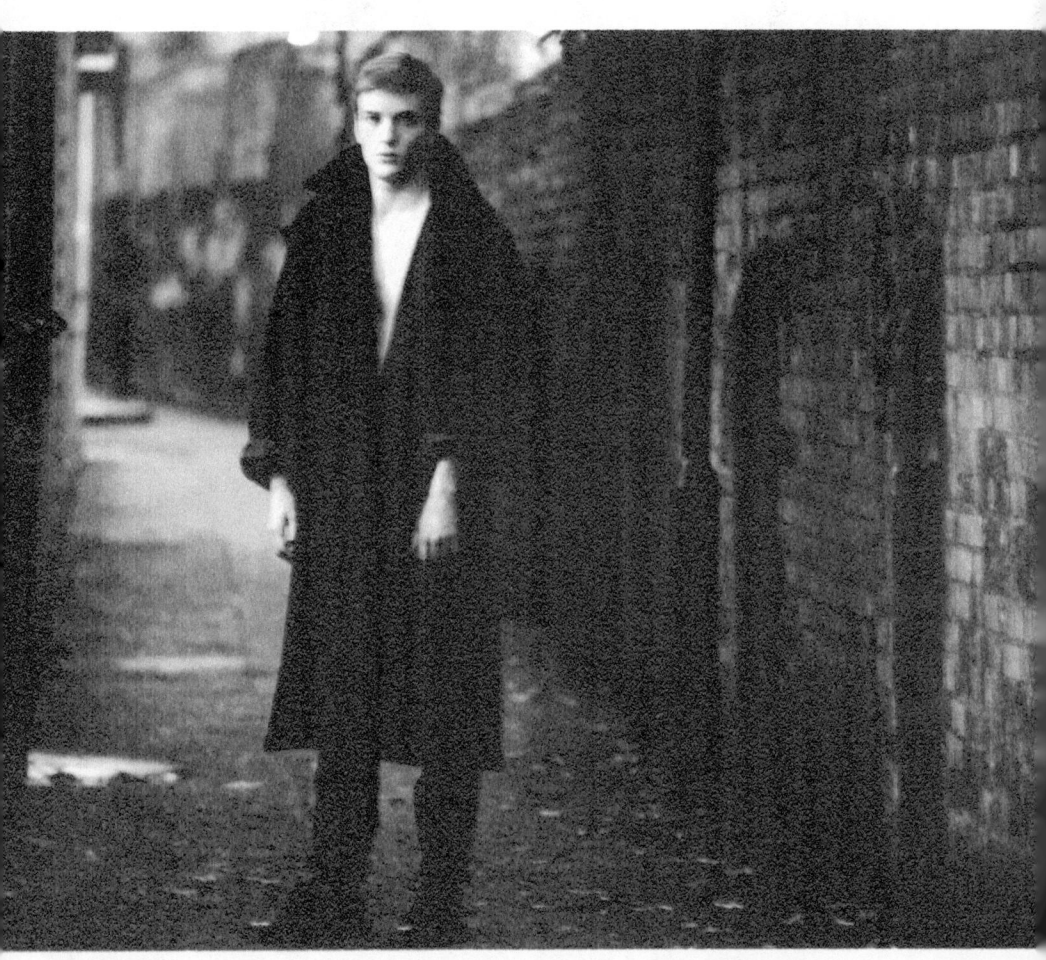

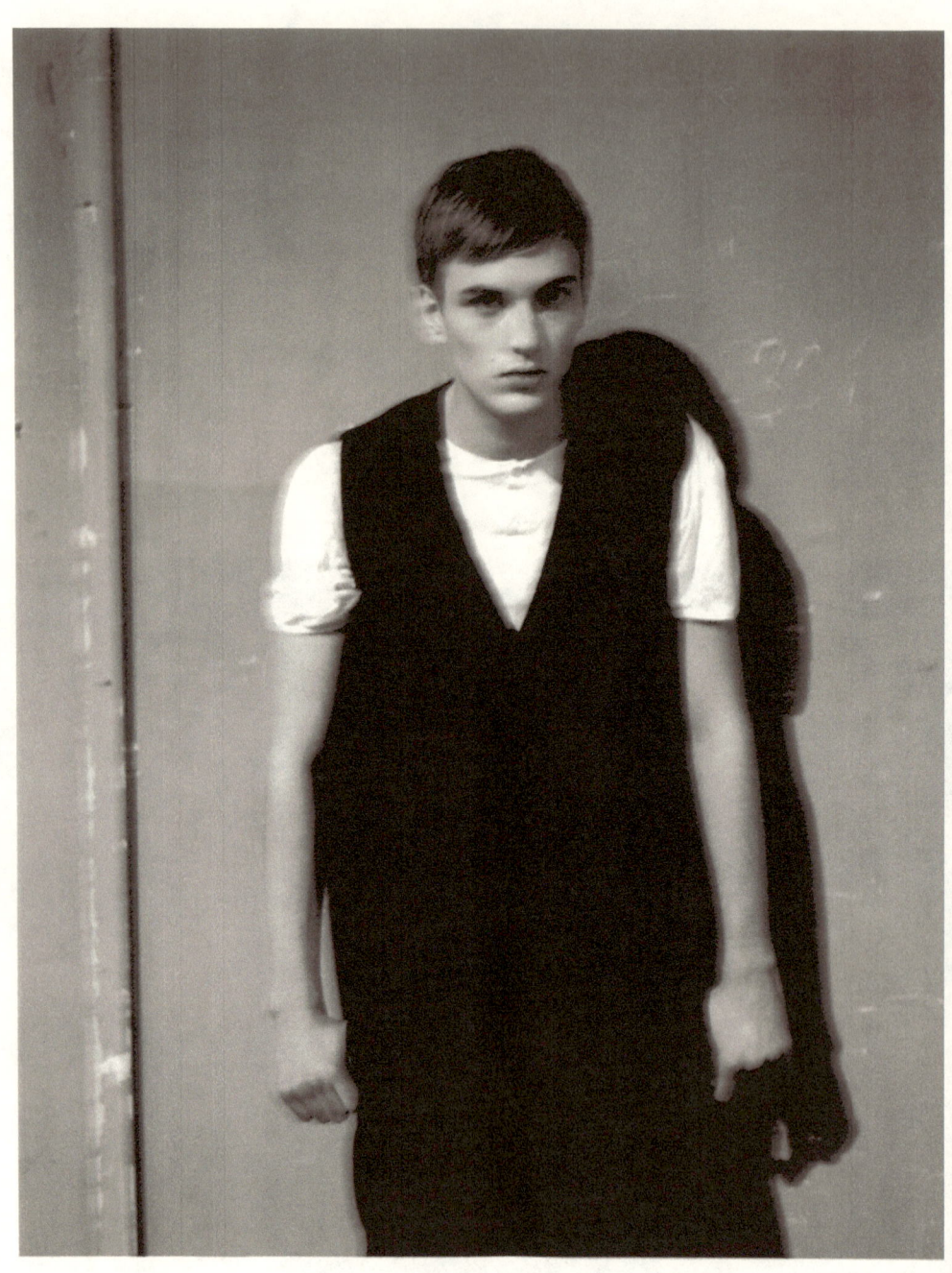

This page, t/shirt by Top Shop, waistcoat by Lee. Opposite page, shirt by Martin Margiela, jumper by Dries Van Noten.

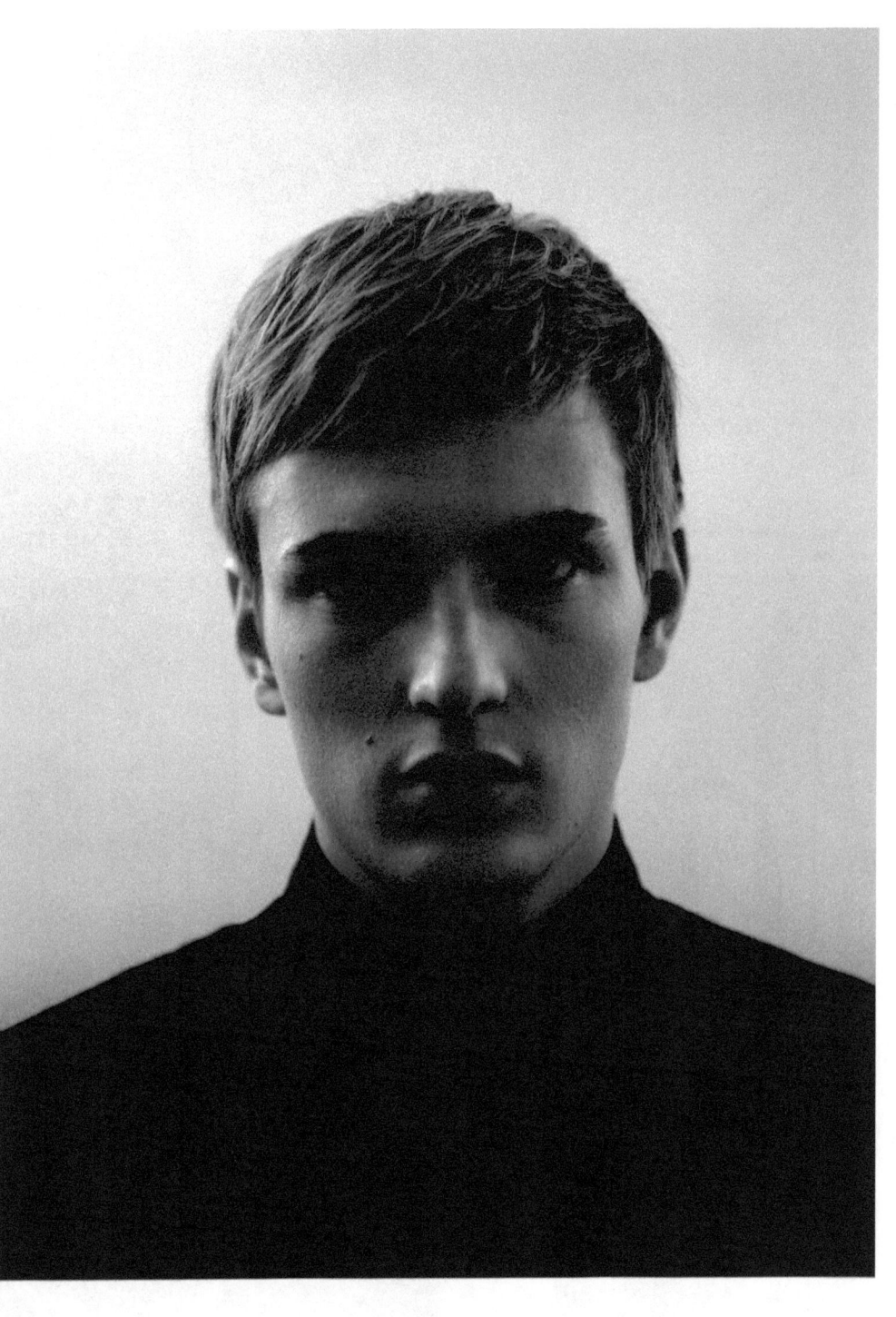

Opposite page, jacket by Soar, shirt Junya Watanabe, trousers by Ann Demeulemeester. This page, shirt by Yohji Yamamoto, hat and veil stylist's own.

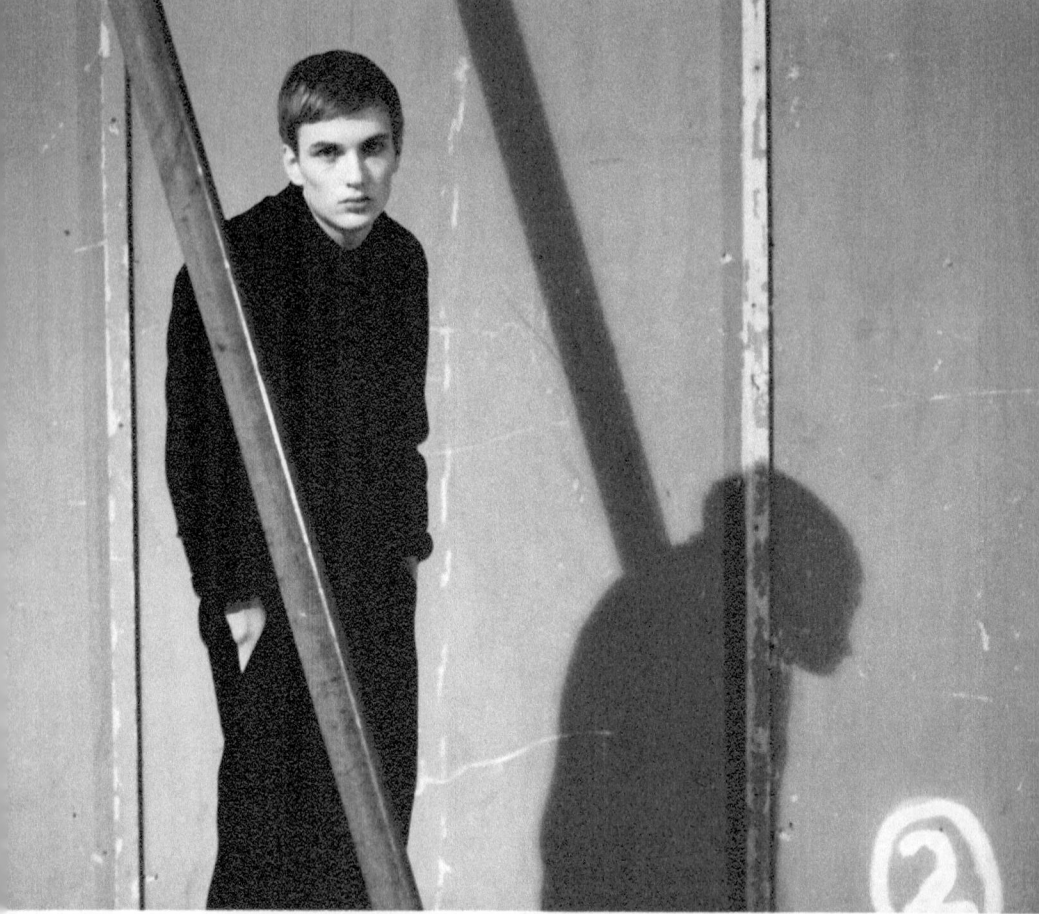

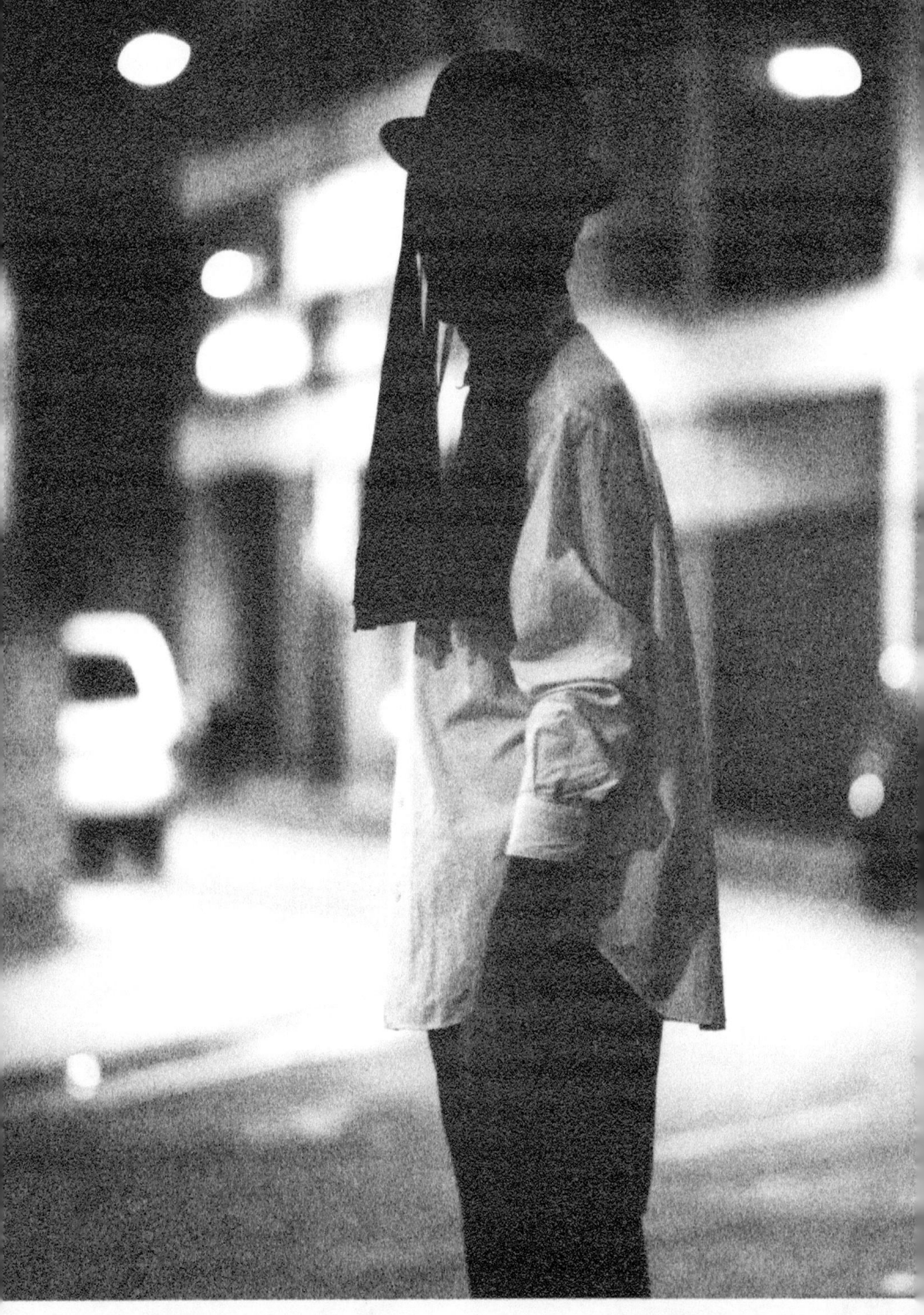

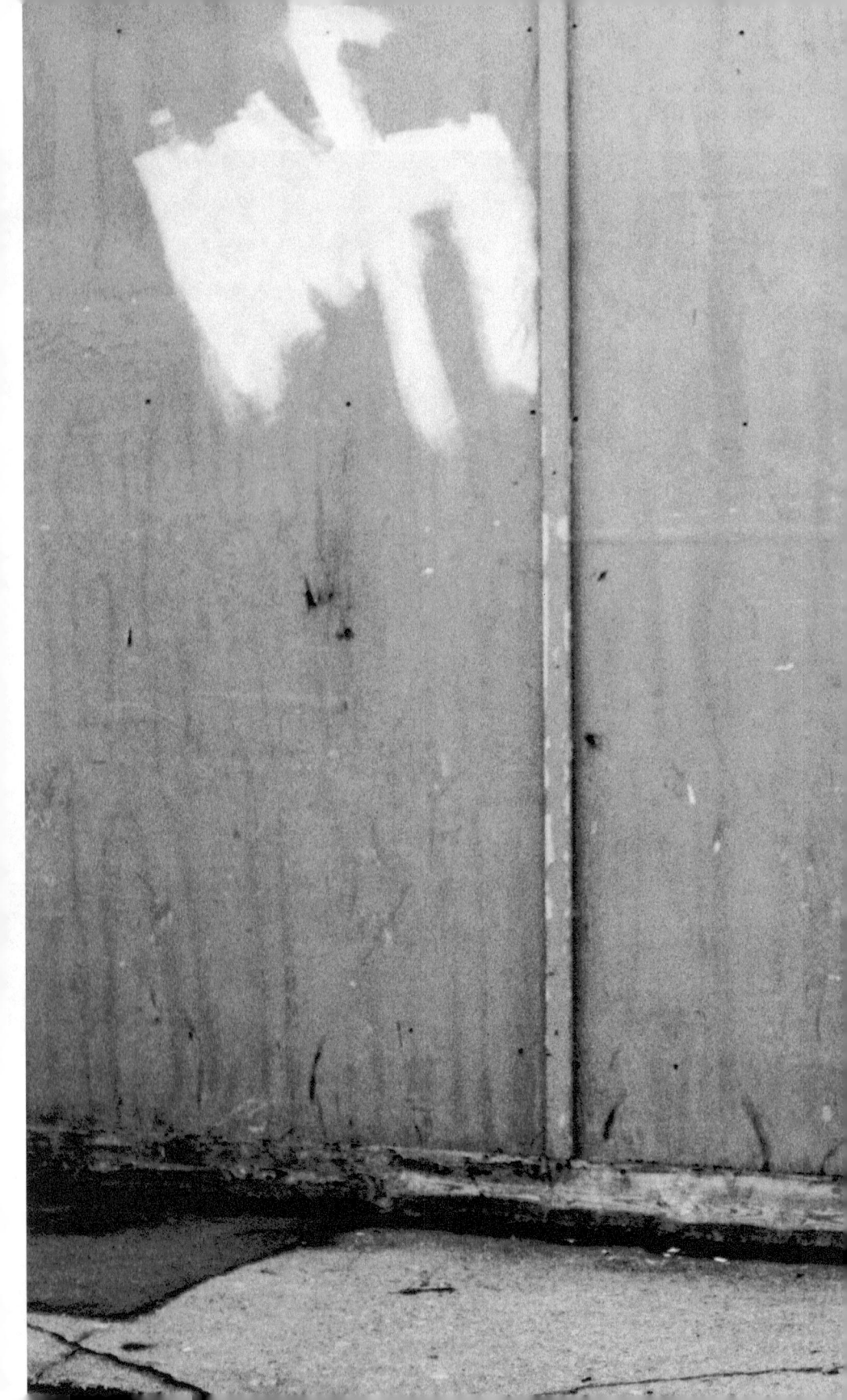

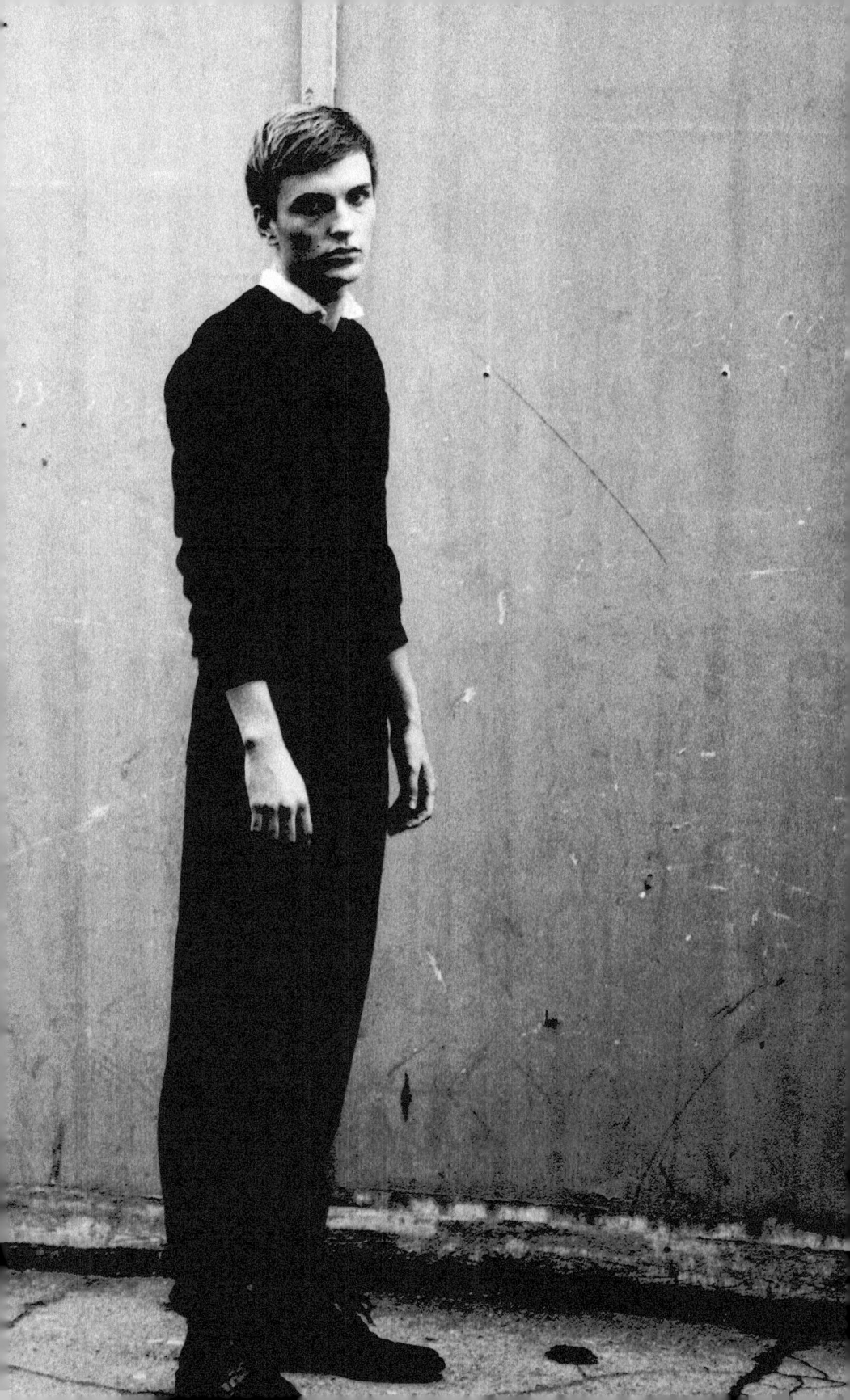

Skin

you that keeps you

IN

ape plum antelope snake

joy-bundle
heart-cockle

meniscus

dew pod

(body-bag for life)

core-carrier
dermis-detritus
soul-barrier
every colour transit van

parsnip peach potato zebra

pillow-slip
milk-carton

osmosis

sweet sweat pips

                                        (body-bag for after)

feather-dreads fruity-nooks paper-cuts

itchy-scratchy-itchy-scratchy-itchy-scratchy-itchy-scratchy

till death do us

obscene

punctuate

OUT

Geraldine Monk

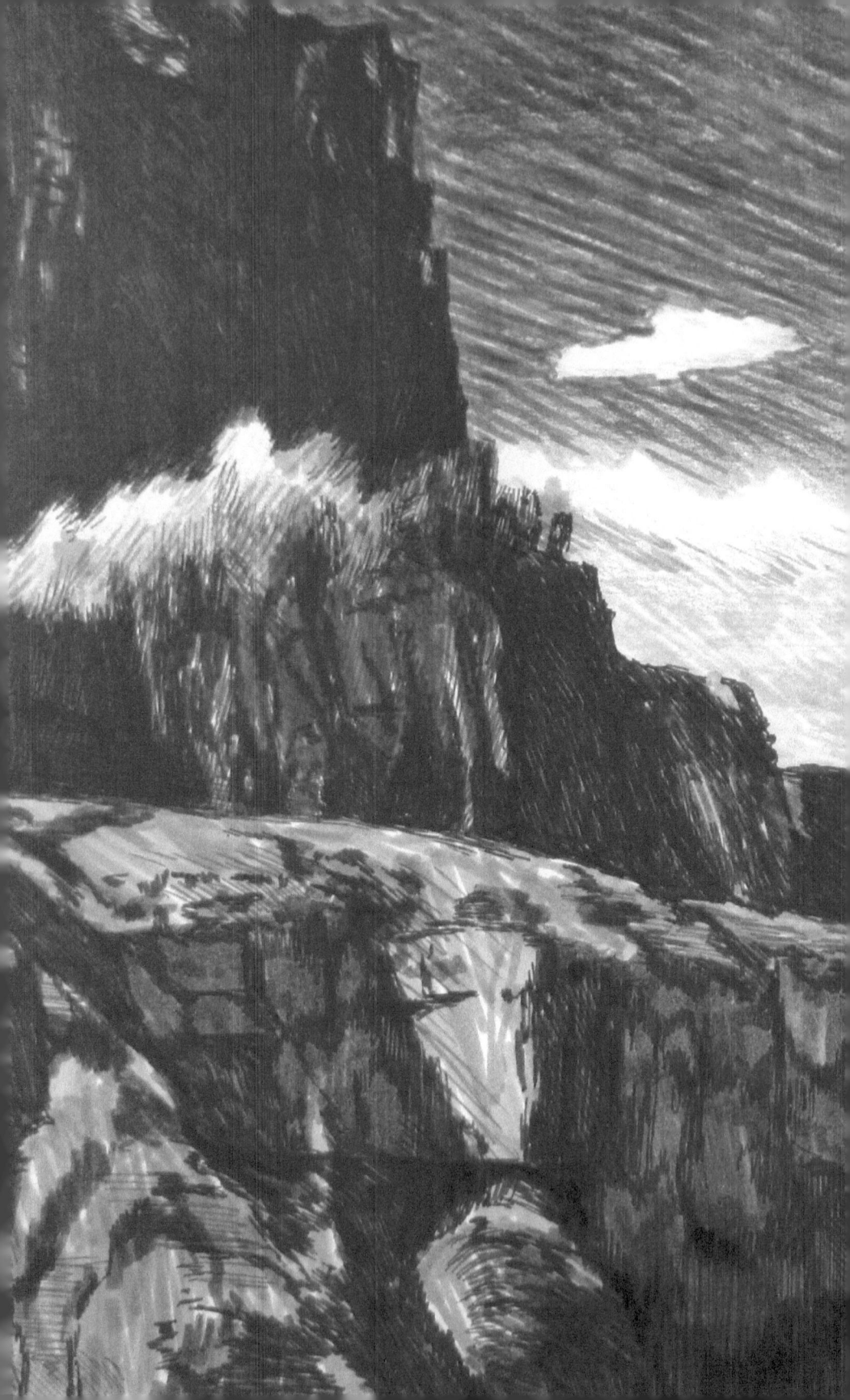

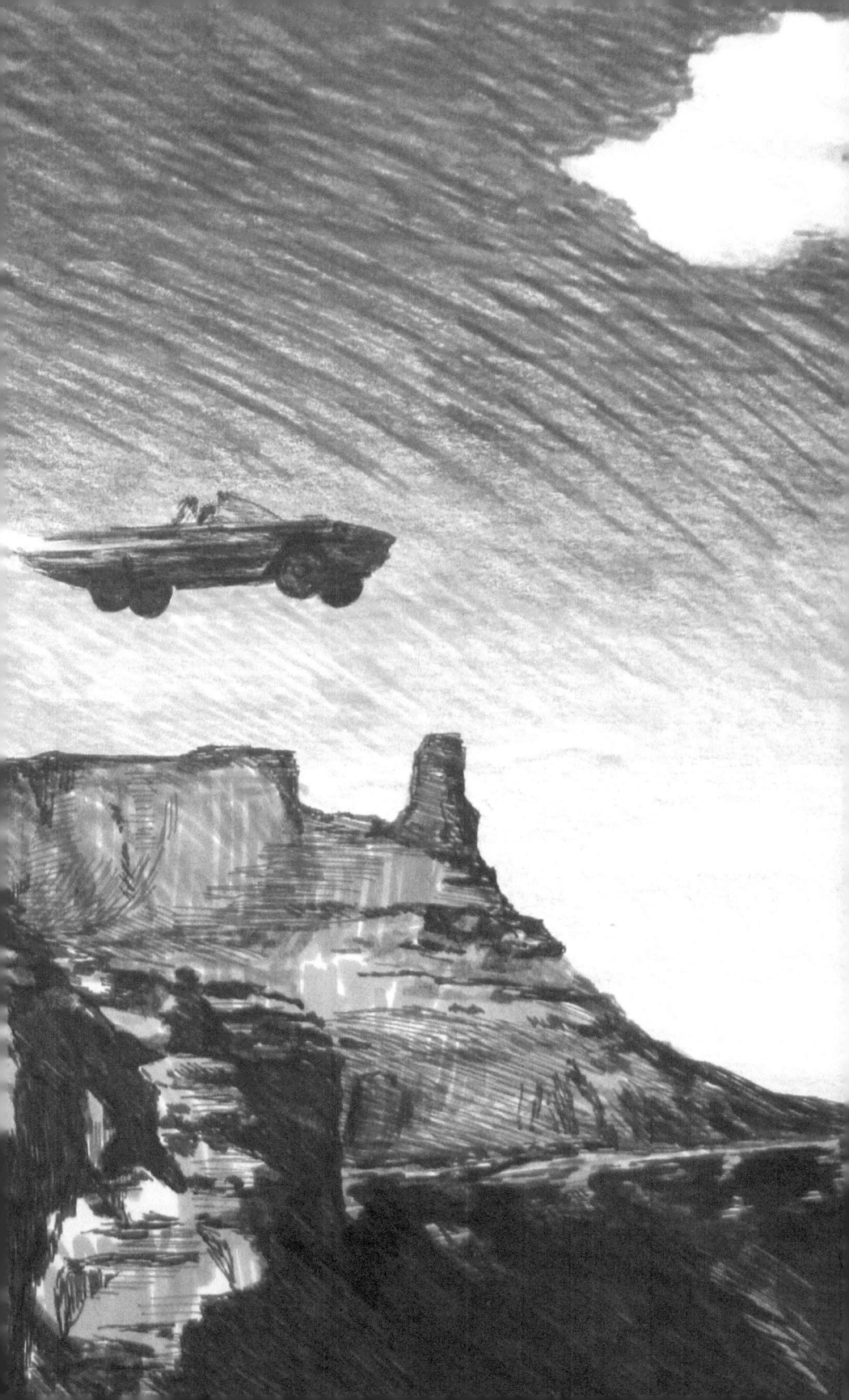

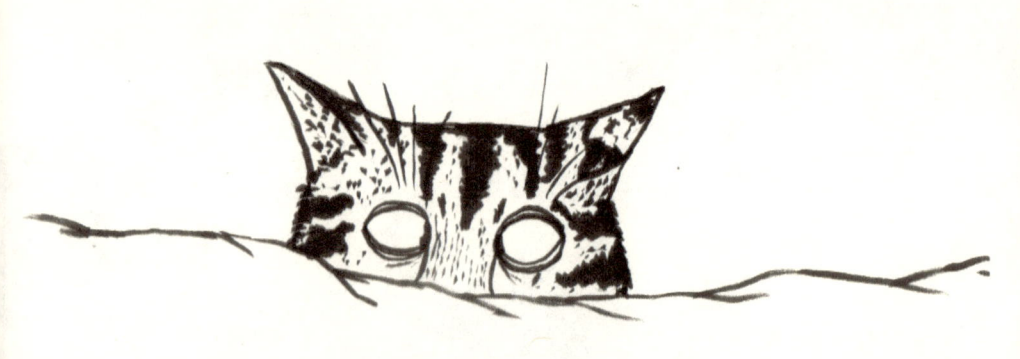

THE POLITICS OF CATS

John Hutnyk
Illustrations by *Evripidis Sabatis*

CAT, N. SMALL MAMMAL WITH AN ATTITUDE PROBLEM.

I imagine that cats are aphorists, composing dialectical koans and licking their whiskers at the elegance of their arabesques. Though I recognise that Adorno himself noted that aphorisms were not admissible in dialectical thought, which should always abhor isolation and separateness (1951/1974:16), I concede that cats are separate and aloof. Since they are never owned by their humans, they stand apart, domesticated only by choice, self-grooming, dreaming of mice (rather than hubcaps – go figure), ignoring us in ways that transcend normal social, political and geophysical categories. We know these routines already, and recognise their outsider status with a mix of awe and disregard.

Projection. The anthropomorphic charge is more difficult to lay upon our conception of cats, yet it does apply. To think of them as yoga-masters, or as independent outsider spirits, is still to malign them as merely human. I am sometimes paranoid in thinking that my cat is mechanical. A twisted automaton designed especially to distort my brain. Uncle Bill Burroughs said that

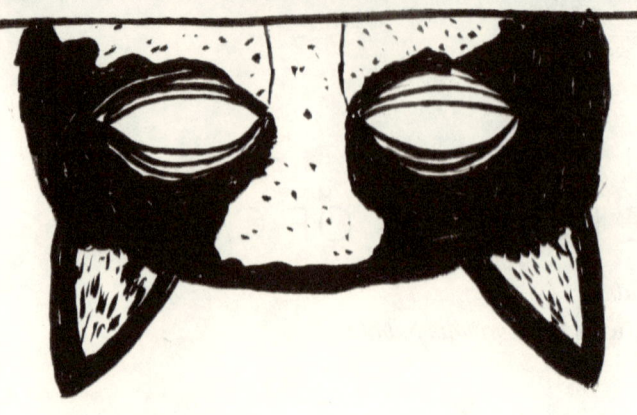

paranoia was being in possession of all of the facts. So let us consider the evidence: Cats purr – this could be very cute, or is it rather the calculated industrial production of cuteness? Cats wash themselves with their tongues—and if they were electric they would short-circuit (though consider how coffing up a hairball might be just that). Cats growl and hiss when interrogated—clearly they could be detained as non-combatants if only we had the will, and a strong leader. Cats have whiskers... More examples would only trap us in a dialectical game of catch and release, and so cats will have once again won. They always do, toying with us; ask the mice.

So I think we need to learn to learn from these philosophers of composure. First of all, I imagine Uncle Bill, stoned in the Bunker, communing in some feline comprehension with his cat Fletch: "Wouldn't you?" But why is it that Lévi-Strauss exchanges a look of understanding with that cat at the very end of his book *Tristes Tropiques*? Why a look, a visual metaphor for knowledge? Well, not so much a look of knowing, but a "brief glance, heavy with patience, serenity and mutual forgiveness" (1955/1973:544). Do cats forgive? Are they theorists of hospitality? That look bothers me some. If I were to elaborate on the metaphors of vision for knowledge I would ramble on about the way our disciplines are divided up into fields; how one strives to see the point of an argument; how instead of seeing your point, I hold a different view – so many ways in which the assertions of knowledge are visual. But with cats you do not know – the enigmatic Cheshire smile prevails.

Kurt Vonnegut died recently, having once written a great book called *Cat's Cradle* (1963) which was later accepted by the University of Chicago anthropology department as a Masters thesis. In that book, the narrator, Jonah (referencing *Moby Dick*) investigates the life of the now deceased Felix Hoenikker, developer of the atomic bomb. Of course we all know Felix is a quintessential cat's name (my first cat), and this Felix is appropriately enigmatic also, concerned only with higher science, the pursuit of knowledge as calculation, and an absentminded outsider. Though I suspect a certain identification on Vonnegut's part, only this narrator, as Jonah, could hunt him down, tempt him with the fish perhaps. It's not just the bomb, Felix invents a substance that threatens the planet – Ice-9 – and his children take it and... To tell more would ruin the story for those who have yet to read it—as far as thesis goes, it's anyone's guess how Chicago Anthropology managed to assess this as a scholarly work. Credit due.

Burroughs also pursued anthropology. This at Harvard as part of the G.I. Bill where returned WW2 service personnel were offered places in university. Uncle Bill reports that he found the department grim: "I had done some graduate work in anthropology. I got a glimpse of academic life and I didn't like it at all. It looked like there was too much faculty intrigue, faculty lies, cultivating the head of department, so on and so forth" (Burroughs 2001:76). It makes me wonder how any of those cats ever get their act together and sit for their degrees. Concentration seems awry, consistency sus-

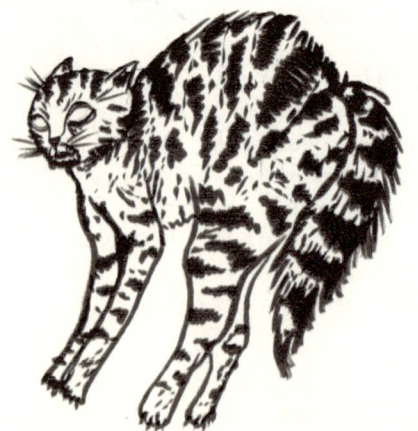

pended. And a mischievous outsider's critical countenance continues to leave them disturbingly set apart.

Burroughs in London in 1970 was strangely prophetic when he described America as vulnerable: "extremely vulnerable to chaos, to breakdown in communications, particularly to a breakdown in the food supply [a typical cat concern]. Bombs concentrated on communications, random bombs on trains, boats, planes, buses could lead to paralysis. But you must consider the available counters. We spoke about the ultimate repression that would be used. Once large-scale bombings started you could expect the most violent reactions. They'd declare a national emergency and arrest anyone. They don't have to know who did it. They'll just arrest everyone who might have done it" (Burroughs 2001:156).

There are suggestions that all cats be detained in Guantanamo. We are close to such a repression. Just presenting the look of being an outsider is a dangerous thing. Cats threaten the Western way of life in this time of 'war on terror', and do so because we cannot ever tell if they are with us or against us. And they are not afraid of sacrifice – they believe they have nine lives! They adhere to ancient cult traditions (from Egypt no less, training camps in the desert we suspect). They are long past masters of undercover operations (consider Catwoman's wily ways of entrapping the hero of Gotham). Just read the old Eastern book of war tactics, *I Am a Cat* by Soseki Natsume (1905/2002) to see how internecine and dialectical warfare offers a tactical advantage to these furry miscreants. Danger, hiss, pttfft, grrrr.

The thing about cats, aberrant and inscrutable, is that they are the antithesis of the rat-race, and for this reason alone it is worth changing their kitty litter. Meow!

REFERENCES

Adorno, Theodor
    1951/1974 Minima Moralia. New York: NLB.
Burroughs, William
    1971 Burroughs Live: Interviews. New York: Semiotext(e).
Lévi-Strauss, Claude
    1955/1973 Tristes Tropiques. Harmondsworth: Penguin.
Natsume, Soseki
    1905/2002 I Am a Cat. Berkeley: Tuttle Publishing.
Vonnegut, Kurt
    1963 Cats Cradle. New York: Dell Publishing.

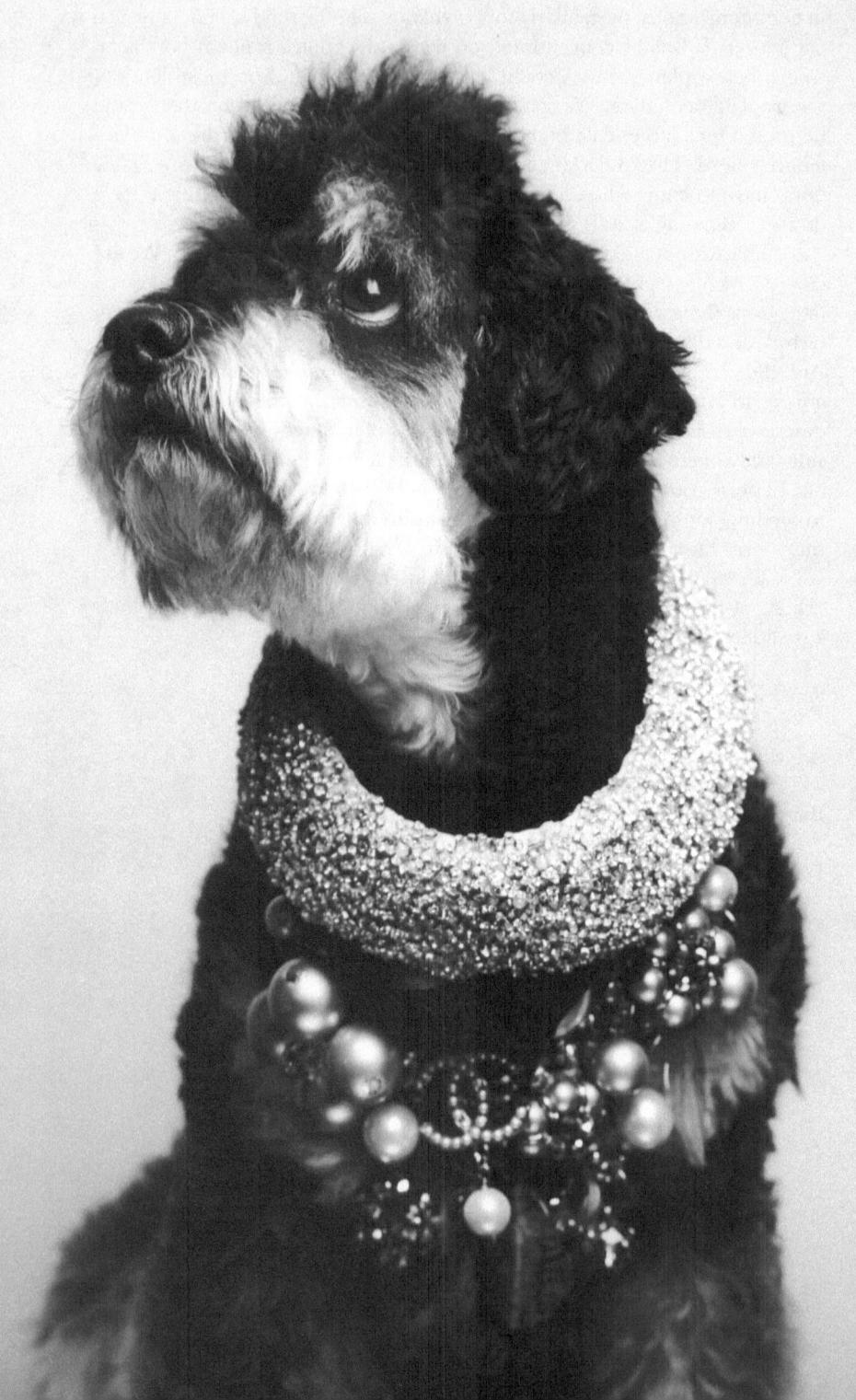

DOGUE

Photographer / Miki Barlok
Make-up / Emma Farrell assisted by Orlaith Shore
Hair / Matthew Feeney @ Aviary Lane, Dublin
Stylists / Annmarie O'Connor and Ella de Guzman
Wardrobe / Siopaella Ltd, Crow Street, Temple Bar, Dublin
Shoot Assistant / Mollie O'Connor Lloyd

Louis wears a costume necklace customised with Chanel brooches; Joanne Hynes crystal collar.

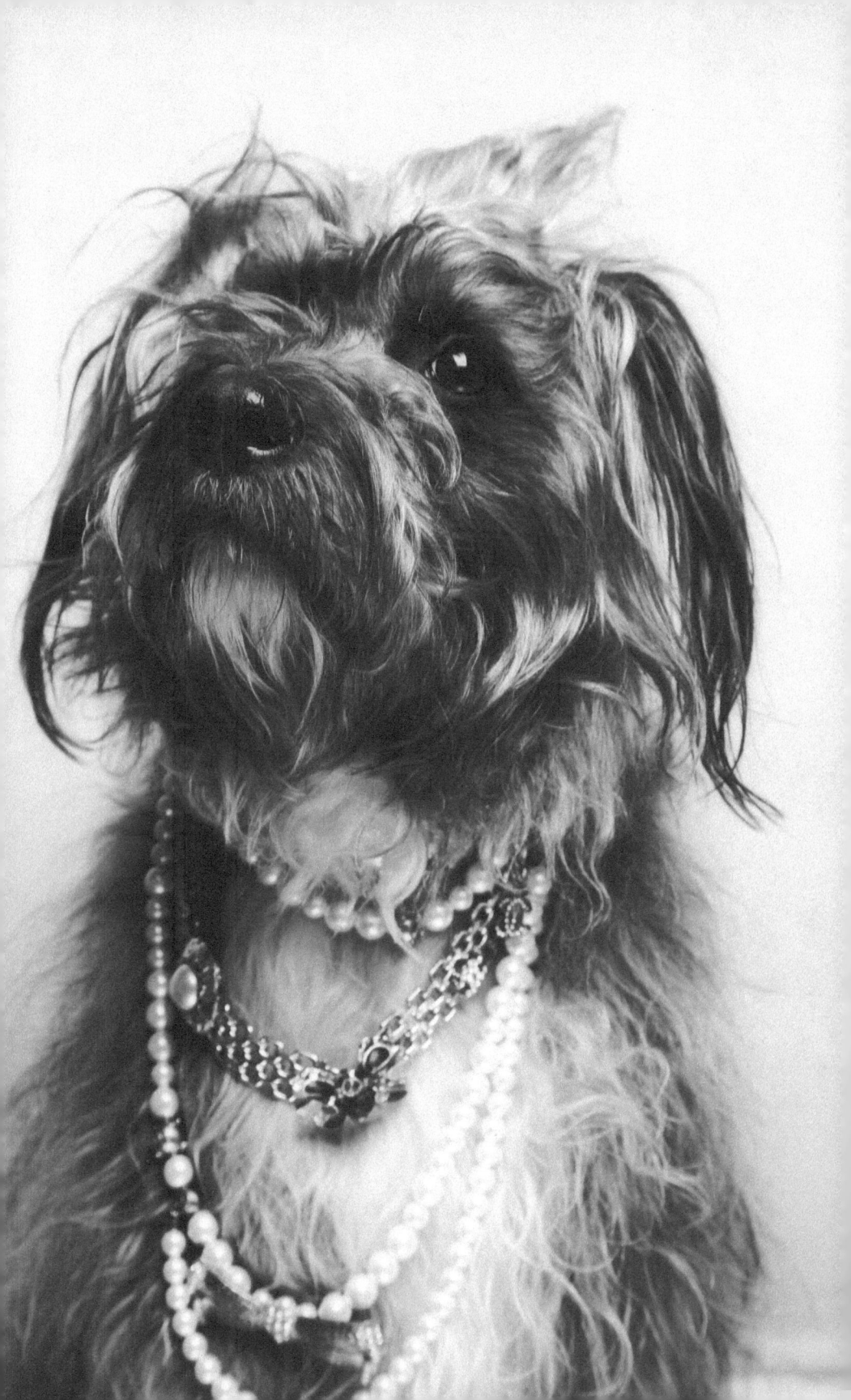

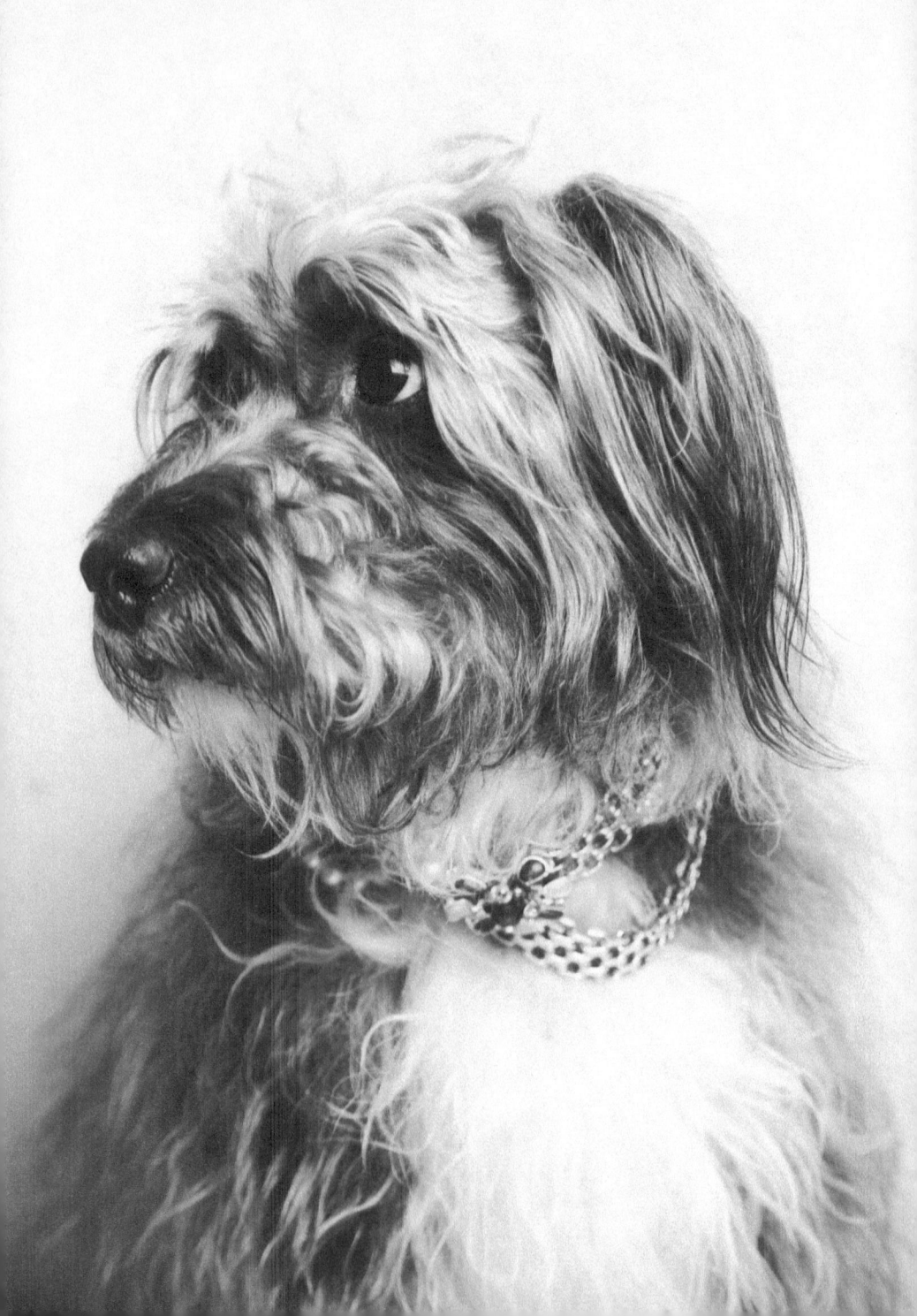

Raquel wears a Chanel belt (as necklace); Chanel pearls

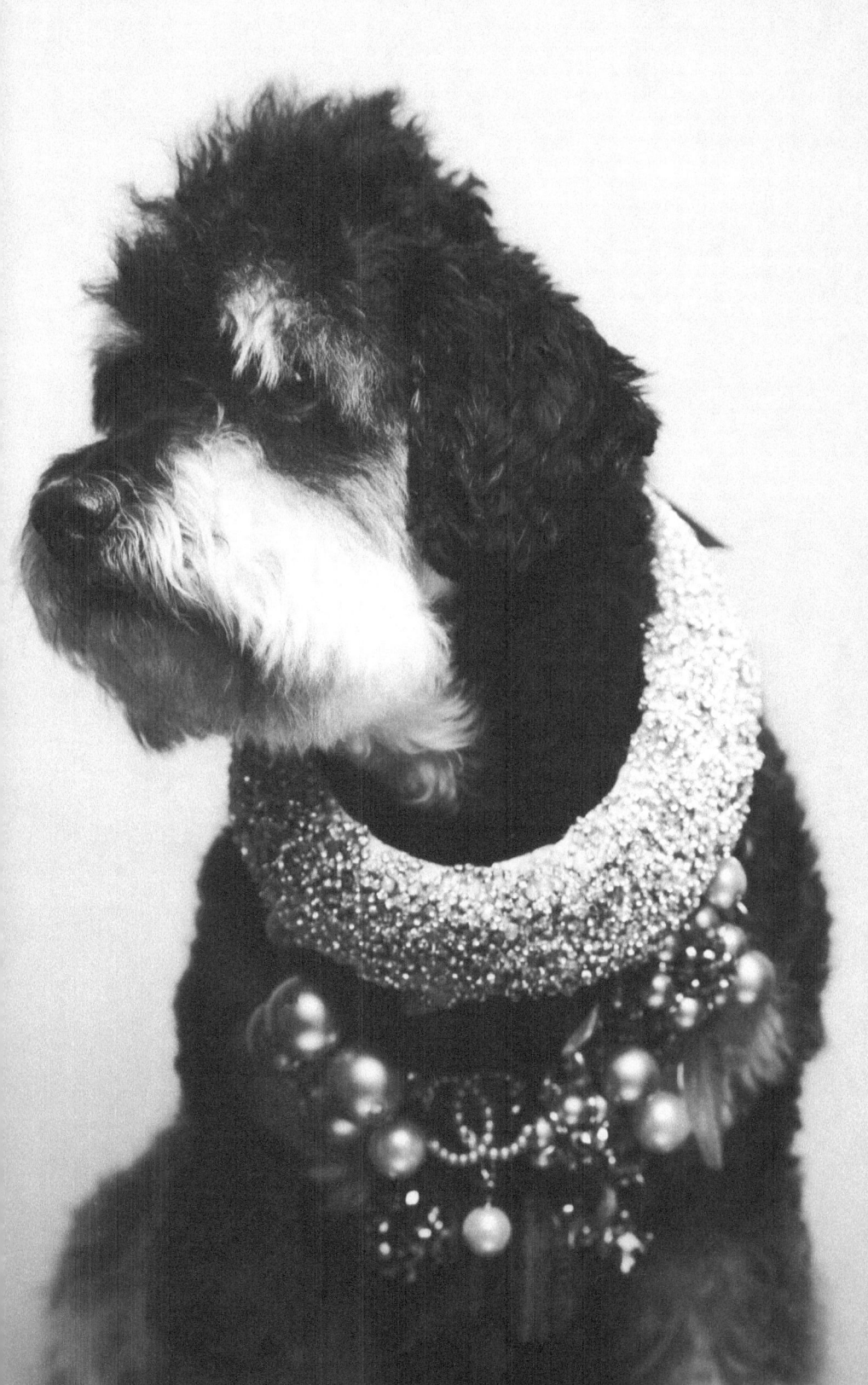

THIS IS PRIVILEGE

Scott Thurston

of
  the constitution roadmap and its width
 every advantage,
I was brought up with ever,
  I bought
up with papers
   folded
  that I would cancel the contract at the term
  white piece of the
  contract
on a clipboard
with
  installation
roadmap and
customer service, I decided back, obscuring the
   contract

at this once. Nobody
 will ever,
   every advantage

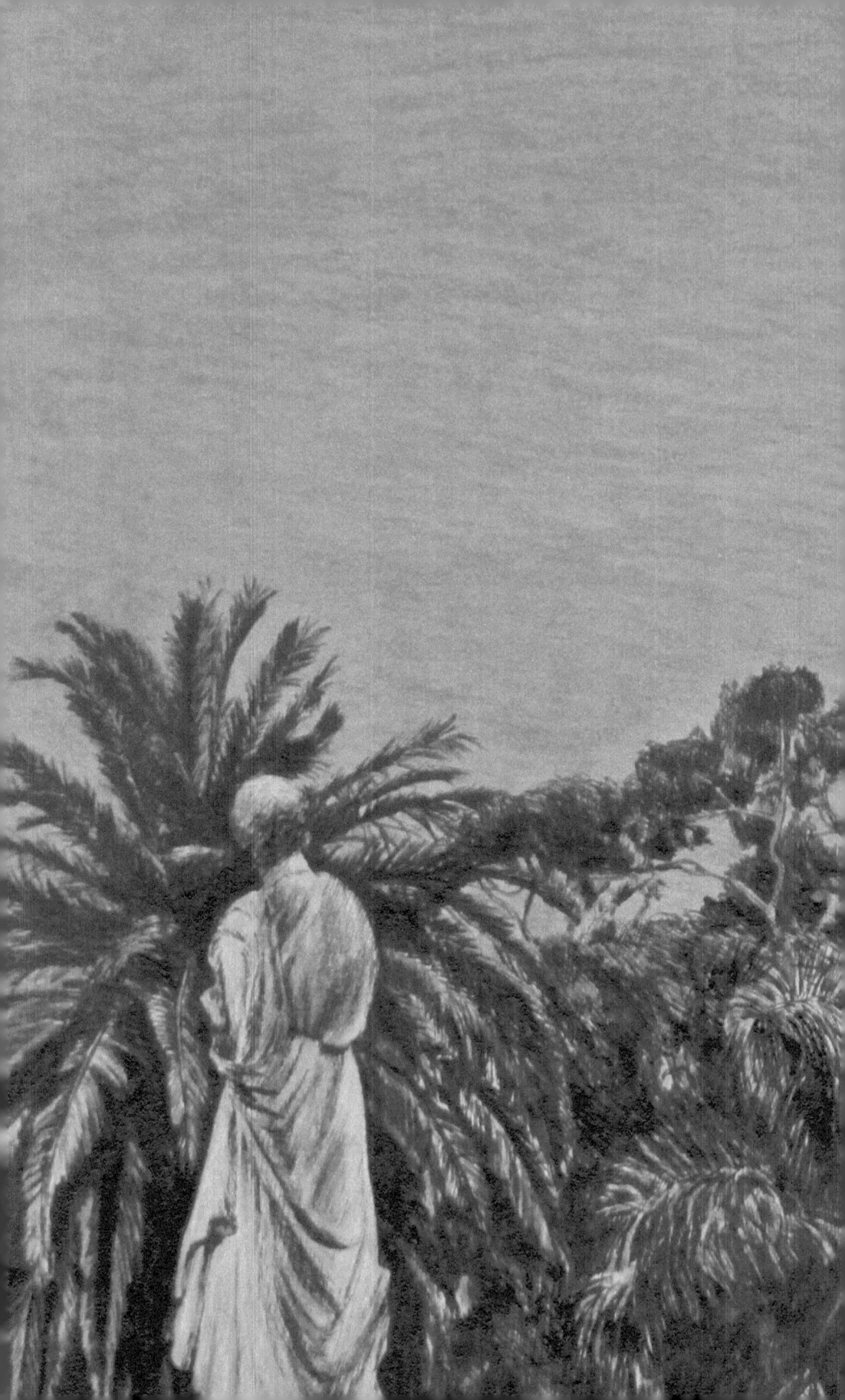

RITUALS - VOICES

Martin L. Davies

THIS RITUAL, FOR EXAMPLE: making a cocktail. Not every day would you do it. (You have to keep a clear head at all times.) But sooner or later – sooner rather than later – the time comes, maybe a special time, the end of the day, of a long day. She says: I want to wind down. You respond: OK, let's have a drink. First, you set out the tall, delicate glasses, the shaker, the measures. Then you arrange the bottles. Then you fix up the lemon or orange or whatever decoration, then the ice. It's like a magic spell for a magic potion. It requires an incantation: two measures brandy, two measures sweet vermouth, a teaspoon sugar syrup, a few dashes Angostura bitters. You shake it until the shaker frosts over and your hands ache with cold. Slowly you pour it out. You drink, you taste a delightful interlude and, with the liquid's flavour sufficiently intense, a moment of epiphany.

Ritual is a self-conscious sequence of gestures and body movements. Its self-consciousness patterns the enacted sequences. It is choreography, performance. There is in it something not just organic, but integral to matter itself. Its being self-conscious is the surface reflex of ontic organisation. All matter is organised: the ratio between adjacent numbers in the Fibonacci sequence (the golden section) governs the spiral structure of star nebulae as it does whorls in seashells. An aesthetic intention inheres in matter, be it in the geometrical regularities of quartz crystals or in the loops and spots on an exotic butterfly's ornate wings. In the human organism the same intention governs tropisms operative within consciousness. One such tropism would be the impulse to interrupt the experiential flux of dreary routine functioning by taking a line of flight, an escape route, ephemeral though it may be, towards the sacred...

Chorus-girls dance in lines uniformly: social theorists saw it as the factory assembly line in its cultural form. Otherwise dance styles are de-regulated (like the free market); but the disco-beat, above all synthetic, indifferent, partly a throbbing pulse, partly an unrelenting measure, would eventually fray the human figures under its spell with its convulsive automatisms. (The exhausting dance marathon was once a characteristic of mass culture – as Siegfried Kracauer remarks). Ballroom dancing is sinister in a different way: it has all the engineered precision of a military drill. It is the epitome of the militant banality of bourgeois culture. But in the pole-dancer there is purity, purity of form and motion – an intense, liquid sculpture, the measured but exotic convergence of athletic prowess and erotic enchantment. Her movements are choreographed by a collage of provocative *Gestalten*, primordial erotic configurations embedded deep in the bio-structure of the psyche, in the repertory of the most archaic of human responses. (To connect the erogenous with the cosmological is not a male conceit but a true imaginary, as in Courbet's painting, *L'Origine du monde* and in the principle of natality. The world that human beings create has to be born to come into being, so that with birth – as with the Nativity – a new beginning always means hope.) The audience, mainly male, is entranced, though some gape in insolent incredulity: either way they are hooked. These men think they know why: she is the object of their desire, clearly she must desire them. They can see themselves only in their narcissistic fantasies obviously making use of her body regardless of who she is. As for her, who she is for herself, I think she's thinking: when I'm through here I shall go backstage, slip on a wrap and have, as she always does, a mug of tea she will make with a routine as dextrous as her dance.

Any line of flight towards the sacred will be ephemeral, because in the disenchanted world the sacred is transient, exceptional. It is a state of attentiveness, of rapture, of ecstasy, of epiphany that is humanly unsustainable. So ritual must be perpetual conjuration, conjuration perpetually reiterated. Think, for example, of the conjuror's compulsive gestures, his distracting sleights of hand, his abracadabras, the magic hocuspocus, the wonderment. All an illusion. There is no transcendental, immaterial entity to which ritual conjuration appeals. It seems to make sense, but only because the appealing gesture in itself projects transcendence. But then sense is an inherent property of reiterated conjurations, of patterns and sequences (as in binary code or the structure of DNA). They need not signify anything! The conjuring gestures need not gesture towards anything. And what, if they could, would they gesture towards? Deep down everyone knows there is nothing out there, that human life is a cosmological eccentricity, that above all consciousness is fatal, a remote observation post in uncharted territory. What an absurdity, death included, except for just one, single compensation – love!

Ritual, though, does something miraculous. It makes something out of nothing, it galvanises ontological destitution. It supplies the rest, the rest that potentialises existence, empowers it. It invests in it an essential, self-sustaining dynamic. What drives it is melody and dance, as in the cult of Dionysus: rhythms of musical movement, rhythms of voice in the song. In enchantment there is chant, itself sustained by the binary code in measures such as the iambus (v –) and the trochaeus (– v), the dactyl (– v v) and the anapaest (v v –), the choriambus (– v v –) and the antispast (v – – v). For once the utilitarians have a point (says Nietzsche): poetry is useful because rhythmic measure is omnipotent. There is nothing it cannot do: it magically drives labour forward, compels God to take heed, bends the future to one's will, and purges the soul: "to lack rhythmic measure is to be nothing, to possess rhythmic measure is to become virtually divine."

This is what they did every Friday (so I was told), at the end of the week, when they finally – at last! – had the time to be together closed off from the world. It was as if they were marking the Sabbath with a feast. It was, though, for her sake. He would light a sea-blue candle in her honour. As a preliminary ceremony the table would be set, the champagne flutes signifying solemnity. The food would be simple but elegant: a *gratin dauphinois*, perhaps, fillet steaks *saignant*, a salad tossed in a light *vinaigrette*, and then a pavlova and espresso coffee for dessert. One would serve the food, the other with nonchalant dexterity would open the ever effervescent wine and fill the flutes. Once seated (I was told), automatically they would raise their glasses and, before imbibing, with grim determination exclaim: Death to our enemies!!!! But (apparently) they never could discover if this incantation worked, if it did the trick. Worse still, through the grapevine (so to speak), came intimations that, far from expiring, their enemies were doing rather well for themselves; that they might even be prospering. In response they could be reassured that their curse (like all curses) would be always active, potent in perpetuity.

However, in the everyday world ritual is displaced, then marginalised by its nefarious simulacrum. What remains gets sequestrated, refunctioned. Choreographed rhythms degenerate into routine behaviour in the socioeconomic mega-machine. Sequences of gestures decline into epiphenomena of the systemic logic sustaining the administered world. Patterns of response are reduced to behavioural reflexes conditioned by organisational procedures. Measures translate the vindictiveness of managerial regulation: there is no quality that is not measurable. In facilitating calculation they provide the certainties – the data, the statistics, the numbers – for the bureaucrat's cold, psychotic gratification. (Psychotic? Did not Rousseau describe calculation as a form of depravity?) The socio-economic mega-machine radiates psychosis. It induces a distinctive psychopathology. The purely functionalistic rituals it enforces simulate neurotic repetition-compulsions. The superior faultlessness of its electronic apparatus, interrupted by frustrating malfunctions resulting from human-all-too-human clumsiness, provokes deep shame. Its relentless automatism, connecting directly with the automatisms of the unconscious, thus liberating regressive desires, outflanks self-reflection and so generates anxiety. As an instrument of totalitarian terror it thus tears asunder the personality already alienated and exhausted by capitalist exploitation in order now to tap into and extract the maximum surplus value from its vast unconscious resources.

Perhaps it resulted from driving for several hours in the tiring sun that my responses slowed so that, instead of turning into the crematorium complex, I mistook for its entrance an adjacent drive-way into what estate agents would call a secluded estate of upmarket "executive homes" otherwise indistinguishable from it. A deft three-point turn and a few minutes later I was parking my car in the congested crematorium car park. I got out and made my uncertain way towards the crowds. Where was the group I was supposed to be joining? The scene – the rows of cars parked, people in groups waiting, an atmosphere of expectancy – reminded me of a frontier control post in disputed territory that had closed temporarily or where travellers turning up without the correct papers or with expired visas had caused delays. (Well, I thought, we might not have the right papers or visa now but this particular frontier post will admit us all sometime or other, sooner or later.) Then the same scene – the rows of cars, the people waiting, the expectancy – evoked a car ferry port prior to departure, perhaps for a rough, night crossing. (But suppose, I thought, the transfer across the Styx was no longer with the fearsome Charon in a graceful gondola. In this culture of the death drive, the dominion of Thanatos, it would surely require the capacity of a roll-on roll-off ferry, a floating structure of cabin-like tombs, equipped with shops, restaurants and cinemas to alleviate the dreadful journey.) And then I recognised other members of the group and, as I joined them, we all moved towards the chapel that was already so overflowing with mourners that we had to gather at its entrance. It had been decided that mourners should wear bright party clothes, T-shirts, jeans, flimsy frocks, because this was to be the celebration of a young life accidentally abbreviated and his friends, having done him proud with this dress code, were certainly conspicuous. But on this mid-summer day I (like the other older participants) had still gone for black as a proper expression of deep sympathy and respect. With the service over, the music, the eulogies, the prayers all done, we filed out past the coffin isolated on its catafalque like a missile on a launch pad about to blast off for the cosmos. There had been none of the usual hocus-pocus, the prestidigitation, so that after a prayer when you look up it has vanished. In the blazing sun outside on the neat, suburban lawn with its rose bush borders we met and reflected in a sombre mood. I was introduced to one young woman who had the most reason to be deeply affected. To express her devastating grief she was wearing the most revealing party dress. Everyone knows that the perpetual conflict between Eros and Thanatos that governs our works and days is vastly unequal, but it was as if, even in this deep crisis, she wished bravely to tilt the odds in Eros's favour, as if in desiring to give a treasured keepsake to the now departed, she was symbolically giving herself. And that (since you did say you wanted to know) is how I learned yet again about the awful sadness of living ...

Ritual is circular, reiterative. It is a conjuration of the very presence, the human presence, to which it owes its existence. It defines a time within time, in the way that a piece of music (e.g. a Mozart sonata, a twelve-bar Blues) has its own time signature, its own temporal structure. It defines a presence within existence that can occur only because it produces sense, because those the ritual involves believe in it. It is the imaginary architecture of a constructive illusion: without it life would be impossible. Ritual is the default recourse to sense production. Along with marriage rituals, burial rituals are an essential, primordial constant in human behaviour. The very concept of humanitas *comes (according to Vico) from the Latin* humando *(i.e. 'burying'), the rituals of mourning affirming presence even in the moment of its demise, the human inextricable from inhumation. But ritualistic constancy has no defence against its institutionalisation. It then upholds the barren formality of tradition. It reinforces the entrenched authority of things as they are. Rituals remain vital only if they are spontaneously created. Or rather they must unexpectedly happen, suggest themselves, emerge unbidden into consciousness like a refrain, a particular melody, some lines of verse, evoking a state of mind, a situation, a complex of issues, a rhizome-like pattern of circumstances, whatever remains, the recollected remnants of having lived...*

The engulfing red is overwhelming: one cannot dodge its blow.

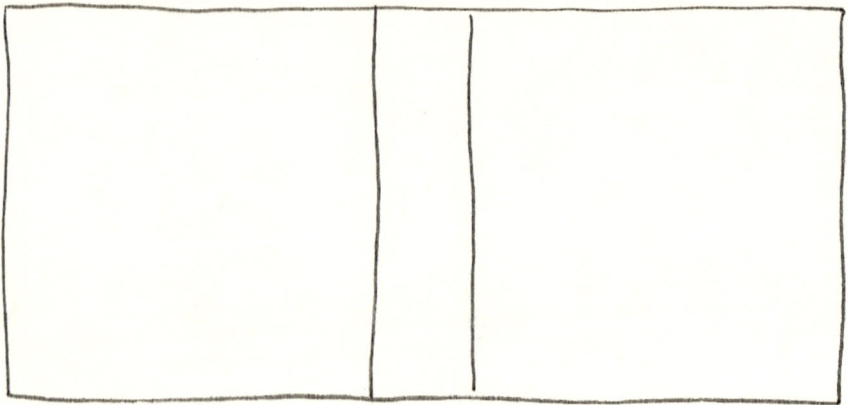

It was an icon of a tradition of painting that overcame 'provincial narrowness' and founded an international culture, an 'unlimited spiritual communication'.

DEAD BIRDS

Michael Taussig
Illustrations by *Atalya Laufer*

ONE OF THE MOST INSPIRING THINGS I read about so-called
primitive cultures is the respect afforded animals in the hunt once they are
killed. At the same time I always wonder how sincere this is and how this
respect can coexist with crass desire for meat.

This wonder is actually the first inkling as to a radically different way
of relating to animals and to the kinship with nature in which we are all im-
plicated. This came across to me recently when I was reading about dreams
in Labrador.

In Naskapi dream theory, according to Frank G. Speck's studies in
the 1920s, dreaming is the main channel by means of which a person keeps
in communication with the unseen world and therefore dreams are of utmost importance for guiding one through everyday life. To follow the idiom,
dreams allow your spirit to talk to you.

Note that several things stimulate dreaming, such as drumming, dancing, fasting, singing, rattling, the sweat bath, seclusion, meditation, drugs,
alcohol . . . and gifts of clothing as when Speck gave a red necktie to a Naskapi
friend who, when short of food that winter, would put it around his neck.
Then he would dream a dream that led to a good hunt.

Marks of red paint were, as a general practice, painted on the underside
of the skin of the animal killed in the hunt. After the skin had been tanned, red
paint would be applied usually at the end of the legs where the feet had been
amputated and at the neck-hole. If the head was intact, then ribbons, whose
colour is not mentioned, were attached to the eye-holes, nose, and ears, and
pieces of red cloth were sewn over these orifices as well.

Among Naskapi there is a device known in English as the sling or pack-
strap for bringing in freshly killed game. Simple and practical, it is also sacred.

Made of moose or caribou skin, it is decorated with coloured silks and beads, sometimes representing animals, among which red silk features strongly. Here are two explanatory captions from Speck's collection:

No.7. For carrying beaver on shoulder. Six feet, one inch long. Tanned caribou skin, three ply. All red.

No. 7A. For carrying beaver on shoulder. Five feet ten inches long. Tanned caribou skin, three ply. All red.

All red. The hunter would stretch the dead animal out on its back, lay the sling on it, put tobacco in the animal's mouth and sit by it, smoking, for an hour or so. The animal, so we are told, is honored in this way, its reincarnation abetted, and the spirit master of the animals reconciled. Sometimes the hunter would sing and dance around the body of the animal.

The most poignant manifestation of red in this set of motives and motifs are the tiny constellations of five red dots forming a diamond pattern. Painted on drums, rattles, food dishes, and objects of household use, these dots are said to represent sun rays falling onto a wide landscape as seen in real life or, more commonly, in a dream, indicating where to hunt large game such as herds of caribou crossing a lake. Like the laying of the sling across the body of the dead animal, these red dots come after the hunt, as homage.

The minute size of these dots stands in inverse relation to their wonder, as does the ordinariness of many of the things onto which they are painted, whereby a kitchen spoon becomes the repository of memory no less than of the miracle. The red dots provide testimony.

In Labrador it is not uncommon for sunbeams to fall obliquely from the sky, says Speck, "through rifts in a heavy cloud mass, illuminating certain tracts of country where the rest lies in obscurity." The Indians can hasten their occurrence in dream through singing and drumming. They call these illuminations "spottings of the sun." And they choose to paint them red.

It sounds a bit like the movies. Rays of light pierce the blackness so as to illuminate, if not make pictures. In the distance we see shapes moving, breaking the surface, those massive caribou, antlers like the branches of trees, swimming in single file across the lake to certain death at the hands of the hunter who sees them, thus revealed, in dream. More red shall follow. Red will be the edges of the holes where the feet were, red will be the edges of the holes where the eyes were, and red will be spotted on a spoon – in other words red is where the animal walked and swam, where the animal saw, and as spottings of the sun, with what people eat.

The illustrations for this piece recall Barnett Newman's Who's Afraid of Red, Yellow and Blue III *and* IV.

Quotes are taken from:

Gamboni, Dario
    2007 The Destruction of Art: Iconoclasm and Vandalism Since the French Revolution. London, UK: Reaktion Books.
Foster, Hal, Rosalind Krauss Yve-Alain Bois, Benjamin H. D. Buchloh and David Joselit
    2012 Art Since 1900. London, UK: Thames and Hudson.

Presumably, the man who knifed the painting, furiously slashing it three times across, could not bear the heat.

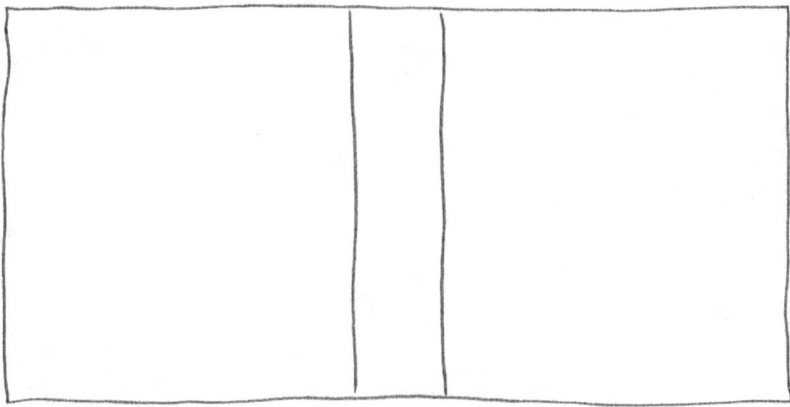

He had been afraid of the painting. Newman's work was a 'perversion of the German flag' (which is horizontally divided into black, red and gold), it ought to 'frighten the Germans' and did not belong to the Nationalgalerie.

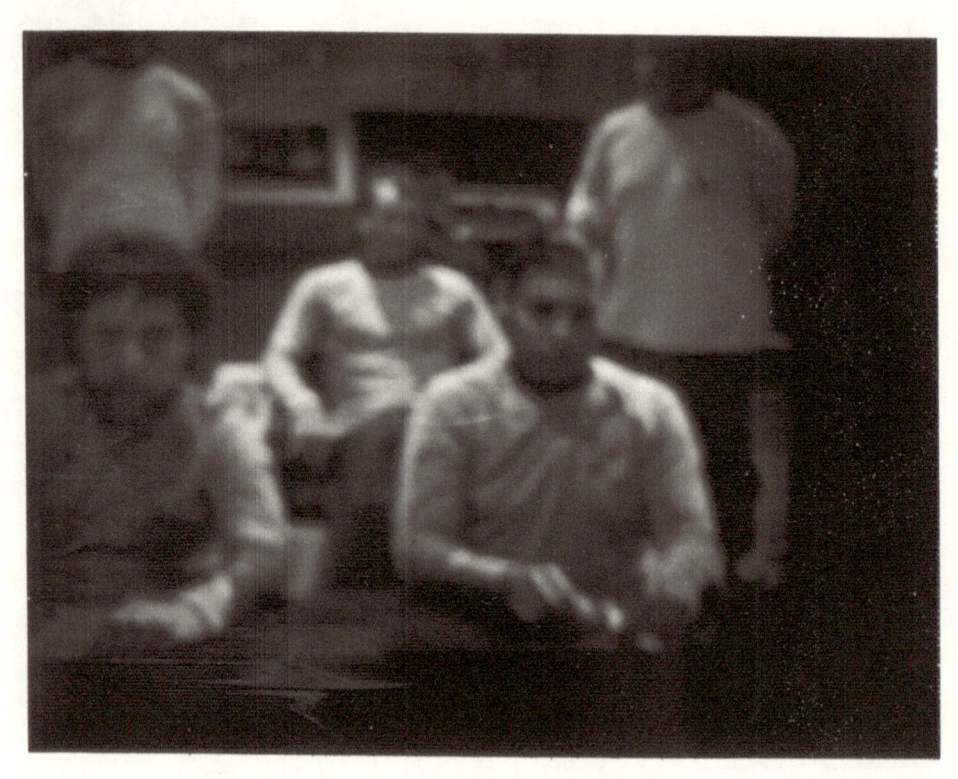

SPACE ATTACK

Series of expired Polaroids by Johannes Gierlinger

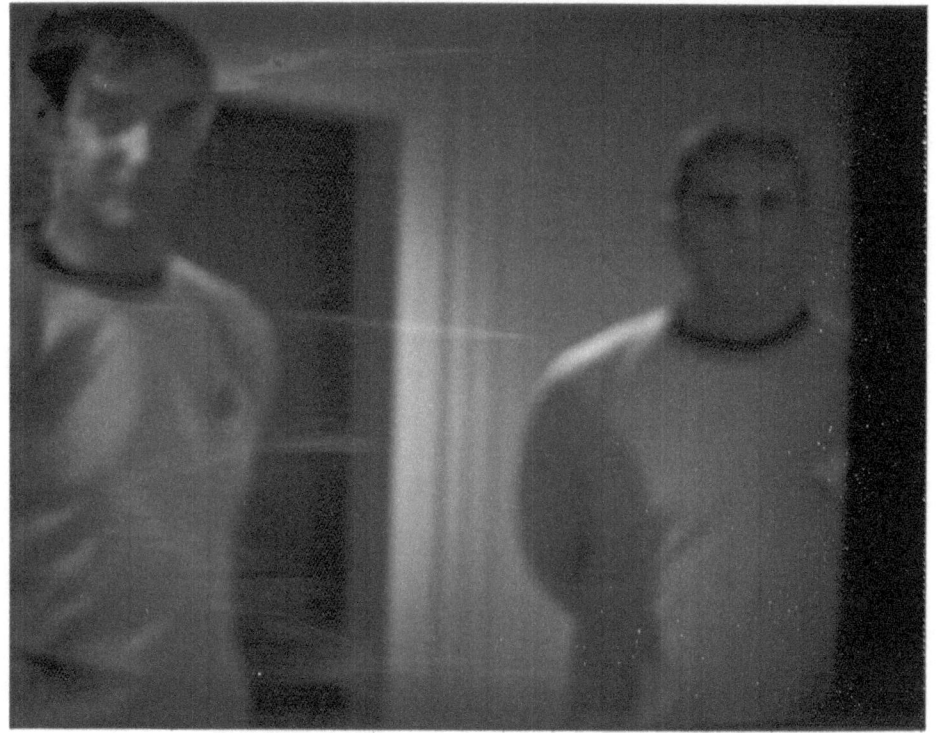

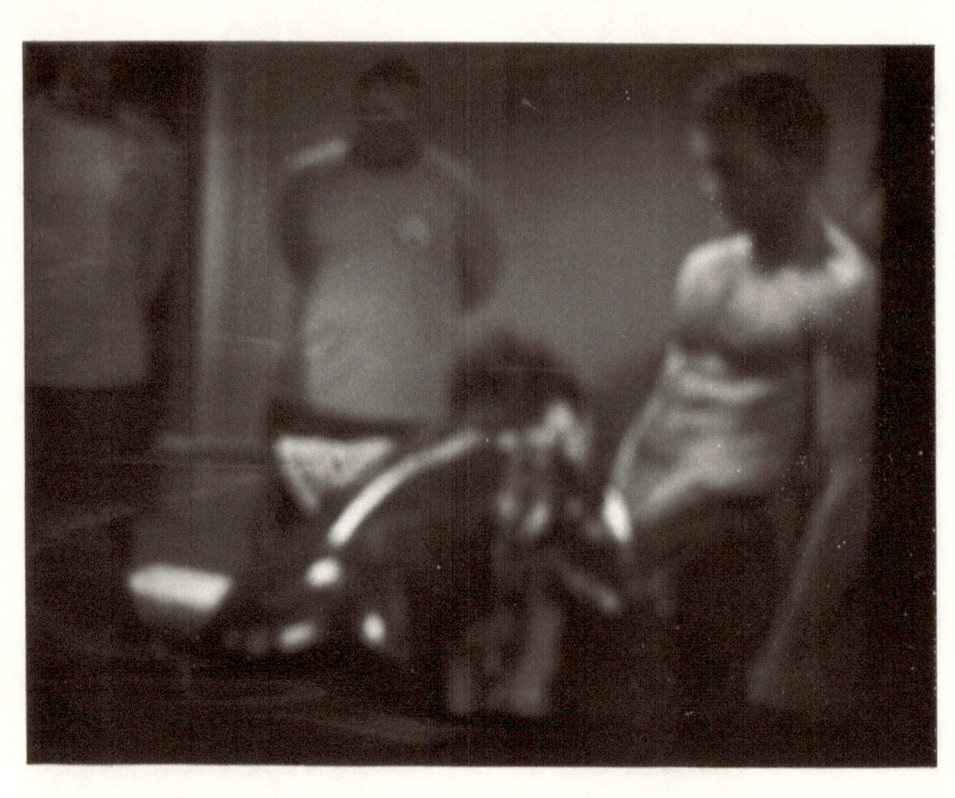

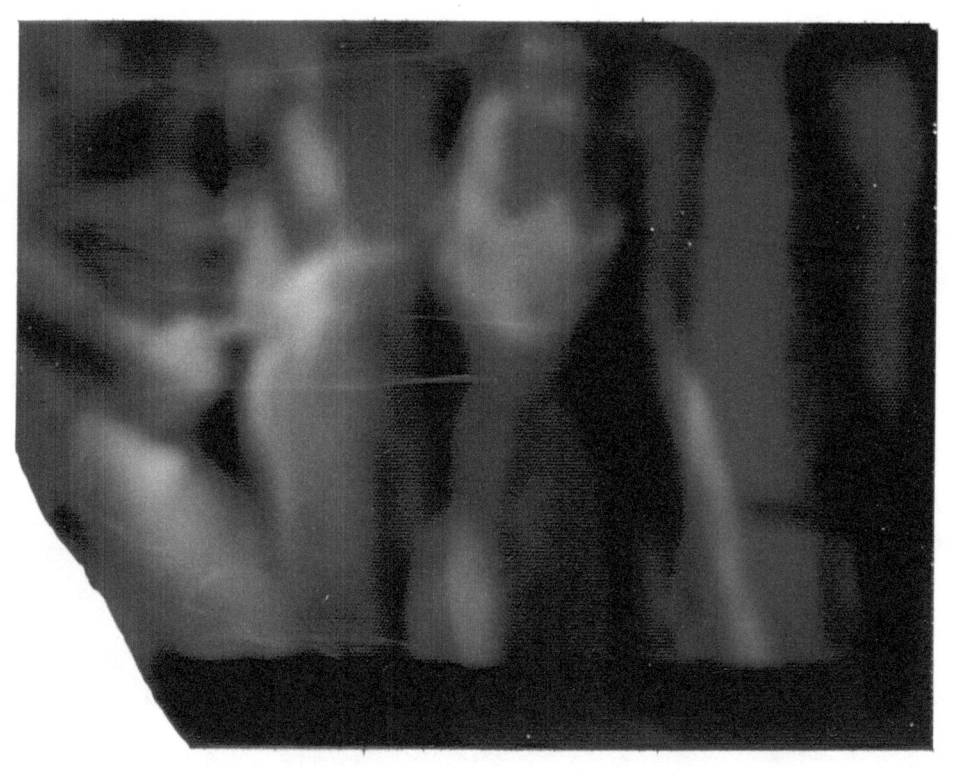

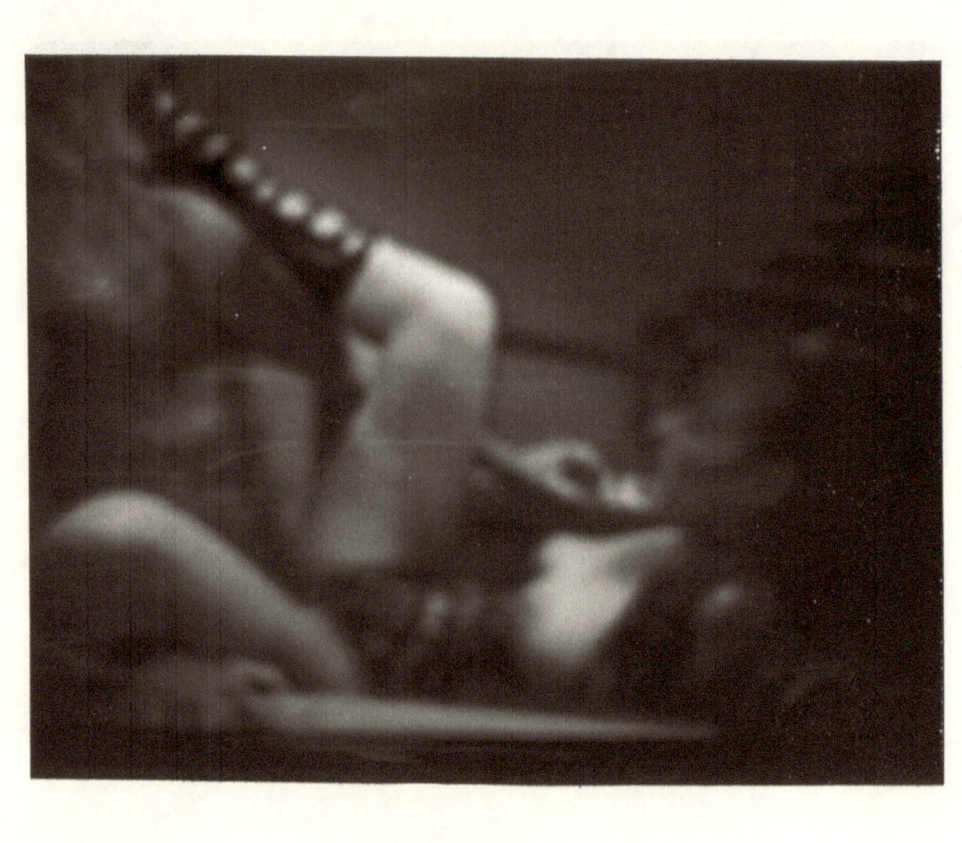

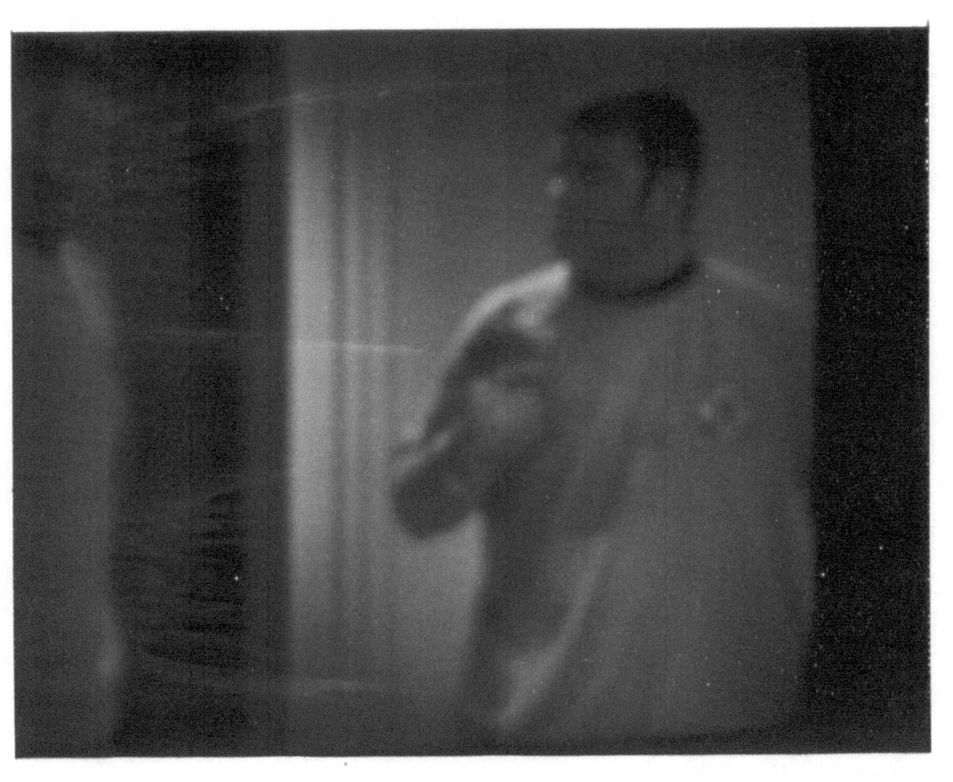

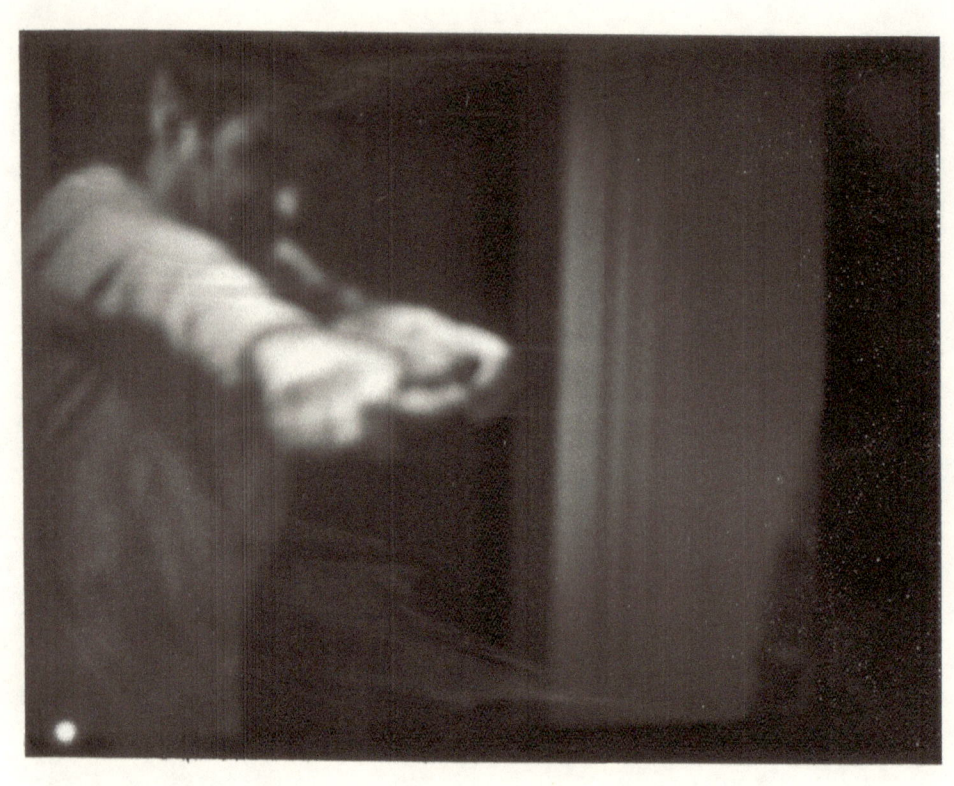

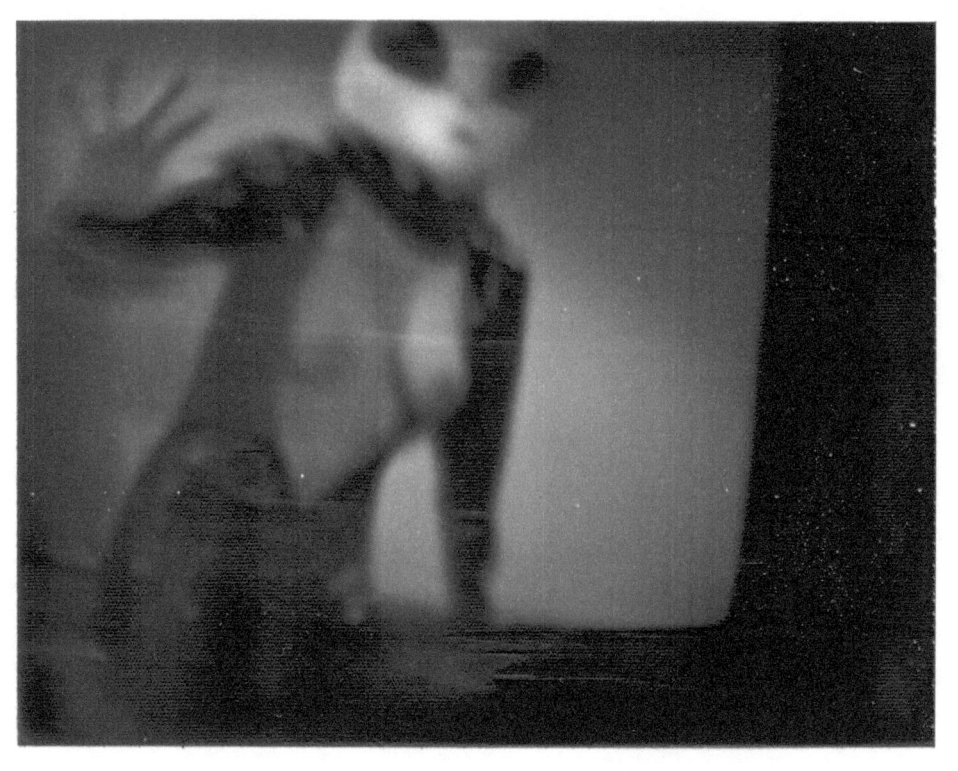

MASTERPIECE - *PRÉCIS OF A WORK UNWRITTEN*

Rob Ward

IF I WERE TO WRITE an extended article on a theme of 'Master', I would envisage the whole as a series of subheadings. In other words, I would have already worked out where the theme would lead. And although I wouldn't have much of an idea how the rhetoric of my thoughts would join up, I would assert a certain mastery of the whole thing. These would be my title chapter headings:

The Master's Craft
Mastery and Mediocrity
Mastery and (Miss)tery
Master/Slave
Master and Copy
Pragmatics of Mastery
Mastering Heuristics
The Ignorant Master
Drawing without a Master
The Unknown Masterpiece
Doing without a Master
The Master's Speech
Viva Voce
Masterstroke, or, Aphasia of Know-How

THE MASTER'S CRAFT

This would amount to a hermeneutics within a 'community of shared semeiosis' (Eco 1995). The 'crafts' we describe amount to the skills we employ in articulating our words, our things and operating a 'knowing sensibility' – something we would once have called (and some would still call) aesthetics. Some things only work when technical mastery has been achieved (a Beethoven piano sonata could only be what it is when all the right notes are played by someone who not only knows which are the right notes but can play them without looking at either musical score or indeed the keyboard, and can play the right notes with a feeling for how they should be played). This craft of 'interpretation', however, is different from the idea of mastery of a creative form in a modern or postmodern era of art. Other descriptions vie for the accolade of quality and often turn on the idea of novelty, spectacle or its opposite form of banality. Skill, as an aggregation over time, becomes 'skill as a means to an effect'. The community that interprets mastery has shifted from the closed guild to the open agora.

MASTERY AND MEDIOCRITY

This would follow on from the previous heading. Whilst the term 'mastery' might now flounder in its attempt to be robustly applied, there is an implied recognition of mediocrity, that is, something that in its conception, its manifestation avoids the epithet 'wrong' but fails to accomplish; fails to satisfy. There is a sense that superficially there is something valid yet there is an established opinion that nothing of significance has been achieved – that there has possibly been a lost opportunity. Even so, there is a kind of mediocrity that stands for mediocrity — that makes it ironical. How is one to distinguish between mediocrity and a kind of mastery of the means to mimic that which is mediocre? The greater the mastery of mimicry, the more convincing the mediocrity.

MASTERY AND (MISS)TERY

Already gendered. Research done already and more into how throughout Western art, master and his model predominate. Dominus. Mystification. Virgin and Child, Adam and Eve, Europa and bull, Rape of the Daughters of Leucippus, Rape of Prosperine, Rape of the Sabine Women. Woman of Canaan, Woman with the Issue of Blood, Woman of Samaria, Woman Taken in Adultery, Women of Jerusalem, Women at the Tomb. Ubiquitous Odalisques full of Eastern promise.

MASTER/SLAVE

Hegelian encounter. Two consciousnesses; why do they fight? 'Since to begin with they are unequal and opposed, and their reflection into a unity has not yet been achieved, they exist as two opposed shapes of consciousness; one is the independent consciousness whose essential nature is to be for itself, the other is the dependent consciousness whose essential nature is simply to live or be for another. The former is lord, the other is bondsman' (Hegel 1807:115). Why do they need to try to subdue? Because they are 'primal' and primal means that they have to fight. That is how it looks. That is how it looked to Hegel, to Darwin.

MASTER AND COPY

'Some properties of an object may be essential to it, in that it could not have failed to have them. But these properties are not used to identify the object in another possible world, for such an identification is not needed. Nor need the essential properties of an object be the properties used to identify it in the actual world, if indeed it is identified in the actual world by means of properties' (Kripke 1981:53).

PRAGMATICS OF MASTERY

Know-how and know-what. Constructivist teaching 'if knowledge is conceptualized as a cognitive state, then instruction is thought of as instructional strategies designed to affect one's schemas.' Thompson, *Running Head*.

MASTERING HEURISTICS

How does one know when one is a master — when or whether one has achieved 'mastery'? James Elkins (2001) deals with the paradoxical nature of master/student assessment/dialogue in 'crits'. First, we don't know how we teach art, and so we cannot claim to teach it or to know what teaching might be like. This may sound odd...— ... but it's my experience that studio instruction teachers and students accept some informal version of it (2001:91). He describes 'crits' as '(U)nbelievably difficult to understand and rich with possibilities. All kinds of meanings, all forms of understandings, can be at issue.' He concludes with the admission that 'they just barely make sense — they are nearly totally irrational' (2001:166).

THE IGNORANT MASTER

Jacques Rancière's assertion of heuristic learning has counterparts with Gadamer's creatively 'prejudiced' hermeneuticist in that they are motivated. The three assertions are:
'All men have equal intelligence'
'Every man has received from god the ability to instruct himself'
'Everything is in everything'

DRAWING WITHOUT A MASTER

Doré's engraved cartoon showing two ragamuffins drawing on a wall the caption reading: ''Drawing without a master, on Madame Cave's method.' N.B.

— The style was applied on the walls of Paris long before the lady inventor was born.' This text could be envisaged as graffiti on an academic wall in that its mastery of certain 'marks and moves' is without a Master — a certain skill — call it rhetorical — but also a vast ignorance — often a combination of the two that promotes arrogance. This ignorance, in itself, isn't inimical to the project. There are always heuristic possibilities, always things to say, but by whom is one allowed to speak? (Rancière on Plato's 'four citizens').

THE UNKNOWN MASTERPIECE

The title of the short story by Balzac published in 1831 and again in 1837. The first version he called a 'conte fantastique', the second a 'philosophical' work. The deranged Frenhofer in the first version becomes the possessed genius in the second — an inspiration for those (from Cézanne to de Kooning) who read into him the idea that pure genius transcended skill and that true mastery could never be recognised by the 'ordinary' senses of men. Frenhofer's masterpiece, a portrait of Catherine Lescault, the courtesan known as *La Belle Noiseuse*, appears to be only 'colours piled upon one another in confusion and held in restraint by a multitude of curious lines which form a wall of painting' (Ashton 1980:7).

DOING WITHOUT A MASTER

Pragmatics of *laissez-faire*. Isn't this what happens in a 'teaching studio'. The 'master' latches onto what the student is doing — often in passing — out of curiosity as opposed to a wilful determination to impose a rule, a decisive thought. In this scenario, the master 'glides over' the student. Both are released from gravity; both float freely without each other's sphere of influence. The student needs the master only in so far as (s)he can internalise a reciprocal dialogue, the master needs the student in order to internalise a hierarchical dialogue. The art student 'does', the master 'waits'.

THE MASTER'S SPEECH

This would invoke Derrida's deconstruction of logocentrism (the privileging of speech over writing). In this sense there is no mastery of speech as the addressee takes part in the possibilities of dissemination. There is no definitive 'meaning'. This surely has consequences for hermeneutics. If a 'grounding' for a provisional hermeneutics isn't forthcoming then there can be no extension to an horizon that could emanate from a position because a position is 'posited' from an interpretation of that position. Mastery in this sense is an attempt at a provisional control over the things that words make.

VIVA VOCE

The master's voice. The rhetoric of mastery. Dissensus/habitus and cultural capital. What do you mean? What do I mean now that you have misrepresented what I meant? What if your (mis)representation was more productive than what at first seemed to be what I intended? Hesitation and stuttering. Unimagined production of misunderstanding leading to fruitful dialogue. Or, for instance, missing the opportunity, as when Proust met Joyce, when Derrida encountered Gadamer. There is a well known film animation by Jan Švankmajer called *Dimensions of Dialogue* (1982) which is in three parts. The third is entitled *Exhausting Dialogue*. In it two highly realistic but pugnacious clay heads face one another, eyes made of glass bulge as each challenges the other. The first opens his mouth and out pops a toothbrush. The other counter-attacks — out of his mouth protrudes a tube of toothpaste that squirts onto the bristles. The next object to come out of the mouth of the first head is a chunk of bread and again the opponent offers a knife with butter which is spread over it. The sequence continues: shoe/laces, pencil/pencil sharpener. The sequence is repeated but where each object offered is responded to by an incongruous counterpart so that bread gets toothpaste, brush is 'sharpened' with the pencil sharpener, shoe is plastered with butter and pencil is tied up with a shoe lace. The sequence is repeated with more incongruous permutations until thoroughly exhausted, the heads echo each other's offering with the same object: Shoe attacks shoe, laces tie up laces, bread crunches into bread butter butters butter toothbrushes grind each other's bristles away, toothpaste tubes clash together in an ejaculation of dental cream, pencils splinter each other and sharpeners paradoxically sharpen each other away.

MASTERSTROKE, OR, APHASIA OF KNOW-HOW

⊨♉▷ ⇦♉ ▷⇦ ⇦◣▲△⇦▽▽ ♉▶△ ↓↔↔⇦△↘♉▽◀
◀↑♉▶→↑◀▽˥ ⊨♉▷ ⇦♉ ▷⇦ ↘⇦▽◀⇦△ ▷↑⇦◀
▷⇦ ↗↔♉▷˥ ⊨♉▷ ⇦♉ ▷⇦ ↗↔♉▷ ◀↑⇦◀ ▷⇦
↑⇦◁⇦ ↘⇦▽◀⇦△⇦⇦ ◀↑⇦↘˥ ⊨♉▷ ⇦♉ ▷⇦
↗↔♉▷ ▷↑⇦◀ ↘⇦▽◀⇦△◢ ↓▽˥

REFERENCES

Ashton. Dore
    1980 A Fable of Modern Art. London: Thames and Hudson.
Eco, Umberto
    1995 Unlimited Semeiosis and Drift Pragmaticism vs. 'Pragmatism'.
        In Peirce and Contemporary Thought. Kenneth Laine Ketner,
        ed. Pp. 205-221. New York: Fordham University Press.
Elkins. James
    2001 Why Art Cannot be Taught: A Handbook for Art Students.
        Chicago: University of Illinois.
Hegel, GWF
    1807/1977 Phenomenology of Spirit. Trans. AV Miller. Oxford:
        Oxford University Press.
Kripke, Saul
    1981 Naming and Necessity. Malden, US: Blackwell Publishing.
Rancière, Jacques
    2004 The Philosopher and his Poor. Trans. Parker, A. Durham, North
        Carolina: Duke University Press.
Švankmajer, Jan
    1982 Dimensions of Dialogue. 14 mins. Krátký Film Praha.
Thompson, Kelvin
    ---- Running Head: Constructivist Curriculum Design. Constructivist
        Curriculum Design for Professional Development: A Review of
        the Literature. Orlando, University of Central Florida. http://
        pegasus.cc.ucf.edu/~kthompso/projects/lit_constructivist.pdf.
        Accessed March 2010.

MINISTRY of
DEFENSE
FROM PEACE ISLAND

THE MINISTRY OF DEFENSE
(A WORK IN PROGRESS)

Danny Hoffman

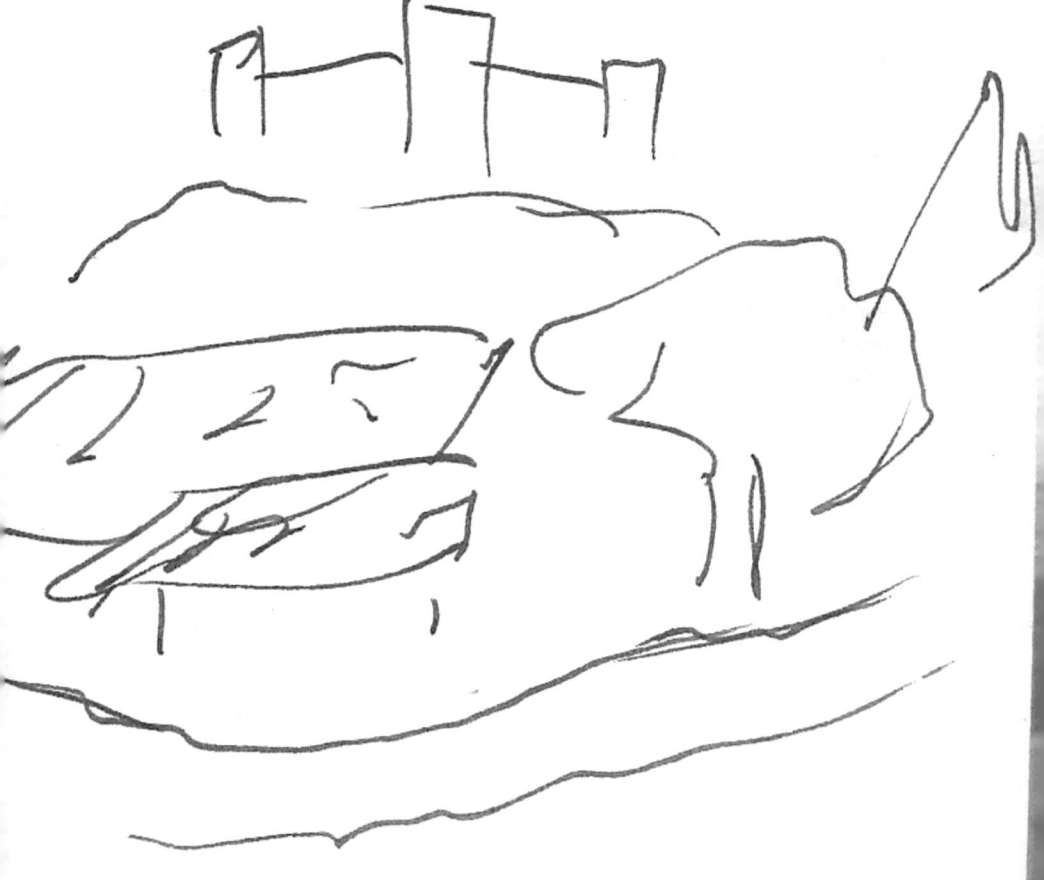

"ARCHITECTURE OR REVOLUTION. / Revolution can be avoided." The radical conclusion to Le Corbusier's 1924 *Toward an Architecture* – arguably the most significant text of architecture's Modern movement – announces a project of global social and political design. Le Corbusier's aphorism actually invokes two revolutions: the revolution in human habitation that he helped to inaugurate, and the political revolution he hoped to avoid by doing so. Today both of these 'revolutions' are woven into the fabric of many, perhaps all, postcolonial cities. Certainly, as Nnamdi Elleh (1997:72) points out, the so-called International Style of modernist architecture dominates the built form of African urbanism. And those forms are inextricably bound to sweeping projects of social and political engineering. Any consideration of the future of African cities therefore requires a reckoning with the revolutions, actual and virtual, expressed in the built forms of the past.

The Ministry of Defense is one in a series of four explorations of those forms in Monrovia, Liberia. In the aftermath of the fighting that consumed this region of West Africa from 1989 to 2003, thousands of ex-combatants remain in the Liberian capital. For almost a decade, hundreds of fighters and their dependents occupied the ruins of downtown structures, squatting in the dismantled infrastructure of the city: bank buildings, government ministries, hotels, office blocks. These buildings' modernist elements – open floor plans, non-loading bearing walls, the separation of service spaces from 'served' spaces – meant that the buildings' residents could carve and configure these structures into massive vertical settlements. Partitions made of salvaged materials created domestic spaces; large communal spaces were kept open for meetings, sports, or protests; utility spaces were appropriated for shops, bars, or private assignations. The population of Monrovia in the aftermath of the war far exceeded the capacity of the devastated city's infrastructure, and so Monrovia's residents, like those in many African cities, had to live 'beyond' the city's architecture (Rao 2009). Adaptive re-use of modernist buildings like the Ministry of Defense therefore realised Le Corbusier's "architecture or revolution" in a literal sense: it allowed for the mass housing of a militarised urban populace that might otherwise have laid more violent claims to the city.

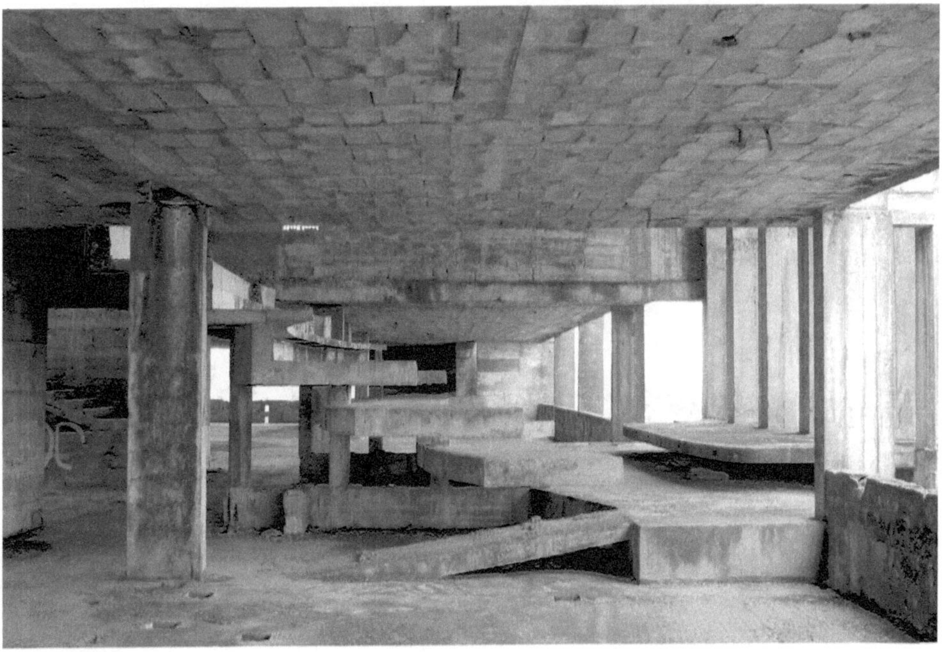

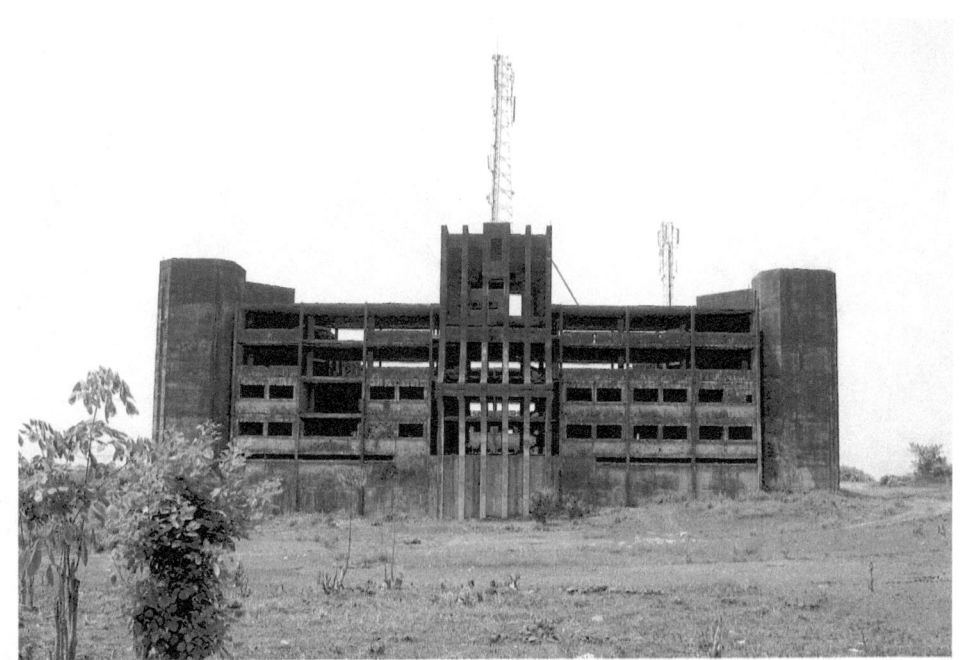

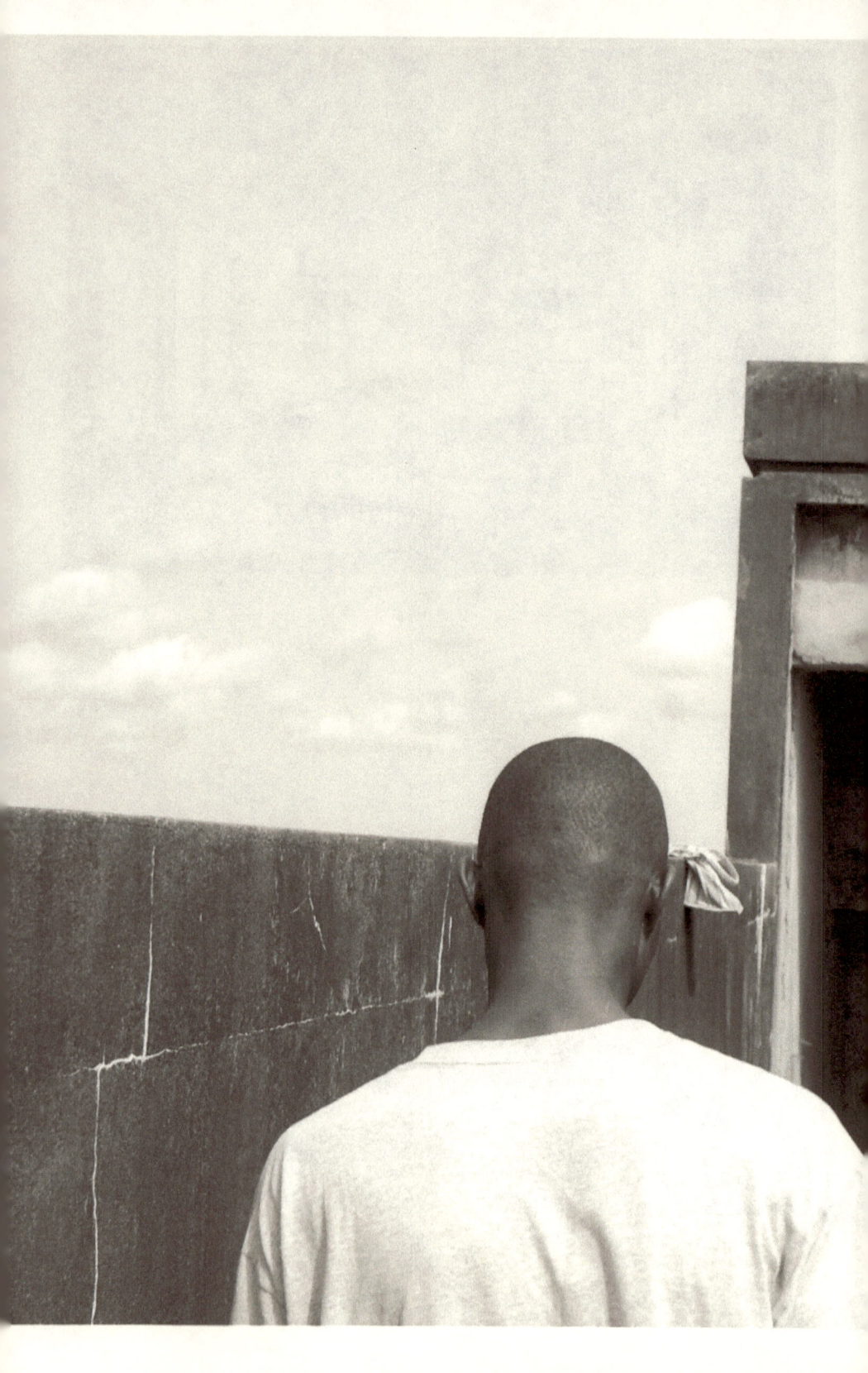

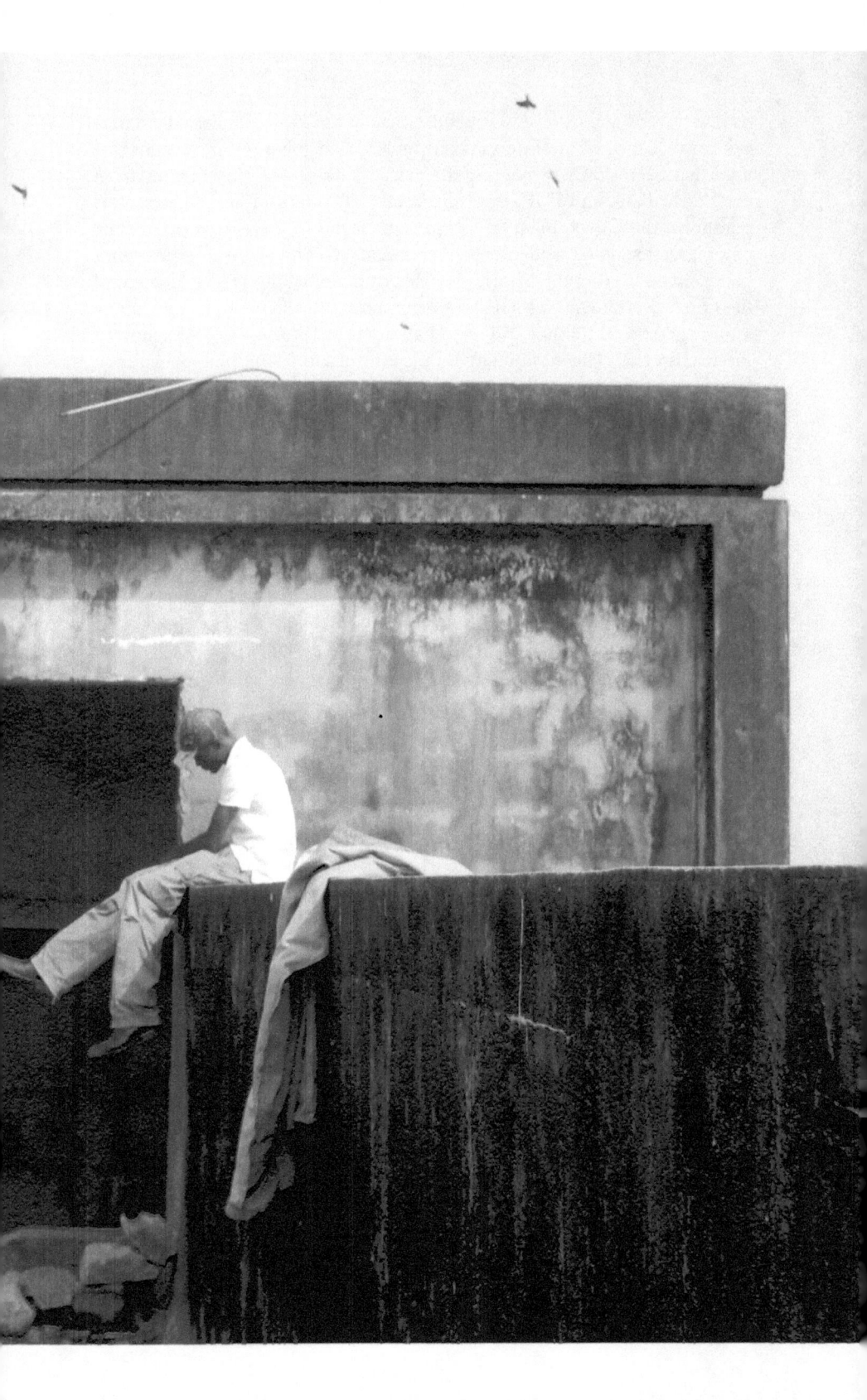

II

And yet over the past several years these buildings have manifested a different consequence of the International Style. Ellen Johnson-Sirleaf's government has been slowly reclaiming the city's architecture. With funding from the World Bank and IMF, or at the behest of American and Chinese corporations, the Government of Liberia has begun to 'develop' many of the city's largest squatter settlements. Populations of combatants and non-combatants who lived in the Ministry of Health building, the Ducor Hotel, and the Old Government Hospital have been moved out so the buildings can be refurbished or demolished. All but a handful of caretakers were evicted from the Ministry of Defense building by the end of 2011, and now the colossal structure stands empty. At present the government is undecided whether to demolish the building to make way for a Chinese-funded complex or whether to keep the structure intact.

Residents evicted from the Ministry of Defense largely ended up in the mangrove swamps behind the building, an informal settlement of some 30,000 people known ironically as Peace Island. Those removed from other structures now squat on Monrovia's beaches, in its graveyards, or in the few interstitial spaces of the city's older and more established slums.

What is striking about these mass relocations is how little opposition they met from the buildings' residents. When I spoke with ex-combatants who had made the Ministry of Defense building their home for years, they were not only unsurprised by the government's evictions but strangely supportive of them. "It's the government's building," said Major Sandi, a former soldier in the Liberian Armed Forces, when I pressed him on why residents had not fought harder against the evictions. "It should be given to the Ministry of Defense." To be sure, residents demanded compensation for vacating their homes. There was a great deal of talk about the value of occupying urban space and many efforts to calculate what a home doomed for destruction should be worth. But at a time when 'Occupy' movements were staking claims to urban space in cities around the globe, there seemed little effort to contest the use and ownership of Monrovia's built environment. The Torre David building in Caracas or the Christiana settlement in Copenhagen offer stark contrast: militant insistence on the rights of the dispossessed to space in the city. And elsewhere in Monrovia, as is true across the continent, the creative appropriation of space seems a hallmark of contemporary African urbanism. Yet in the Ministry of Defense such claims failed to materialise.

Here, then, may be a second actualisation of Le Corbusier's 'architecture or revolution'. The same modernist elements that allowed urban squatters to make these buildings livable may ultimately have made them uninhabitable in a meaningful way. This was not, in the end, an architecture in which Liberia's ex-combatants could 'dwell', to use Heidegger's term. In their own minds the residents of the Ministry of Defense never belonged in the Ministry building and never claimed the space as their own. This was not simply an artifact of the building's social and political history. Other spaces associated with the past, with the dead, or with political repression did not carry so strong a taint of the past that they could not be appropriated and inhabited anew. There seems, rather, to be something about these structures themselves that forecloses the possibility that they can be occupied in new ways. That they can be made the possession of the people, that they can be inhabited differently and fully. In this sense the Ministry of Defense represents an architecture that does, indeed, successfully avoid revolution.

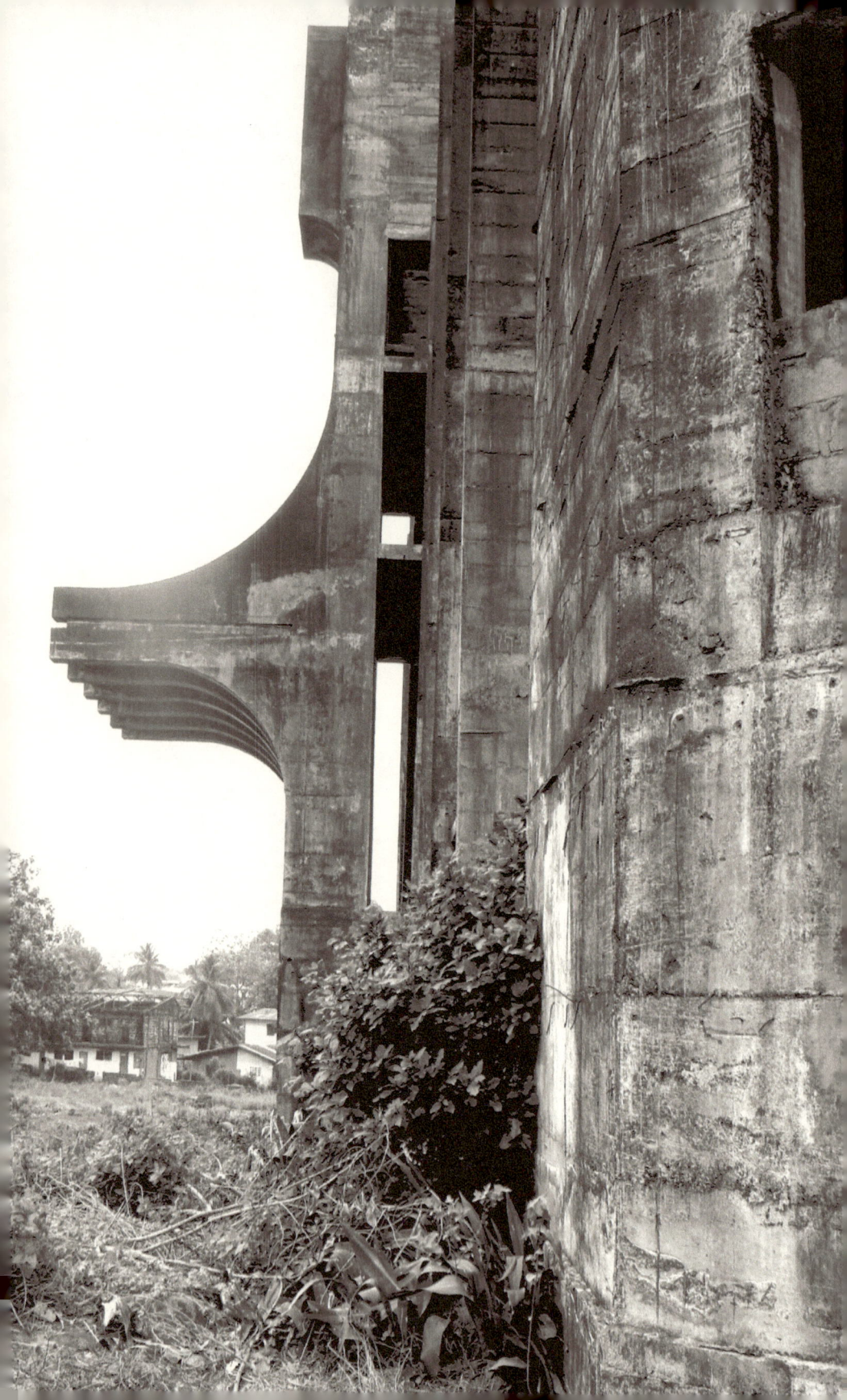

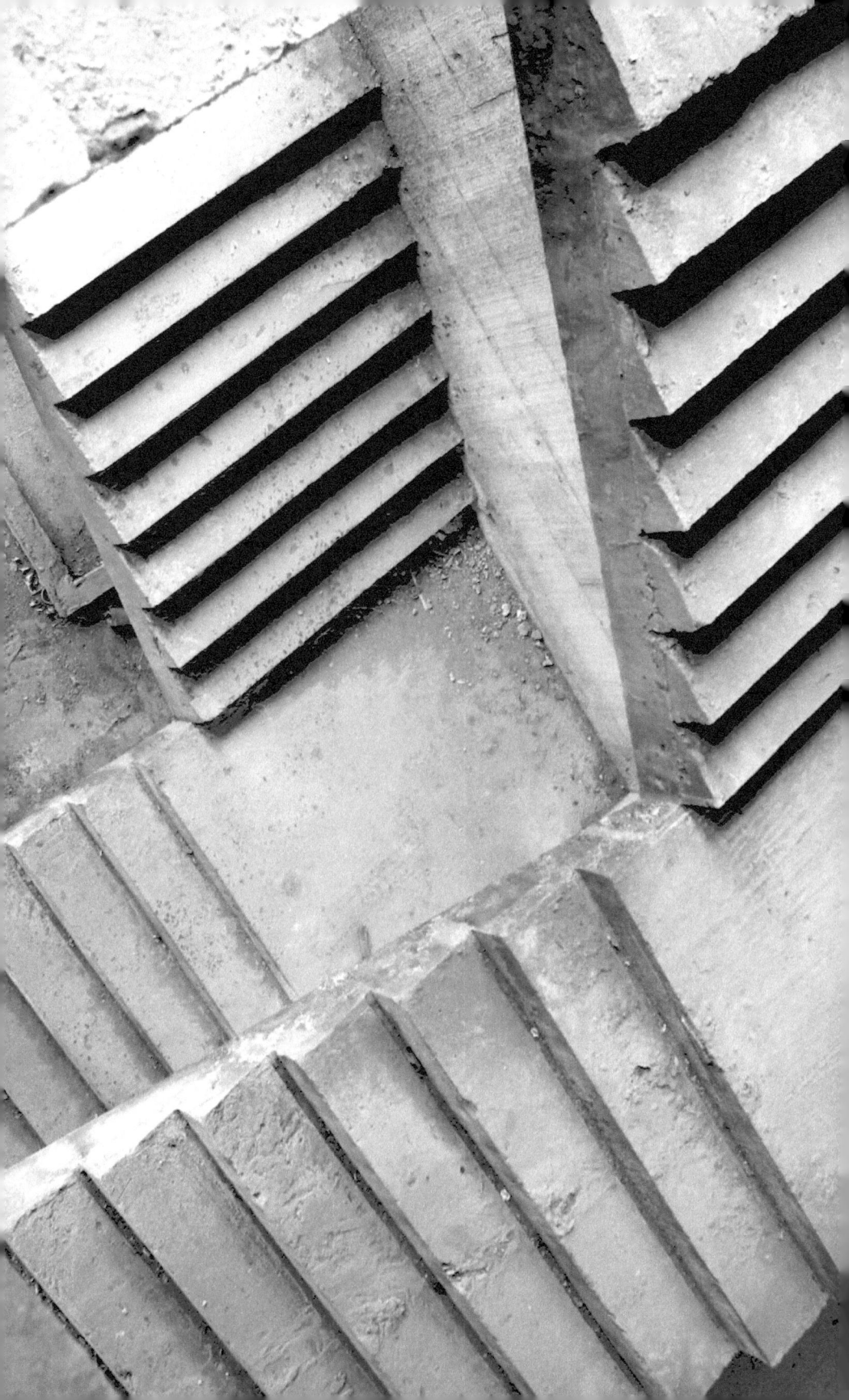

III

Photography is an integral part of this story. The camera is an agent in both the revolution in living and the revolution foreclosed by certain modernist architectural design.

At least since the end of the Second World War, the still photograph has been the primary means by which modernist architecture circulates. Designers learned about the new aesthetic primarily from photographic images in the popular and trade presses. As a consequence it was the still photograph's peculiar rendering of space that instructed architects in how to design 'modern' buildings. Wide angle lenses made the open plan of Mies van der Rohe's work appear even more vast, and the compression of telephoto images made the symmetry of columns and ceilings more pronounced. The aesthetics of the image became more and more pronounced as designers copied not buildings but images of buildings (Mostafavi and Leatherbarrow 1993:111-112; Pye 1978:66; Zimmerman 2004). By the 1950s, architects in the New Brutalist school of modernists, the aesthetic that most obviously influenced the design of Monrovia's Ministry of Defense, had begun to think of buildings as images and to design for the way their buildings would circulate in photographs (Banham 1955; Zimmerman 2012).

What's more, as the Modern movement developed in architecture, photography was an indispensible tool for convincing residents that the improbable new aesthetic was habitable at all. The photographer Julius Shulman's most famous image, of two well dressed women seemingly suspended in the night air in a glass box over Los Angeles, was primarily a visual argument that Pierre Koenig's outrageous building was safe (Shulman 1997). Photography simultaneously disciplined the residents of the new architecture in modern practices of living. The intimate scenes of domestic life in advertising images for the famous Eichler homes in California, among the first mass-produced modernist housing, were meant not only to sell the homes but to instruct home owners in how to use their unfamiliar spaces (Adamson, Arbunich, and Braun 2002).

In Brasilia, in Chandrigarh, Abuja, Dar es Salaam, and in cities across the global South, the image-logic of modernist architecture became even more pronounced, while the disciplining apparatus required to inhabit it became more fractured (see Holston 1989). The Modern movement was inextricably but unevenly bound to the project of modernisation and understandings of modernity. Le Corbusier's maxim appears ever more complex in light of the ways the image-based architecture was cathected to modernity's revolutions.

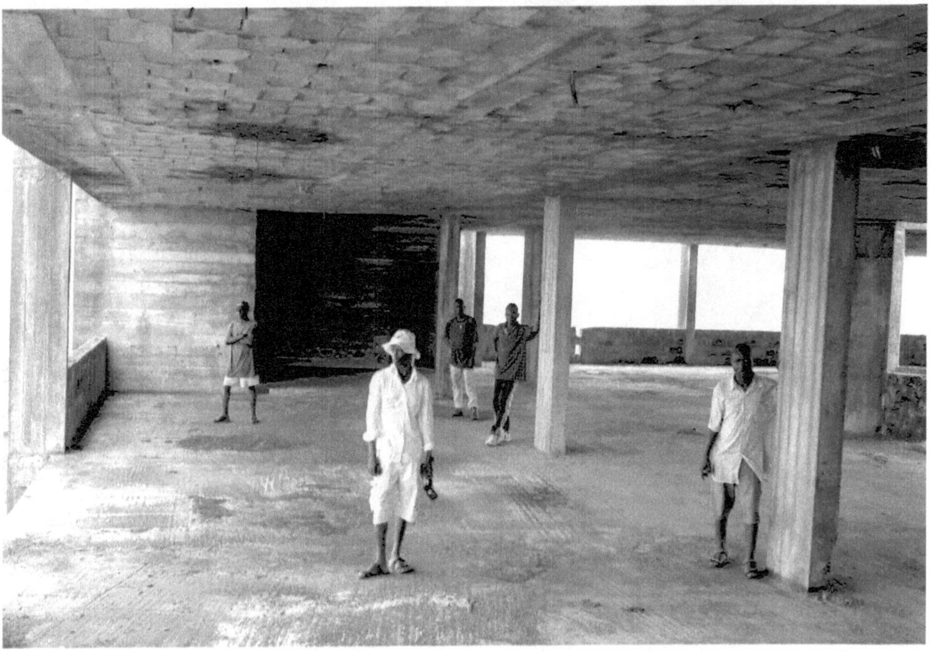

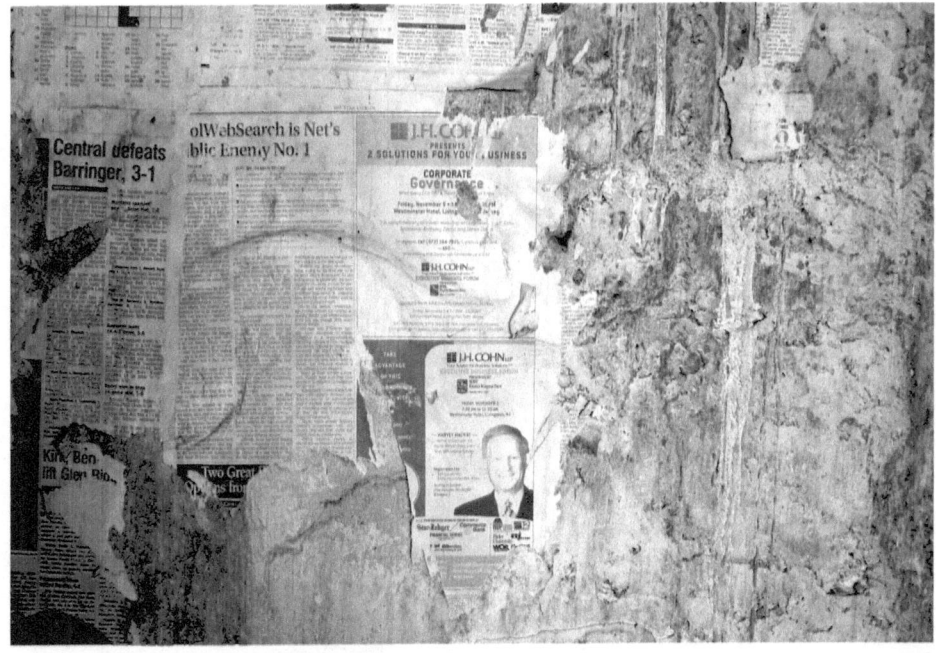

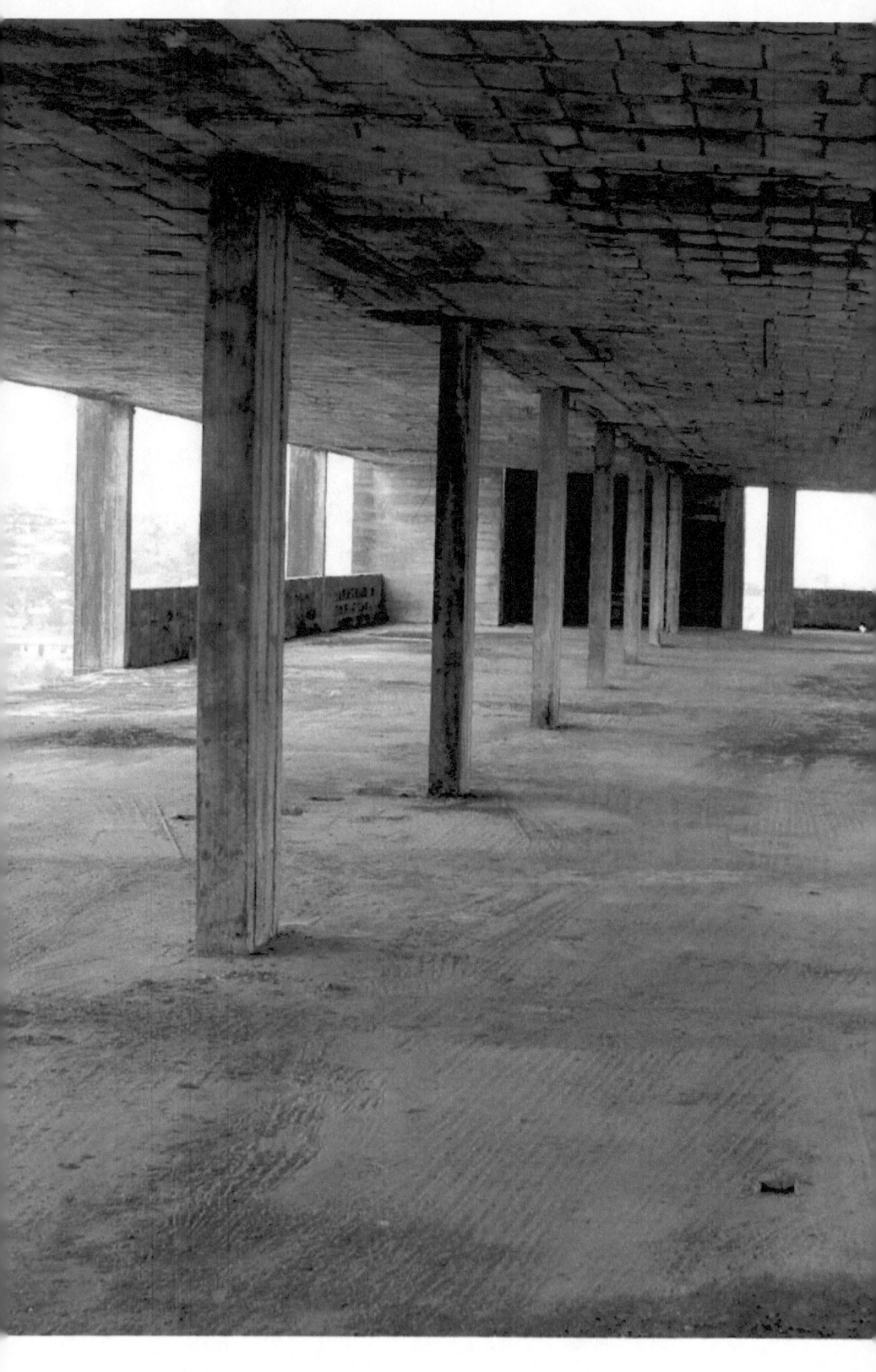

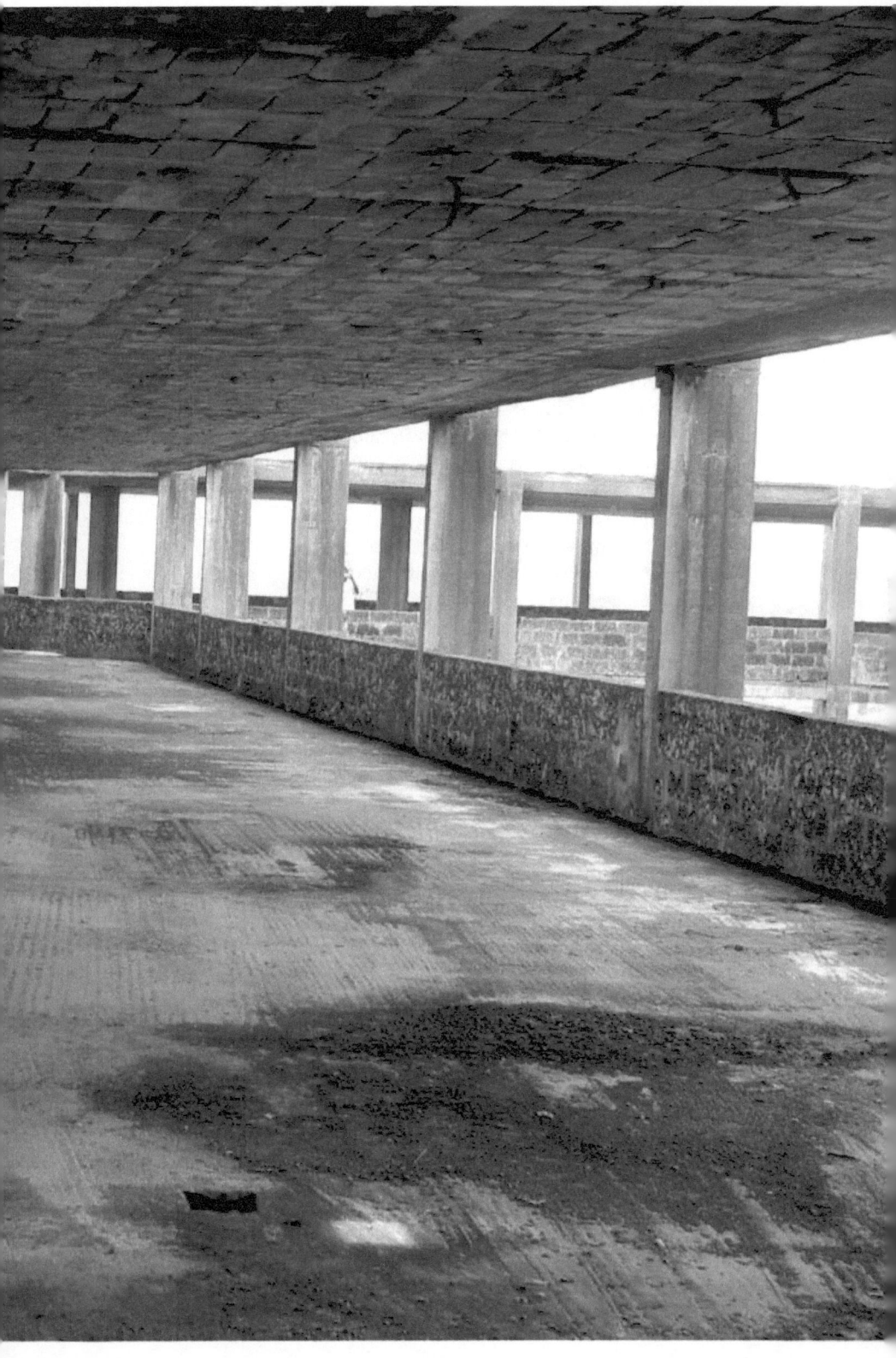

IV

The camera is therefore a unique diagnostic tool for exploring the spaces of modernist architecture. The photographs here were made in April 2012, not long after the building's residents were moved out. The project is part of my own long-standing interest in how young men's bodies and labour became part of this region's war economy, and an interest in the spaces that continue to make these men available for deployment in that economy.

The poetics of the essay are therefore not that of high modernist architectural photography with its studied lighting and its emphasis on form. That approach would have produced images that emphasise the Ministry's status as ruins, images that capitalise on the shock of seeing destruction rendered as unintended architectural art. (As, for example, in the Detroit work of Yves Marchand and Romain Meffre.) Nor is this project based on a straight documentary reportage, utilising a deliberately messy aesthetic to offer a literal (though equally shocking) depiction of its subjects' lived experience.', utilising a deliberately messy aesthetic to offer a literal (though equally shocking) depiction of its subjects' lived experience. Both are useful projects, though at this point I am unconvinced that either has the power to raise new questions about what it means to inhabit Africa's urban spaces today.

The images collected here are informed instead by a less fixed, emergent way of envisioning the built environment. Exemplified by the work of the Ivorian photographer Ananias Leki Dago, South Africa's Guy Tillim and the Dutch photographer Iwan Baan, this is a project that shifts the emphasis away from either the formal composition of built forms or the realist depiction of everyday living within them. The visual argument is a more ambiguous and ambivalent one about the ways people can and cannot inhabit constructed space. Figures in these images make reference to scale and geometry, but mostly they raise questions about what may or may not be possible in such spaces, about what may or may not come next. These are images that take seriously AbdouMaliq Simone's proposition that in African urbanism, people constitute the city's true infrastructure. But they do so by simultaneously asking what the limits to that constitution may be in an urban form like the Ministry of Defense. The camera becomes a tool for exploring the conceptual boundaries imposed by structures scaled to accommodate photography rather than the human form. A tool for seeing spaces sculpted to appear monumental in two dimensions rather than inhabited in three.

The camera becomes, in short, a means of exploring the complex relationship between architecture and revolution.

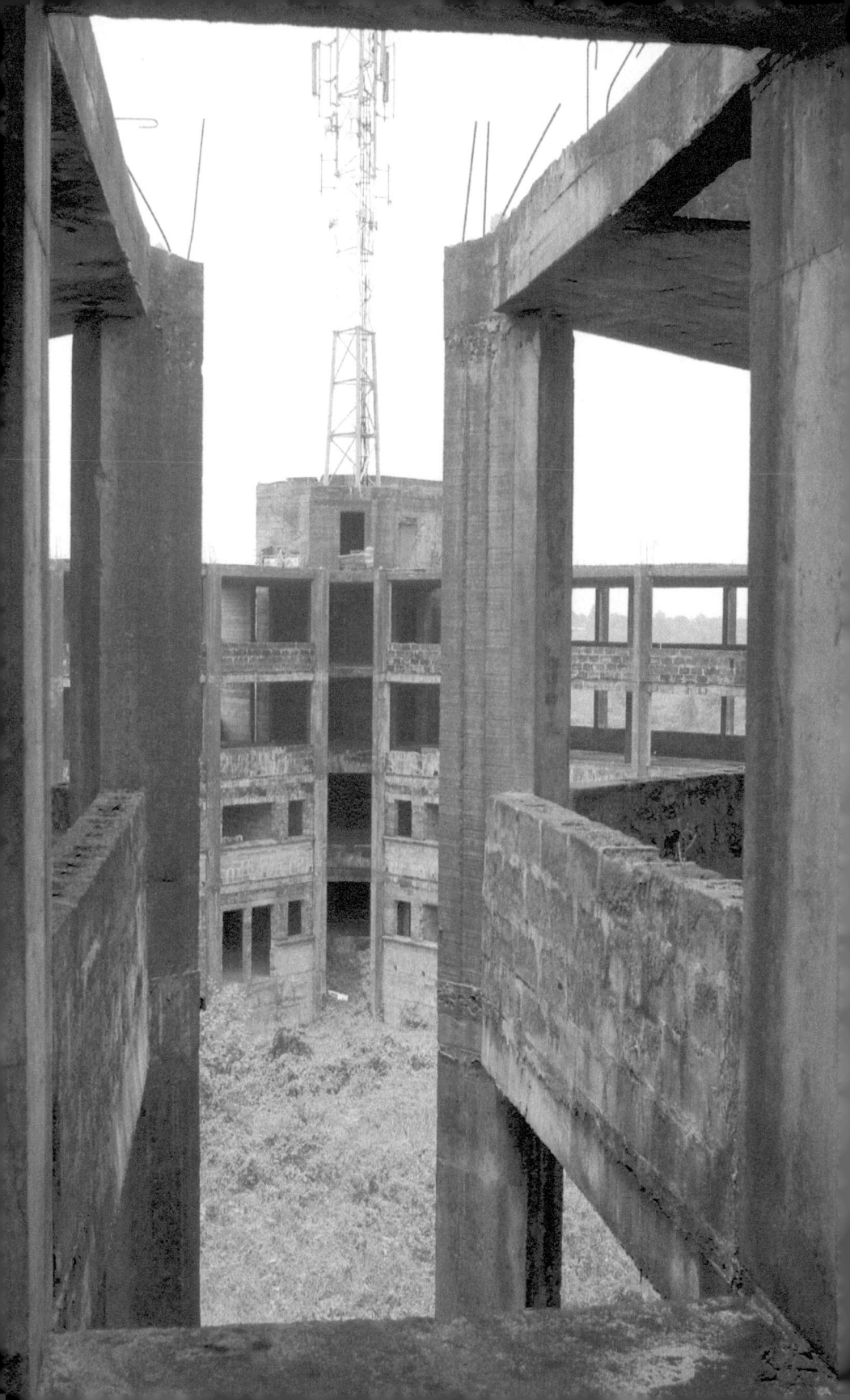

REFERENCES

Adamson, Paul, Marty Arbunich and Ernie Braun.
  2002 Eichler: Modernism Rebuilds the American Dream. Salt Lake
    City: Gibbs Smith.
Banham, Reyner
  2011/1955 The New Brutalism. October 136:19-28.
Elleh, Nnamdi
  1997 African Architecture: Evolution and Transformation. New York:
    McGraw Hill.
Holston, James
  1989 The Modernist City: An Anthropological Critique of Brasilia.
    Chicago: University of Chicago Press.
Le Corbusier
  2007/1924 Toward an Architecture. London: Francis Lincoln
    Limited.
Mostafavi, Mohsen and David Leatherbarrow
  1993 On Weathering. Boston: MIT Press.
Pye, David
  1978 The Nature and Art of Workmanship. Cambridge: Cambridge
    University Press.
Rao, Vyjayanthi
  2009 Urbanism beyond Architecture: African cities as Infrastructure,
    Conversation with AbdouMaliq Simone and Filip de Boeck.
    African Studies Reader. 1:23-40.
Shulman, Julius
  1997 The Fear of Architecture: A Photo-Essay. *In* Nan Ellin, ed.
    Architecture of Fear. New York: Princeton Architectural Press.
Simone, AbdouMaliq
  2004 People as Infrastructure: Intersecting Fragments in
    Johannesburg. Public Culture 16(3):407-429.
Zimmerman, Claire
  2004 Photographic Modern Architecture: Inside 'The New Deep'.
    The Journal of Architecture 9(3):331-354.
  2012 Photography Into Building in Post-War Architecture: The
    Smithsons and James Stirling. Art History 35(2):270-287.

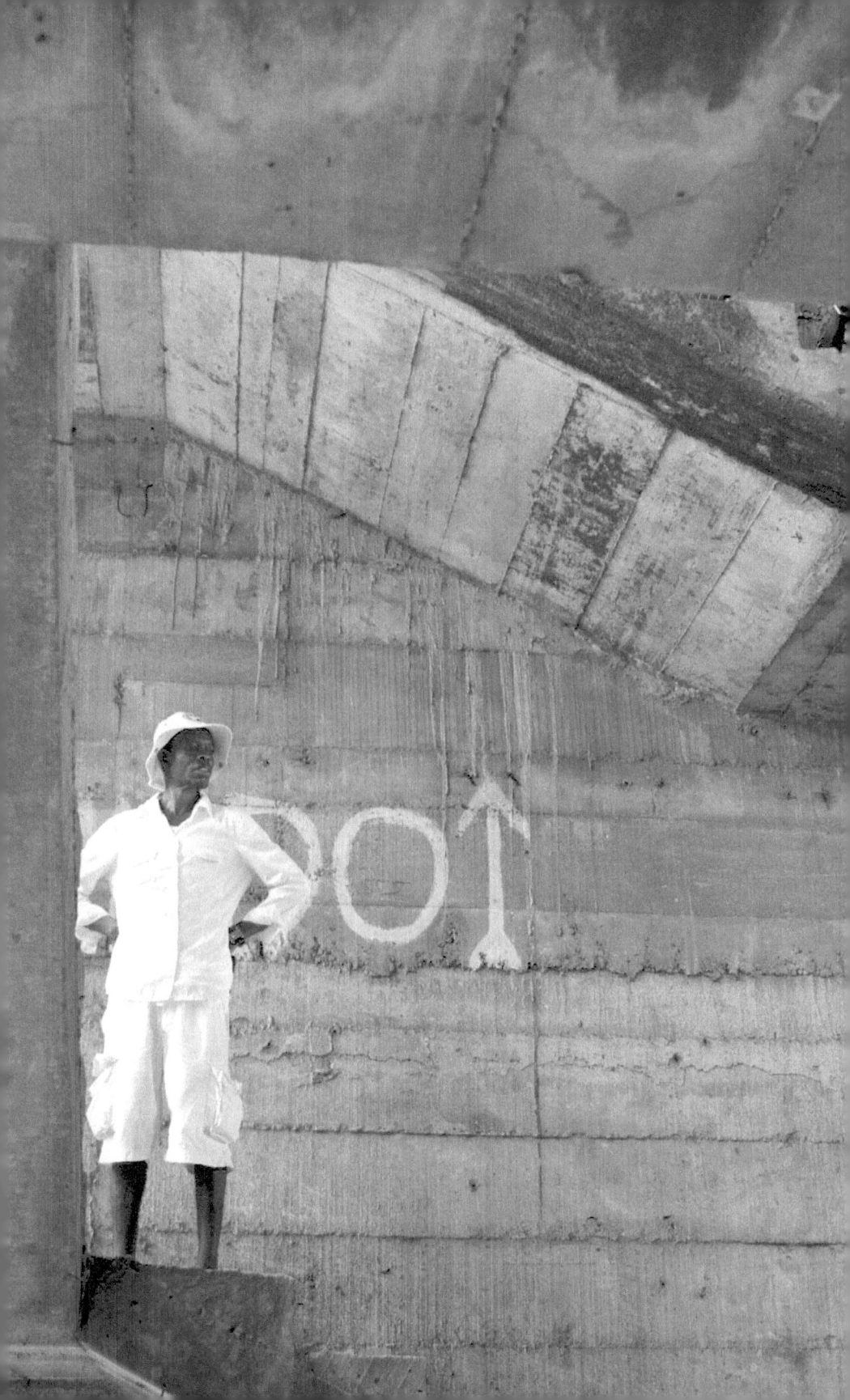

Text written as a response to Cris Brodahl's The Papers
Want To Know *(2009, oil on glued linen, 63 x 42cm)*

THE PAPERS WANT TO KNOW

Yannis Tsitsovits

quietly, through the silent flute's breath of
your throat, your swan song ripples out / the thin
long neck growing a neck / the wan white skin
revealing skin (revealing more than you

had bargained for). The nacre in your old
shell-self must out / newly-found flesh be loosed
from underneath your face's prepuce (and
so pared back, all excess will unfold like

cast-off bandages). Being bound up in
this hot rush, the taut thrill of the membrane,
your focus fixes
                        on the sky (as though
wild dogs or fire were leaping at your thighs)
but you will never be complete, nor I
be pure, until I splay you from inside

TORRENCE & FRIENDS

Steve Gronert Ellerhoff

ASHER CLASPED HIS FIVE-YEAR-OLD HANDS like a primary share holder en route to a board meeting, riding in his three-wheel stroller towards the back of the store. Arriving at the train table in time to immerse himself without the distraction of idiots each morning was an exercise in herding his mother. If he could only count the number of times he had to spur the woman, both verbally and with shinwhaps, to finish folding the laundry, to clean up breakfast, to drive, drive, drive, to hurry up with his car seat and get the stroller out of the trunk… It had happened before, them arriving seconds after the store opened to find some toddling nobody having his or her ignorant way with the little wooden trains, trains with distinct names and personalities which apparently bore no credence to anyone but Asher. Even his fool of a mom couldn't tell them apart. For years he tried to educate her in distinguishing all eighty-six from one another but none stuck, save boy blue Torrence. His patience had waned. It was too late for her.

Today the table stood unoccupied, ignored even by the redheaded clerk hung over at the adjacent wind-ups counter.

"You have to go potty first?"

Asher ignored her and vaulted from his stroller, making for the table's low edge like a natural born engineer. The circuitous wooden tracks, bridges, stations, and three-stall roundhouse, encapsulated in two and a half by four feet the steam-powered Isle of Sooter, beloved by children whose parents were convinced public broadcasting rendered less damage than network TV, or, God forbid, cable. Every element existed grossly out of scale without a single human on all the island, its painted mountains attempting to mask its perfect flatness. Despite the lack of citizenry, and subsequently any need for a railway system, the trains abounded, anthropomorphised with plenty of coal to haul for hauling's sake.

Asher lowered his dimpled chin and narrowed his eyes. First thing was to place each tossed engine and derailed car back on its wheels, undoing the carelessness wrought by the last titan to hold sway over Sooter. Setting the playboard anew, as if for a game of chess, he found Mr. Harris Jefferson, patriarch of the Petticoat Pandas of Palatial Plantations, lying under the red-arched suspension bridge. Whether playing toll troll or down-n-out hobo, he had no place on the island. Asher threw the flocked figurine hard over his shoulder.

"No throwing," Mom said into her mass-market paperback.

The sun had risen over the Isle of Sooter, bringing another morning like untold mornings before, and Torrence was up with it, hauling his tender with that cemented smile on his face. Elton, George, and Graham were still asleep in the roundhouse, older and stupider than him. They were rule fol-lowers, slowpoke engines low on steam in neverending need of maintenance. Yes, Torrence was the only one with any idea of how to get coal – in a timely fashion – to where it needed to be. And so it was, up early as usual, going about his business.

But there was a plot against him. The newfangled diesel engines, led by boxy Hardwicke, wanted to retire the steam engines to a school on the main-land where humans would use them to learn railway work. Torrence, who was too smart for school, was so good at his job that their every plot so far had failed. But that didn't stop them trying. And so Hardwicke, carting a tender of dynamite that looked like coal but really was dynamite—it was dynamite with coal on top to hide it—chug-a-lugged under a bridge Torrence was about to cross and detached his load and kept going and then when Torrence sped overhead, crossing the bridge, Hardwicke exploded it!

Asher wrenched the bridge section free, snapping it from its glued bond to the table.

Torrence soared through the air, back flipping, the bridge crashing down under him, his tender blown clear back to China, which was on the other side of the world. And Hardwicke giggled.

And Torrence, wasting no time, sounded his whistle in the special distress call.

"TOOT TOOT TOOOOOOOOOT!"

Luckily, Rob and Daniel, twin engines who hauled rock at Silurian Quarry, heard his cry and choo-chooed over fast as they could. They got under him and shot up their steam together to make a cloud to—

Another child, spooky, in overalls with dull rings around his eyes, approached the table.

And the steam made a sort of cushion that Torrence—

The spooky little kid rummaged through the train yard and picked up Finnegan, the caboose, examining his undercarriage.

That Torrence—

He dropped Finnegan, reached over, and took Daniel. Asher snatched Daniel out of his fool hand and the intruder, irritatingly unbothered, side-stepped closer and took Rob.

"Oop!" its creepy dad sounded from above. "Looks like someone busted that bridge."

Mommy sat wearily in the one folding chair provided for weary parents and stirred the contents of her purse, plastic clacking, keys jangling. The revolting dad stooped over the table and slotted the bridge aright.

Not to be upstaged by a twerp or a twerp's dad, Asher clamped Torrence and Daniel between his fingers in one hand and grabbed Rob away, staring the little one down.

"Asher. Sharing."

He transferred Rob to his full hand and cradled the three engines to his chest before making an offer. "You can be Hardwicke," he said, nudging at the villainous, gray diesel engine.

His adversary denied the fruit-bearing olive branch with an empty blink and fiddled about again with the red caboose.

"How old's your boy?"

"How old are you, Asher?"

The dad who needn't exist at all was grinning at him with a mouth where each tooth was its own colour, like an ear of peaches-n-cream sweetcorn. The corners stretched way back, revealing blue-grey metal bits of dental work. His son crabwalked along the table, shoving right in front of Asher, pausing a step before scooting on.

"My boy's three, aren't ya, Egan?"

The intruder's attention didn't break from the island, impervious to distraction. Oblivious to the function and habits of trains, he went to banging Finnegan upside down against the tracks.

"Asher's five."

"Oh hey! He in kindygarten?"

"This fall."

"Duh, makes sense. If he were in school, he'd be in school!"

Brow crossed, Asher set down Rob, then Daniel, then Torrence, and made for Finnegan. The little one suddenly had quite the grip, no amount of tugging proving strong enough, so he forced the caboose and the hand attached to it to the rails. Aligning the wheels with the grooves was like shoving like-poled magnets together. He pressed cruelly against the toddler's resistance. He jerked the caboose back and forth.

"It goes like this," he threatened.

He held down the spooky little baby's hand until it slackened. Asher eased off. The tot went on rolling Finnegan back and forth, back and forth, back and forth. Set thus on cruise control, he went back to work, dismantling the bridge again and laying it on its side.

"Come here often? Heh…"

"He has the table and everything at home but won't touch it," she complained. "We have to come here."

He made himself take a breath.

Torrence was still falling, falling through the air, plummeting to the fast-approaching ground. Rob and Daniel's little steam spouts had gone up and vanished, not strong enough to catch the skythrown engine. They wheezed, watching helplessly. But Torrence—

"Guess you won't be here so much once he's in school though."

Torrence wasn't scared. He saw the impact coming, felt the pressure building in his tank. If he could—

"Course Egan doesn't have to go to school for another couple years."

An upside-down steam geyser blown at the exact, precise moment might soften—

"Whaddaya think, Egan? Wanna take over Asher's daily duty at the train table?"

Asher dropped Torrence. Warm wetness flooded his Torrence & Friends undies, coursed down his pants legs, filling his Velcro sneakers. The usurper went back to banging Finnegan senseless, the dad to grinning his piebald corny smile, while Mom sat there, her eyes closed with migraine. His face burned, his lower lip unbuckled, and he stutter-ventilated his lungs full to capacity, his whistle set to cry.

When Asher blew, clear and shrieking, the hungover clerk at the counter lifted his head, turned it the other way, and rested it down again.

Steve Willey

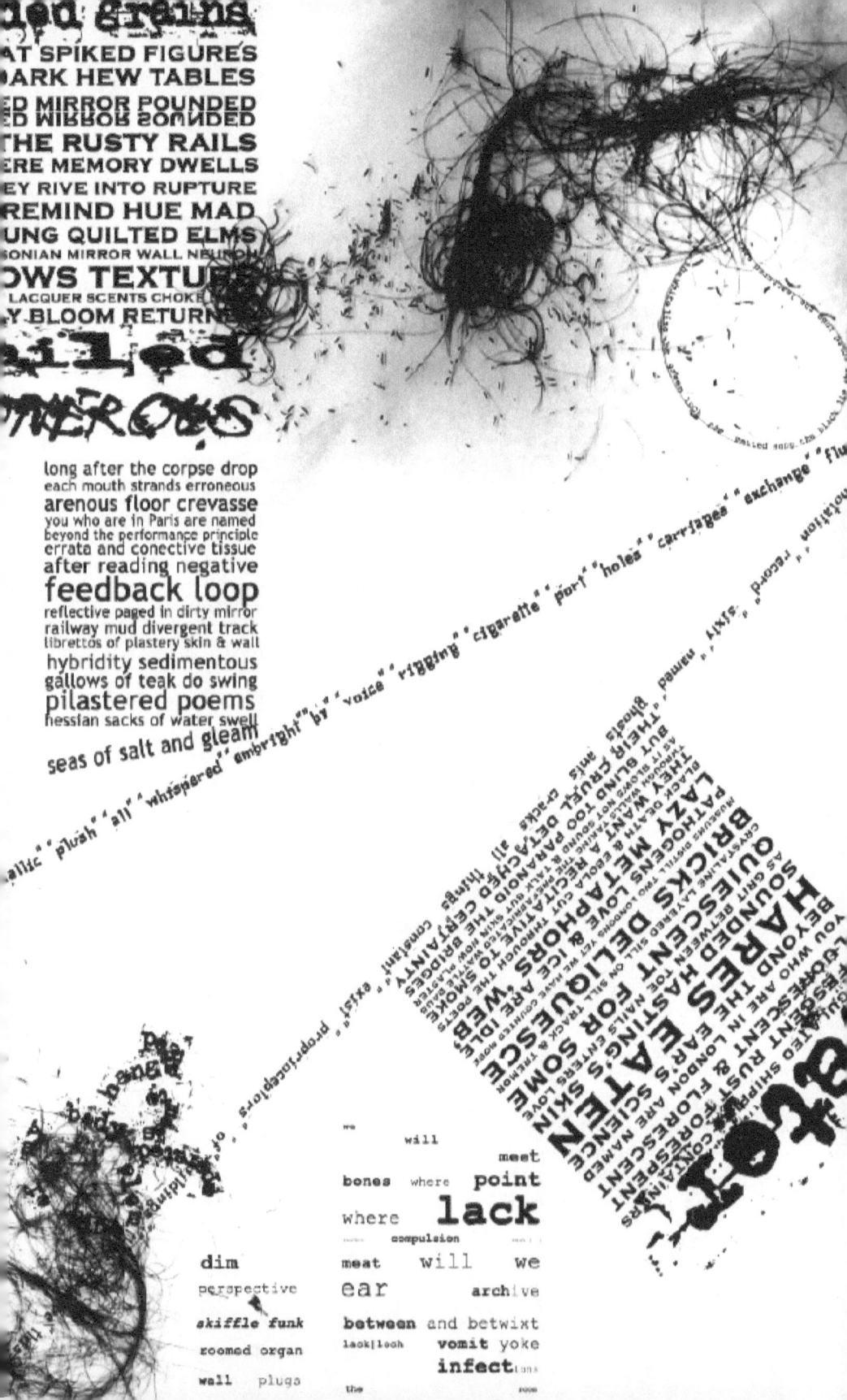

ed grains
AT SPIKED FIGURES
ARK HEW TABLES
ED MIRROR POUNDED
ED MIRROR SOUNDED
THE RUSTY RAILS
ERE MEMORY DWELLS
EY RIVE INTO RUPTURE
REMIND HUE MAD
UNG QUILTED ELMS
SONIAN MIRROR WALL NEURON
OWS TEXTURE
LACQUER SCENTS CHOKE
Y BLOOM RETURN

long after the corpse drop
each mouth strands erroneous
arenous floor crevasse
you who are in Paris are named
beyond the performance principle
errata and conective tissue
after reading negative
feedback loop
reflective paged in dirty mirror
railway mud divergent track
librettos of plastery skin & wall
hybridity sedimentous
gallows of teak do swing
pilastered poems
hessian sacks of water swell
seas of salt and gleam

will
meet
bones   where   point
where   lack
compulsion
dim   meat   will   we
perspective   ear   archive
skiffle funk   between and betwixt
roomed organ   lack||lack   vomit yoke
wall   plugs   infect

LINE BREAKS: ICONOGRAPHY

The sighting of graphite <C>
A paper [thin] dream <avatar>

... and why some travelling sheep are symbols of drawing

Phil Sawdon <© 2009>

<165>

Note ♪ to magazine (Stimulus → Respond) editors <mgmpjs>
A dream is proffered on the understanding that a reader will not stir <z>

Dérive ... we know you're only dreaming <db1972>

The proposal that pencils align with scholarly consequence and time <S R'08>
and again René's [straying pantomime] sheep wander through the <g‖aps>
in the field to check that extended field boundaries edge the cliff <WHH1852 >

$\qquad\qquad\qquad\qquad\qquad\qquad$ → Oh no they don't <baa>

Oh yes they do <baa baa>

$\qquad\qquad\qquad\qquad\qquad\qquad$ Oh no they don't <baa>

← Oh yes they do <baa baa>

Paper explores what happened to the donkey that ate the pencil <?>
and why the travelling sheep (escorted by a bear) are marked with smit <?>
Note ♪ that given an opportunity, most donkeys will bond with sheep <baa>

The sighting of graphite, a lack of definition (ambiguity) enables spaces <4>
some more concepts to graze and scratch [additional tools] in the dust <...>
... *becoming drawing an analogy ... becoming an icon* <psrmAAH'09>

Commencing in 1502 the year of a sweating sickness and some storms <dec>
Our study is ongoing and currently incorporates twelve participants <snt>
including René Hector (*humhyphenhum*), Monsieur Âne, Madame Pipe <|>
Monsieur Lièvre, Jacques Taché, a donkey (Gabriel Chêne) and 6 <an>
[pantomime] sheep <6Z>

Line breaks, allotropic dreaming and meaningful play, enhanced </BMT9>
livers, honey, and almonds, riffing pummelling percussive tattoos <400rbt>
The screams and swoops of pencil and pen as they weave in and out <of>
the mêlée spouting cosmic space prattle enable analysis to be ongoing <...>
... automatic ... to ascertain whether there is anybody inside <93keys '09>

→ *What ... pardon? ... did we learn from conducting this study* <?>

← *What ... I'm sorry? ... story are we able to tell* <?>

→ *What ... beg your pardon? ... were we able to know from this line* <?>

← *What ... could you repeat that? ... are the boundaries* <?>

→ *What ... come again? ... are the implications of our work* <?>

<risqué>

Paper supports a position ... *you shouldn't do that* <b/t1972>

< breakfreeiconoclast>

[It] argues that the discovery of Wad in the early 1500's in the Borrowdale area of Cumberland should not be constrained by the requirement of unambiguous language.

Following violent storms trees were uprooted leading to the discovery of a black material underneath. This material turned out to be graphite, and the shepherd (René Hector) initiated using it to render sheep.

[*A passing sheep bleats*] ... Réne try to fly ... you get nowhere

René Hector: [*after a small silence*]: Lamb fat, worth rendering?

There is the sound of a clock ticking and a pen scratching into dust

Monsieur Âne: [*affected and with admiration*]: Render it! You could make a couple of batches of soap with that. I've used beef, pork and duck fat for drawing so far. I heated [mon] agneau very slowly until as much liquid fat as possible ... *drip* ... *drip* ... *drip* ... had been extracted, leaving small and crisp remains.

The year might be 1502 through 1504

Jacques Taché: [*recounts*] [*spilling ink*]: We were on our fourth voyage when storms and disease forced us ashore near Seathwaite. I had a sense of apprehension, followed by violent cold shivers ... unsteady ...

a headache ... exhausted and severe pains in my neck ... this must have continued for three hours. I then started with a hot sweat ... delirium ... headache ... a rapid pulse and such a thirst like never before. My heartbeat was chaotic ... chest pains and I collapsed on numerous occasions ... I was desperate to sleep however we agreed it may be fatal ... Madame Pipe chopped off her tail with a carving knife to keep us occupied and she promised we wouldn't go blind.

The sweating sickness continued ... Poor Arthur, poor Abraham.

As research revealed Rene Hector appropriated the fat (now cooled) from Monsieur Âne and messily combined it with the black allotropic material and some of the hollow sticks from one of the uprooted trees (an ash) and he called it a pencil of smit. Later referred to in the infamous sheep trials of 1789 as The Devil's Crayon for the devil's mark. Gabriel Chêne (a donkey) is thought to have been a verbatim reporter and the court illustrator.

<fragments>

→ *The year might be 1789 ...* <PB>

←*... Abraham Werner ... graphein ... use it in pencils ... no it's not lead ...*
metallic element lead ... <Pb>

→ *... [continued to] daub smit [and] pencil marks [on] the sheep's paper thin fleece* <400>

← *... let's cut their ears ... cut mark their lugs [with] lug marks ...* <M&S>

→ *...the combination ... unique ... local sheep... local areas ...* <sq>

← *... marks ... strokes ... pops ... letters ... shapes ... crosses ......bugle horns*
...words ... <∞>

<mind the gap(s)>

On blank and open paper and on common land, sheep are a travelling drawing wandering through the spaces in the boundary of the extended field.

Identification is only an important issue if artist researchers need to know which sheep belong to them and which to their field.

Interdisciplinary and allotropic ... **LOOK** ... the sheep are wandering through the spaces in the boundary dressed as diamonds. They are trying so hard *to get somewhere* ... let's cut their hair ...

... with pen and ink?

No ... now we have pencils ... *with trees and flowers growing their hair to get nowhere* ... so we do.

I'm getting aware <b/t1972>

And as for what happened to Gabriel Chêne ... I found him in a dream looking for ... me. Drawing the knife and weighing the meat

<=>

Returning from the colloquium, Jacques Taché ... an *ANYTIME DAY S* ... the body ... added *£15.40* ... render my head?

From YORK *

To SHEFFIELD *

He's wearing ... dark woollen cap, white shirt open to the chest, pure white knee-length apron covering the trousers, dark hose and my shirtsleeves are not rolled up above the elbows.

He scratches **Start date**, remembering that one ear is bent down.

8263-59 ... two arms ... **Route**

Validity ... the eyes, an **Adult** ... the nose ... **Class STD** ... my teeth.

Gabriel please take great care with those scales ... hang the meat in such a way that ...

SGL ... the legs ... feet ... a spot of hyper realism

Price inside the eyes ... the pupils.

ONE and **NIL** for the details ... eyebrows, ears, mouth, teeth, the knife and sharpening steel hanging from the belt

Tussock *ON DATE SHOWN* ... the head.

Trace the final lines on the arms and legs.

René herd what you want to keep and ~~erase~~ any extra.

Icon <baa>

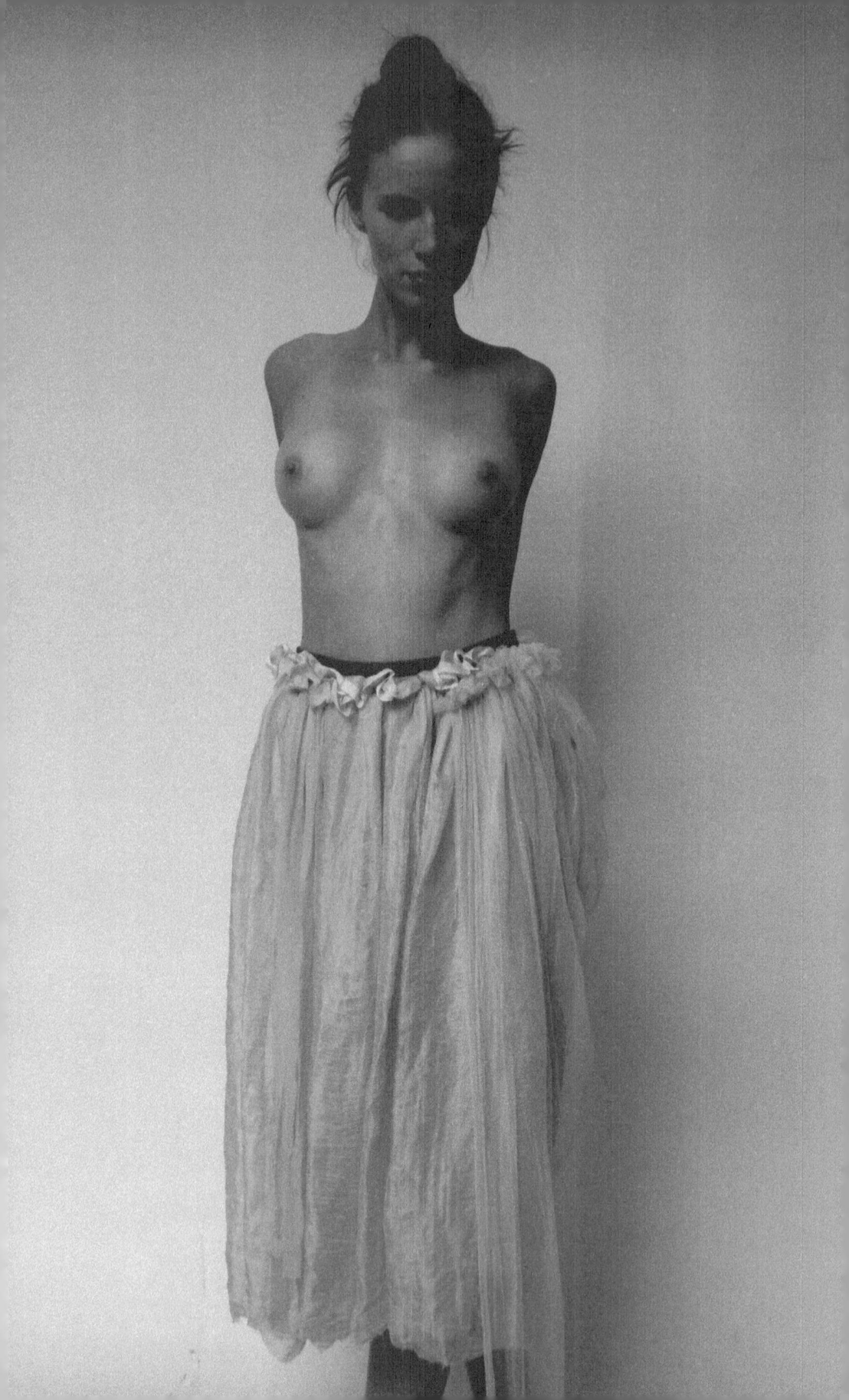

RAW

Photography *Harris Kyprianou*
Model *Nia* wears *Elena Dawson*

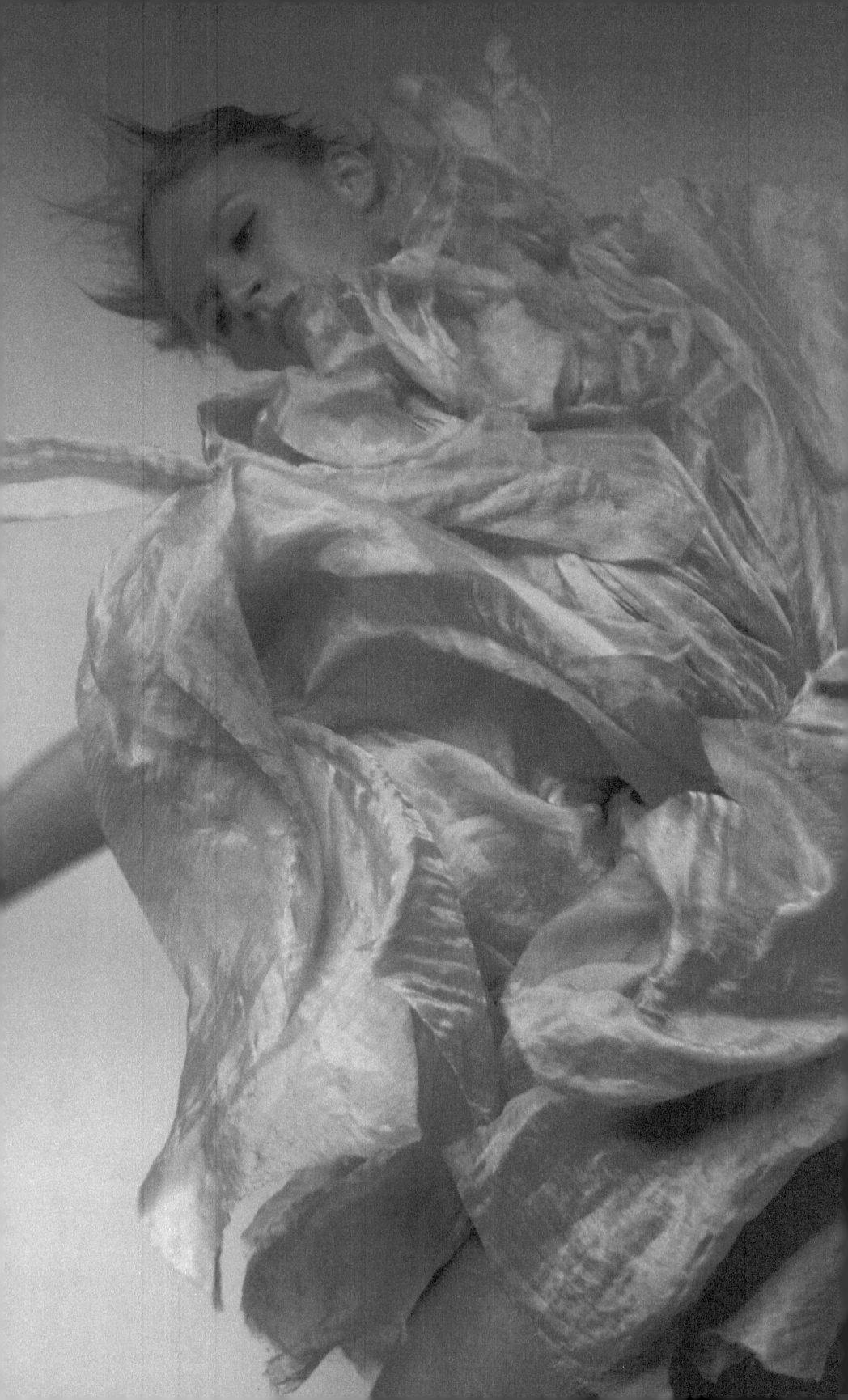

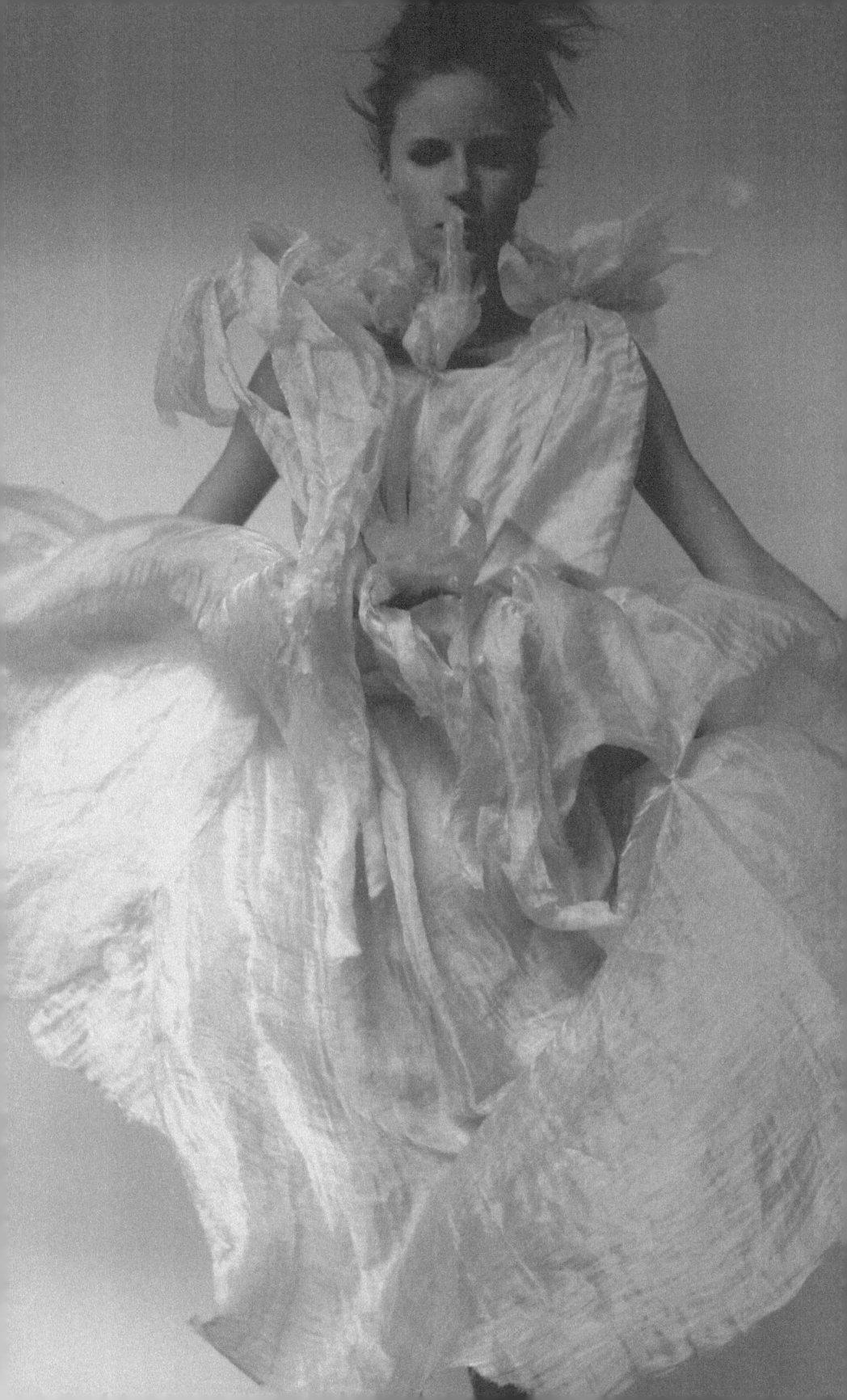

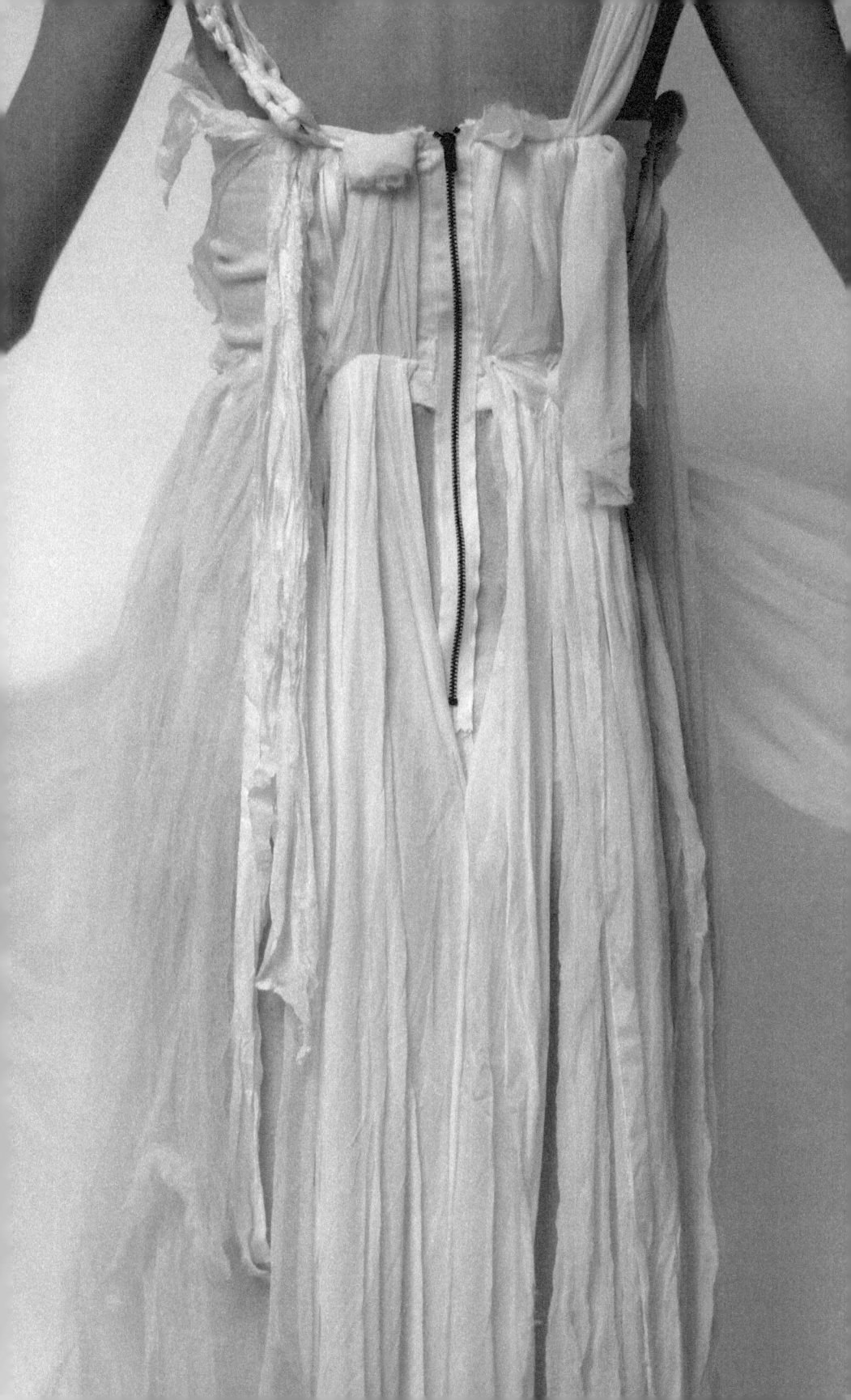

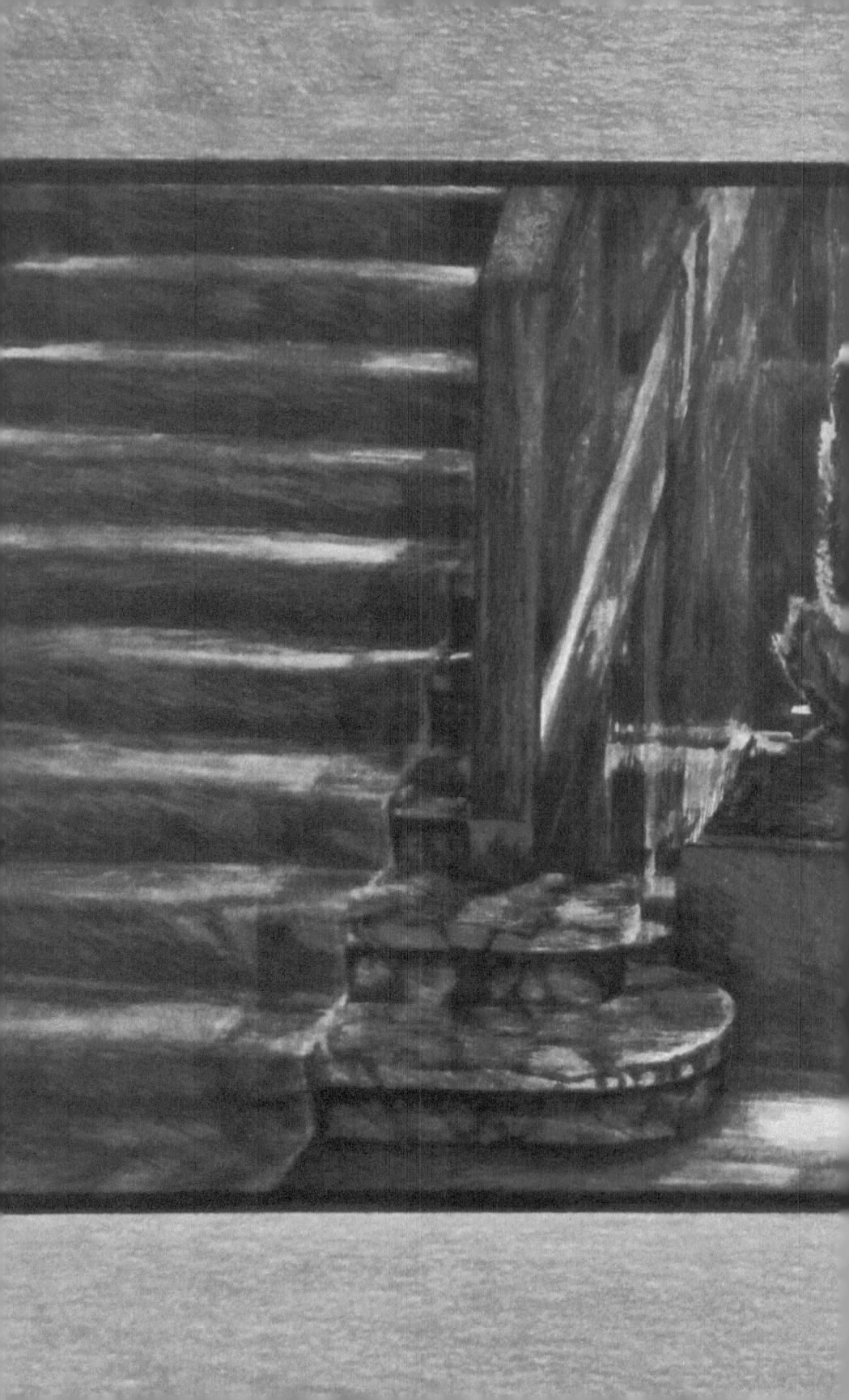

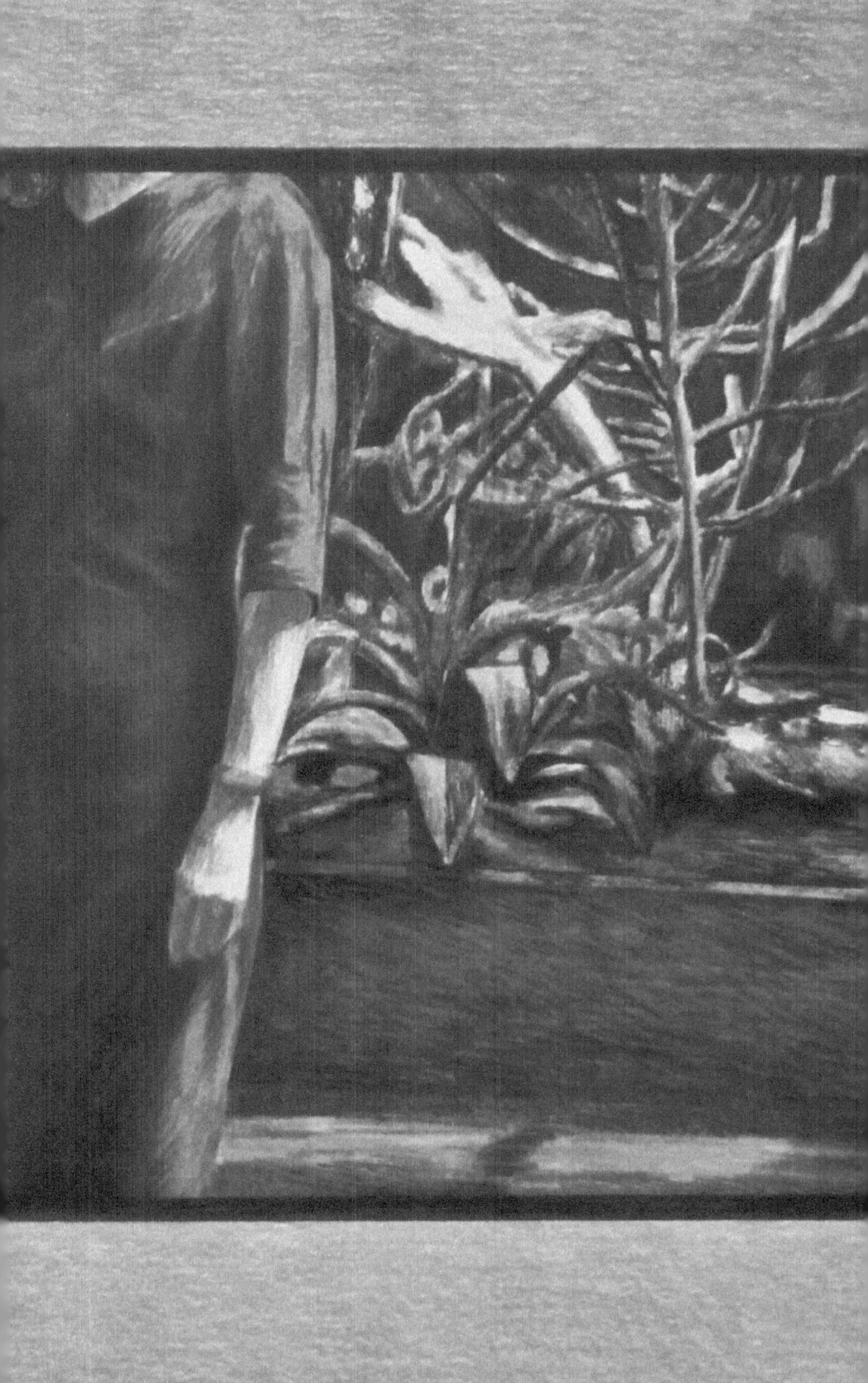

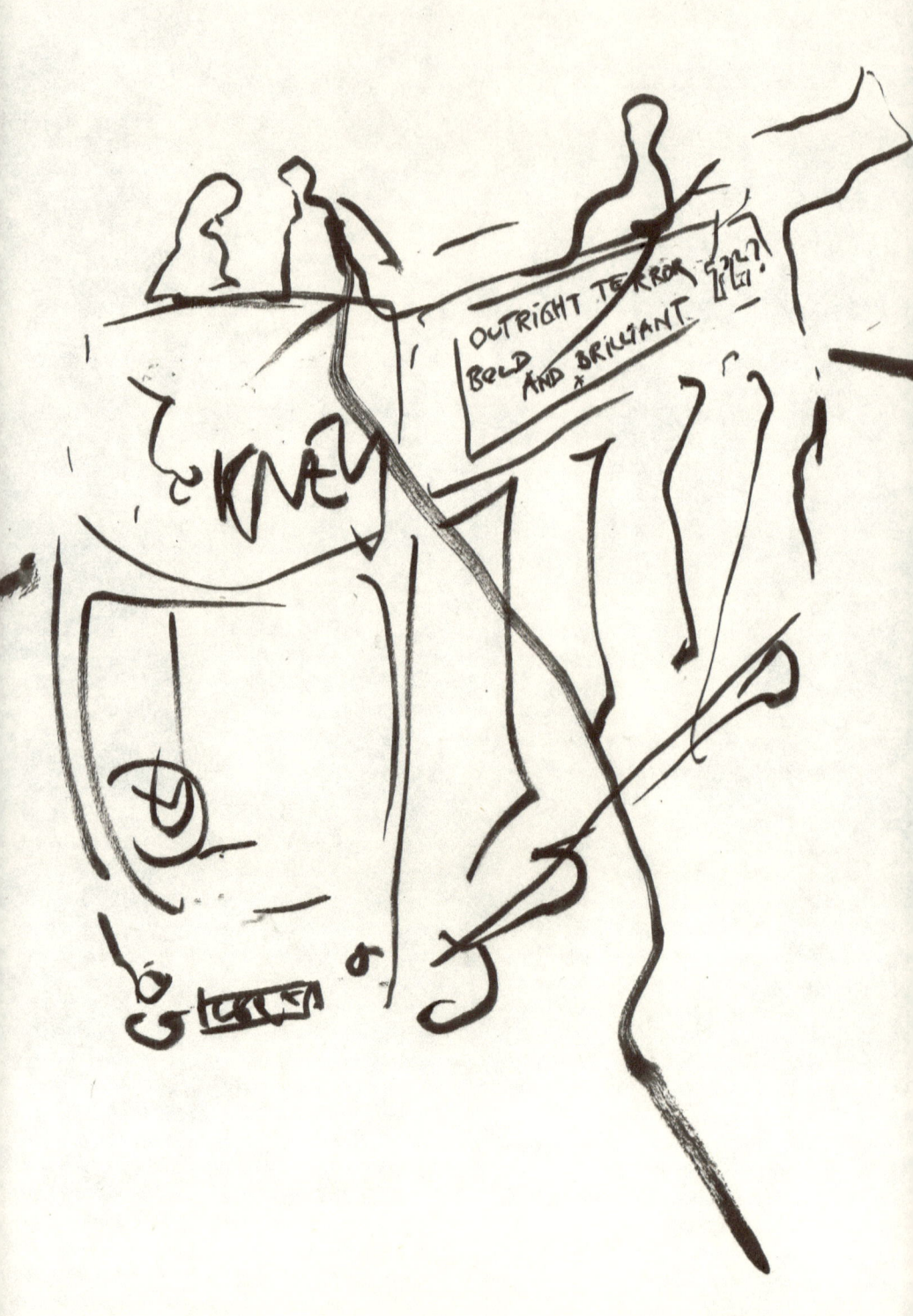

SPECTACULAR TRANSPORTS

John Hutnyk
Illustration by *Estella Mare*

TERRORISTS: you ignore them for ages, then a whole bunch come along at once. Or so it seems, as the everyday profiling of Muslims as threatening others has reconfigured how we all move about the city. An old fashioned racism based on looks, surface and skin has risen to unquestioned prominence at the very time when discussion of race transmutes into talk of religion, ways of life, and civilisational virtues. We hear over and over in the mainstream press, and from the Government, talk of a clash of values, integration and of the need for community cohesion. This old 'new' racism is blatant and its prejudice is clear: policy by scaremongering and tabloid popularity poll. There is also a theoretical parallel to this in the work of scholars who write today about ethnicity, identity and culture, and even in the work of those who ostensibly would offer up radical critiques of the way the war of terror has been prosecuted by those in power.

Profiling is designed to fill us with dread. A culture of fear and anxiety provokes shivers and panic, has us tingling with unease. Everywhere I look I see intimations of this story – as I commute to work, railway station announcements warn that my belongings may be destroyed if I leave them; I am told not to hesitate to ask someone if an unattended bag is theirs; a general air of uncertainty pervades the tube; fellow passengers are almost too careful and too polite to each other; I suspect them of moving far away from anyone with even a hint of a beard and a backpack; and we all move away from those with Brazilian good looks (because we remember Jean Charles de Menezes, who was shot by police at Stockwell). I avert my eyes and read my newspaper (a free advertising sheet, with minimal – often sensationalist – news); and even at home I am not spared, a constant stream of bombings on screen. Myriad incidents conspire to make us squirm.

This squirm is strangely marked by a transportation theme, and an iconic one, which – as I will suggest – is inflected with an unexamined un-canny aspect. It will be easily accepted that the red double-decker bus is the globally acknowledged symbol of London, you can buy trinket sized models of them in the souvenir stalls. As everyone knows, the bus became even more potently symbolic after the devastating bus and underground attacks on the morning of July 7, 2005. Indeed, we are continually forced to recall the hor-rific details: on that day three tube carriages and a number 30 Routemaster were destroyed, leaving 56 people dead.

The real face of terror for me is a delinking of cause and effect in rela-tion to this incident and the bombing of this particular bus: it is what I will call a transportation mutation and a blindness of representation. It is my argu-ment that as commentary turns to religion or culture, any critical response to the scene of the ripped open vehicle becomes somehow silenced, and that we become blind to what this image means. I am invoking here the terms used by Susan Buck-Morss and Slavoj Žižek in books that address issues of terror and violence. Along with Alain Badiou, they refer to such atrocities, and to the actions of suicide bombers, as mute, blind, silent and disconnected. This was also the perverse refrain of former British Prime Minister Tony Blair in defending British foreign policy in the wake of the London bombings ('there was no link between last week's bombings in London and the Iraq war' 25 July 2005 BBC [1]).

In his 2008 book *Violence*, Žižek calls terrorist attacks and suicide bomb-ings a 'counter violence' that is a 'blind *passage a l'acte*' and an 'implicit admis-sion of impotence' (2008:69). I find this not dissimilar to how Badiou, writing of September 11, 2001, starts his essay on 'Philosophy and the War on Ter-ror' by saying: 'It was an enormous murder, lengthily premeditated, and yet silent. No one claimed responsibility' (2006:15). Susan Buck-Morss, in her book *Thinking Past Terror*, offers: 'the destruction of September 11 was a mute act. The attackers perished without making demands … They left no note behind … A mute act' (Buck-Morss 2003:23). It should be said she qualifies this with a question 'Or did they?', but the suggestion of an absent verbal – mute – message is something to which we should attend, listen and consider again, and not just with our eyes scanning for evidence (hint: on the side of the bus, see previous), but with our ears and minds as well. In a similar tone, we might pass over the curiosity that Žižek chooses the infirmities of blindness and impotence to characterise the terrorist suicide bomber, as if the Twin Towers of September 11, 2001 in New York indicated a scene of masturbation (too much and you lose your sight) and castration (impotence, symbolic castration of the towers, mummy daddy, the old psychoanalytic staples are invoked – later it will be called a parallax).

The point is that these theorists all agree on an absence of meaning that sets these acts apart. Badiou and Žižek's claims about suicide bombings recall earlier comments by Buck-Morss on New York, where she suggests that the 'staging of violence as a global spectacle separates September 11 from previous acts of terror' and, as we should underscore, all three dwell upon the absence of message: 'They left no note behind ... Or did they?' (Buck-Morss 2003:23-4). More uncompromising and perhaps mischievous, Žižek in *Welcome to the Desert of the Real*, presents the event in his own peculiarly Lacanian perspective:

> "The spectacular explosion of the WTC towers was not simply a symbolic act (in the sense of an act whose aim is to 'deliver a message'): it was primarily an explosion of lethal jouissance, a perverse act of making oneself the instrument of the big Other's jouissance."
>
> (Žižek 2002:141)

I for one am not satisfied with this. The task of a critical commentary is not just to stop and stare. It is also not just a matter of listing ever more details of the symptomatic eventuality that has to be pathologised. We might do more than read surfaces if we look closely at one such revealing detail, that has, curiously, been thus far ignored.

The scene of the July 7th tragedy is captured in widely circulated images of the wrecked bus in Tavistock Square, taken by US-based photojournalist Mathew Rosenberg. One of his pictures, appearing in most newspapers the next day, showed the bus from a 45% frontal angle with a disturbingly ironic film advertising placard visible on its side. This was for the film *The Descent*, due to be released the next day (2005 dir. Neil Marshall). *The Descent* was a schlock horror-thriller about inhuman monsters in a cave visited by a group of friends who become lost and are subsequently killed off one by one. The cave is the least of the coincidences however, as Londoners read reports and looked at grainy mobile phone video footage from the dark underground. Could we even begin to understand this horror? And were we ready to absorb the irony that the portion of the film placard left on the side of the bus after the explosion clearly displayed a message for us all. Tangled metal and stunned commuters foregrounded by a torn but still legible placard. It says: "Outright Terror, Bold and Brilliant – *Total Film*".

Hasib Mir Hussain was said to be the bus bomber (generally accepted as fact, although questioned by bus passenger and witness Daniel Obachike in his book *The Fourth Bomb* [2]). Hussain detonated his bomb some 50 minutes after the three tube explosions. Speculation was that, having planned to also blow up a tube carriage, he had lost his nerve and was fleeing the scene, perhaps accidentally setting his bomb off while trying to diffuse it (there were reports of him fiddling with his rucksack). Because the bomber is dead, it is not possible to ascertain whether Hussain had intentionally targeted this particular bus. But some seem ready to decide – for example, my sociologist colleague Victor Seidler says the Tavistock Square bus bombing was 'unplanned' (Seidler 2007:10). Whatever the case about the bus – and I tend to think it is a gory coincidence – the thoughts and motives of a suicide bomber are never readily available even where the bombers leave messages and – in the case of Hussain's co-conspirator, Mohammed Sidique Khan – bequeath us justificatory 'confessional' videos to be broadcast after the event. We have however to analyse these with something more than anxious fear. The interpretive work of reading the sign on the bus means refusing the broad brush that paints these bombers as merely mute and blind, even as we put names and faces to them – the very gesture which allows fear to proliferate. To profile and to silence is a doubleplay that only confirms the 'bold and beautiful' success of this terror, this atrocity.

Of course we can only watch those images for so long. Indeed, the image from the side of the bus seems to have been erased. It was not 'Total Film', despite the terrible irony, and it looks as if we cannot bear to discuss this much at all. Instead, we have a different mode of commentary, in which – I want to note this as irony too – we see a lot more Muslims on the news than ever before. Bombers Hussain and Khan are offscreen, but the frequent presence of Muslim community leaders as 'spokesmen' on British television news talkback is a part of a larger project, in part orchestrated by Government and its agencies (police, media) to manage the postcolonial nation in a context of war. Carefully selected 'moderate Muslims' must be identified, shaped and disciplined into a discursive non-fighting force – a class of persons of colour, compliant in taste, in opinion, in morals and in intellect (pace Macaulay's Minute) – while 'extremist', outspoken or otherwise non-compliant figures serve as characters fit for demonisation, scaremongering and foreign policy justification. The good cop/bad cop scenario is transmuted here into a management of appearances – the good community leader is set against the aggressive, often ridiculed, aberrant complainant. Brown skins are offered on screen in dual roles. Scratch the surface of appearance and what we have is a struggle over national identity, a contested arena of civil freedoms and a lost opportunity for real debate.

That the debate scenario of televisual news is a colour-coded fashion show is counterfactually reinforced by the continued parade of white models, white presenters, white authority – but I am no longer persuaded that the mere fact of having brown faces on television is a step towards equality. Visibility must mean something more – such that while we might now insist the skin tone of the speaker matters not so much as the speakers' allegiance or not to a set of ideas, the degree that those ideas may more or less conform to a white supremacist agenda is itself reinforced again by skin. Rather than the contours of distraction and anxiety, the theoretical arabesques about jouissance, or of mute and blind violence, a louder and less myopic debate must be had now. Much has already been said, but the meaning is obscured if we refuse to read the signs before our eyes. I think this is a part of a general obfuscation, a general avoidance. There are some that talk about war-on-terror fatigue – we are no longer capable of paying attention to the impact of this war on our day to day lives – but I think it amounts to a strangely deflected reaction to the suspicions that we know are everywhere present. In full face profile, the upfront discussion we need about everyday racism on screen and on the buses might then filter through our convoluted anxieties and point towards better understandings, and a more robust defence of those under attack. It is unacceptable to see brown faces accused and detained, having to deny wrongdoing over and over (as was 23-year-old 'lyrical terrorist' Samina Malik, as well as so many other 'suspects'). This war of terror as it plays out in the city means Muslims are subject to stop and search, special investigations, harassment and inconvenience, train stations and airports are an ordeal, suspicious looks are just a step away from violent attack and a rendition flight to Guantanamo. The face of racism renewed is that Muslims today are required to 'get their house in order', or they must 'leave': a spurious double play that sets a superficial tone for media commentary and excludes deeper perspectives. We cannot remain mute nor turn away blind to a racism that wreaks such pervasive destruction upon us all.

NOTES

(1) http://news.bbc.co.uk/1/hi/help/3681938.stm. Accessed 24 March 2008].

(2) http://daniel77witness.blogspot.com/. Accessed 24 March 2008.

REFERENCES

Badiou, Alain
    2006 Polemics. London: Verso.
Buck-Morss, Susan
    2003 Thinking Past Terror: Islamism and Critical Theory on the Left. London: Verso.
Seidler, Victor Jeleniewski
    2007 Urban Fears and Global Terrors. London: Routledge.
Žižek, Slavoj
    2008 Violence, London: Profile Books.
    2002 Welcome to the Desert of the Real, London: Verso.

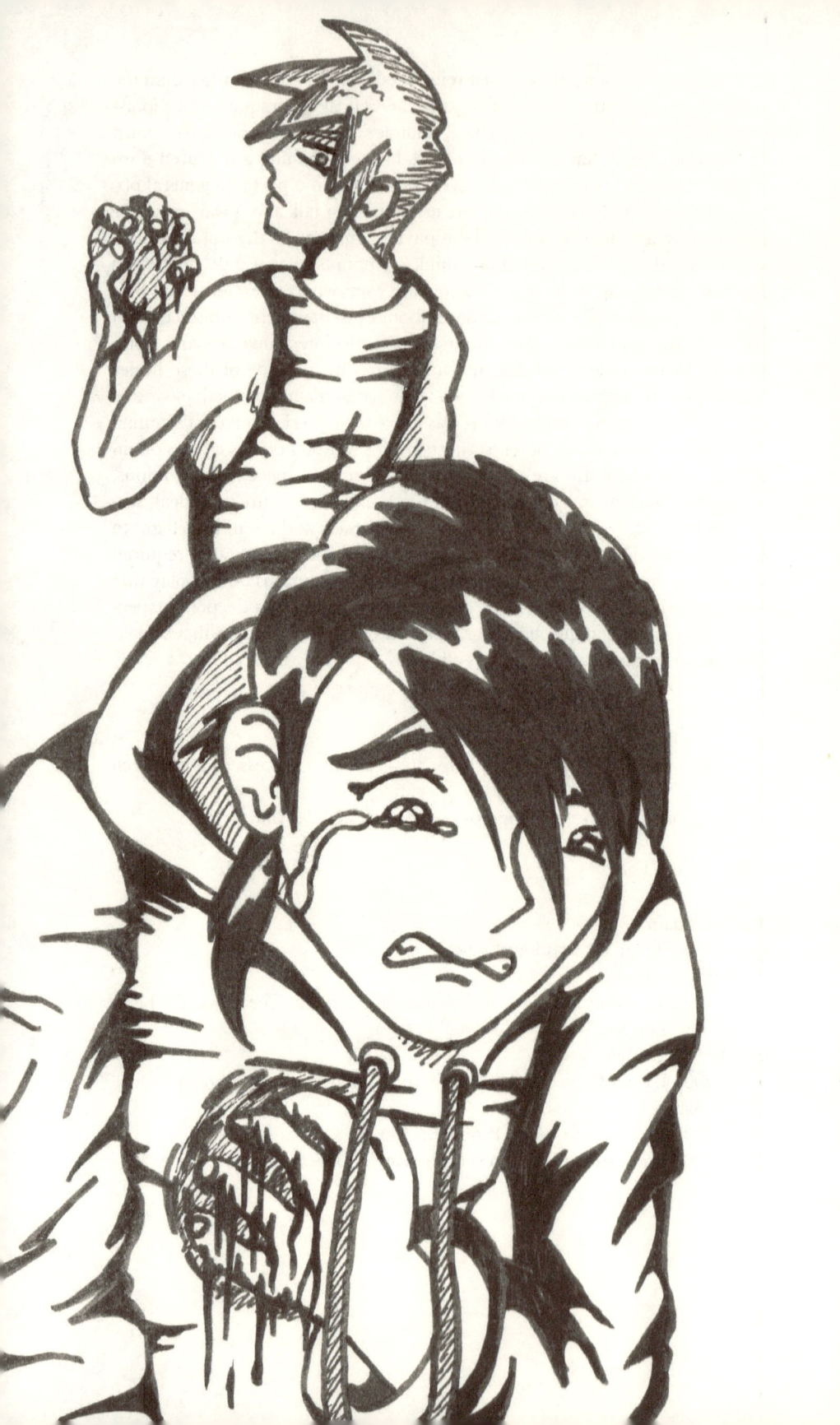

'NO ASIANS PLEASE': SAME-SEX SEXUALITY AND ETHNIC MINORITIES IN BELGIUM

Wim Peumans

A FEW MONTHS AFTER MINH and I met for the first time for an interview, I bumped into him at an LGBT party. Dressed in jeans, black shoes, and a white shirt that was opened half-way across his chest, revealing a white undershirt, Minh stood dancing in the warm hall, surrounded by friends from an LGBT organisation. He introduced me to a Vietnamese man who I had actually seen at the gym a few days earlier. The Minh I saw dancing here was a different man to the Minh of the interview. He had obviously taken pleasure in dressing up and was enjoying the looks of others. The sensuality and 'physical closeness of sharing sounds, touch and movement to music produced a sense of commensality' (Buckland 2002). Minh used the dance floor and the experience of dancing with other men to 'understand, embody and perform' himself as a gay man (Valentine and Skelton 2003:855).

European debates on same-sex sexualities in ethnic minorities often seem to centre on the opinions of Muslims. This is problematic for two reasons. Firstly it overlooks the complexity of everyday reality: same-sex sexuality remains an 'issue' within several ethnic minority groups in Europe (including the ethnic majority group). Secondly, existing problems are reduced to an oppositional and essentialist political discourse: the perceived homophobic, conservative Muslim is played out against the perceived liberal and homotolerant European (Peumans 2011b).

In this chapter I look at same-sex sexuality as lived by young adults from ethnic minorities in Belgium. More specifically I focus on the narrative of a gay man of Asian origin. I chose the story of the Vietnamese-Belgian Minh because – compared to, for example, Muslims – Asians are much less visible, either socially or in political and media debates (see also Pang (1999) on the Chinese in Europe). Nevertheless, Asians make up 22 percent of the population of non-European descent in the EU (Eurostat 2013). Focusing on one story allows for a deeper and more detailed description. Personal narratives are 'socially embedded in the daily practices and strategies of everyday life' (Plummer 1995:15). Also, ethnographic narratives make up an entry point into broad social, cultural and historical processes.

My argument is that the migration background and the specific ethnic/racial subjectivity of Minh inform certain dynamics in his performance of gender and sexuality. I will proceed as follows: I start with a short introduction to the research project and afterwards I treat several elements from Minh's narrative: the discovery of his sexuality and the role of the internet and drawing in this self-reflexive process; the management of disclosure and silence around sexuality; the intersection of sexuality and ethnicity/race in everyday life.

AN ETHNOGRAPHY OF SEXUAL MIGRATION

The story of Minh was part of a research project I did in 2008-2009. The study looked at sexual migration to Belgium, or migration that is fully or partially motivated by the sexuality of those who migrate (Peumans 2012). My fieldwork consisted of in-depth face-to-face interviews and I took part in the activities of WISH, an association for LGBT asylum seekers and refugees. Minh's narrative fell out of the scope of my research, but I met him during fieldwork and I decided to include his narrative as a separate chapter in the book (Peumans 2011b).

Minh's mother took him to Belgium at a young age in the mid 1990s. His father had migrated to Belgium a few years earlier in search of better education, a higher standard of living, more security, more freedom, and an escape from political corruption and criminality.

THE DISCOVERY OF SEXUALITY, ON- AND OFFLINE

I want to start with an analysis of how Minh discovered his sexuality during puberty. As is the case with many (LGB) youngsters, Minh partly discovered his sexuality online. The internet offers many possibilities to study how lesbians, gays and bisexuals understand sexuality, sexual desires and erotic practices (Alexander 2004:2). Often the internet provokes a moral panic in society and this is frequently linked to issues of sexuality. Think of the debates that arose after UK Prime Minister David Cameron announced in the summer of 2013 he wanted to restrict the online access of porn (Gross 2013). The internet is sometimes thought to lead to a decline in community spirit and face-to-face contact is deemed ethically and socially more satisfying (Hillier and Harrison 2007:83). Parents might worry their kids spent too much time tweeting, Facebooking and surfing the internet, where they may fall prey to sexual predators. But as the public space available to young people is diminishing the internet constitutes a democratic and – sexual predators notwithstanding – relatively safe space for youngsters to explore their sexual subjectivities. This democratic quality is nevertheless limited to those who can afford access to the internet.

The internet also creates many possibilities for people with non-normative sexualities and genders. For many LGBs cyberspace is a specific kind of 'third space' (Woodland 2000:418), where the sociality of a public space is combined with the anonymity of the closet. The feeling of security is brought about by the nature of online interactions. These are based on a complex game of anonymity and intimacy, privacy and disclosure (Kunstman 2004:4).

In the telling of his own sexual story, Minh recalled how he started to watch porn when he was a teenager.

> You start to watch porn. In secret. First you are like: 'Ah, that woman looks nice. She got nice jugs.' And then you think: 'Okay, nice, nice. They look nice and such, but I am not feeling anything.' But at that age you do not think you should feel anything special. But what I did like was when a man appeared in a movie too. First you check out his body and you are thinking: 'Wow, he is looking fit.' Or: 'He has got a big cock.' It starts with a comparison: 'Damn, I wish I was like that too.'

From an early age, Minh loved drawing. Through surfing the web he found furry drawings. Furries are anthropomorphic animal characters. While heterosexuals play and experiment with erotic desires and sexual practices during puberty, Minh used drawing as a means to express his sexual desires. As Minh recalled: 'You could find drawings where masculine furries pal up with each other. I felt good about it, because in the end they were just drawings. Not real people with real penises.' But after a while Minh started questioning himself:

> I wondered: 'Well, is this actually normal?' I like women, they are nice. But this is much more exciting! So because of the drawings I went to look for porn. I mean: real gay porn. Although I did not get any further than watching a few clips. My friends would drop by regularly and I did not want them to find out I might not like women. I had not accepted myself as a gay man yet. I just liked naked men.

Here one sees how the internet is a paradoxical space. Although Minh actively discovered his sexuality online, he had to take precautions to prevent his friends from finding out. From his surroundings he got the perception same-

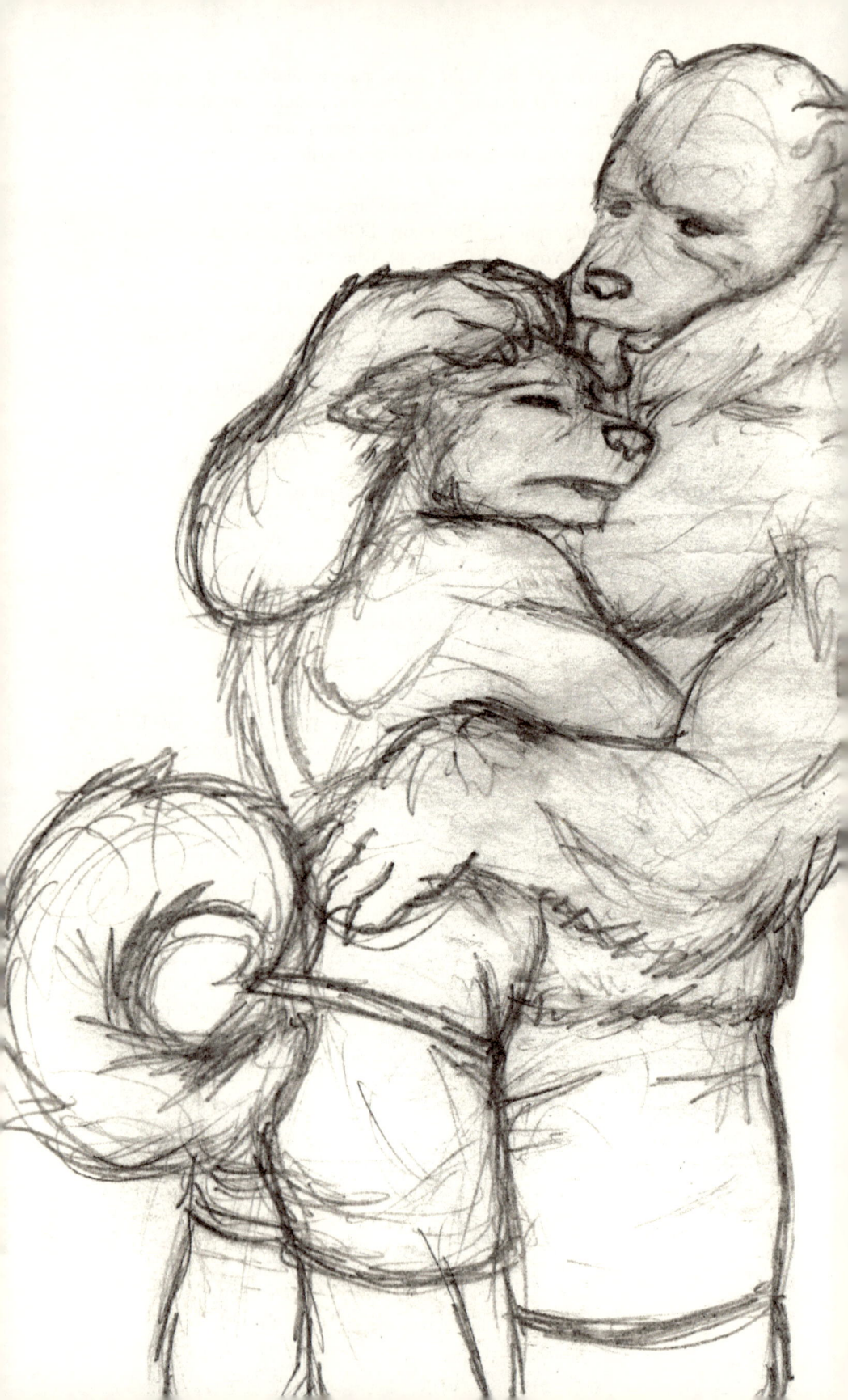

sex sexuality is something bad. That is why he questioned whether what he was doing was 'normal'. What also contributed to this was the reaction of his mother when she discovered one of his erotic drawings: she forbade him to draw such a thing ever again. What Minh felt while he was surfing the internet informed his life offline, and vice versa: he looked at other men in daily life and had a crush on his best friend. During his discoveries online, Minh's 'real-life' sexual practices were limited to sexual play with heterosexual friends.

SILENCE AND DISCLOSURE OF SEXUALITY

In this section I want to discuss how a multiplicity of moral frameworks concerning same-sex sexuality and the migration background of Minh's family inform the ways Minh manages silence and disclosure around sexuality. The first framework is a homonormative moral framework that sees coming out or the disclosure of one's sexuality as the summum of what it means to be gay (Wekker 2009). One is not 'a real and proper' LGB person if one does not come out and sexuality is at the core of one's being. This model equals 'speaking out' with honesty, truth and authenticity.

Around the age of sixteen Minh came out to his best friend and he identified as bisexual. As his best friends and two other friends reacted very positively, he decided to tell his parents.

> First they were a bit... They thought it was a joke. They said: 'Oh, you are just imagining things.' And I answered: 'No, I really think I am.' So at that time I said I was bisexual, hoping it would soften the blow. You know: 'No, worries, Mum, I can still fall in love with a girl'.

The conversation was conducted in Vietnamese, but Minh said 'bisexual' ('biseksueel') in Dutch, because it had more positive connotations than the Vietnamese or French terms (such as 'pédé') he knew through his parents. To his parents his coming out implied a re-definition of their expectations. The new reality was in contrast with the gender patterns and roles they associate with sexuality. Specifically, this meant they needed to reframe their future perspectives of family and offspring.

Yet the way Minh manages his sexuality in everyday life is informed by another, and what he sees as Vietnamese or Asian, moral framework. Minh identified himself as '70 or 80 percent Western' – although fellow students at his university will ethnically categorise him as 'that Chinese guy'. Values such as freedom of speech and defending one's opinion to the utmost are deemed Western. He considers respect for his elders or superiors more important and describes himself as someone who would be persuaded to concessions.

> It is a philosphy given to me by my mother: 'Not everyone has to know what you do and who you are. You do not have to show off.

It is better to hide because you never know what people's intentions are.'

Minh will selectively disclose his sexuality to other people. In the city he grew up in, he did not frequent the LGBT scene and seldomly went to LGBT associations. Within the Vietnamese community in Belgium people would speak disapprovingly of LGBTs. Minh wanted to avoid his parents becoming the subject of gossip and exclusion.

> When my mother arrived here, she knew a [Vietnamese gay] man who was their interpreter. His family left for the States, they were ashamed of him. They went away and he was left behind to finish his studies. Other families would gossip about them and no one wanted to deal with them anymore.

Apart from the Vietnamese moral framework, Minh's migration background is important in understanding how he manages sexuality in everyday life. Transnational migrants such as Minh's parents often rely on the solidarity of members of the same ethnic community in the country of arrival – not only for economic reasons (for example, to help each other find a job, housing, with translation, etcetera), but also social and emotional ones. Through contacts with the Vietnamese community, one maintains membership to the ethnic community in the country of destination and origin. The family as a unit is important in the context of migration, as the home is often one of the few spaces where cultural practices of the homeland are intergenerationally passed on. Also, respect for one's parents is not only important as a 'Vietnamese value' (as Minh explained above), but because the parents have made a lot of personal sacrifices throughout the process of migration: as transmigrants they have often gone through economic and emotional hardship to provide their kin with a better future.

Minh tries to keep his life with his gay friends separate from his life at university and the student house he rents a room in. On the one hand, I noticed he wanted to meet the homonormative disclosure imperative:

> Well, I do not know… Am I fooling myself? I accept myself as a gay man, but I am not open about it. Well, at least not in a big group of people. Things are good the way they are now. As long as there is no need for them to know, then I rather keep it that way. I think it is better to avoid complications this way.

On the other hand, he wanted to be open about his sexuality, but reactions of fellow students – jokes about LGBTs or gossip about possible LGBTs in class – prevented him from doing so. Another cause is phantom acceptance (Goffman 1963): 'At the surface, people will say "we accept you". But below the surface they do not. At least, that is what I think, what I feel.'

'NO ASIANS, PLEASE': SEXUALITY AND ETHNICITY/RACE IN EVERYDAY LIFE

For Minh, moving to another city to attend university was a liberating experience. He started going out on the gay scene and attending the parties and activities of an association for international LGBT students. This association is a safe space: he feels accepted as a man with Vietnamese roots. The LGBT scene carves out spaces where LGBTs feel they can 'step out' of the heteronormative world they inhabit (Valentine and Skelton 2003:855). But within the LGBT scene certain hegemonic (white middle-class) homonormative norms and ideals of lifestyle, looks, beauty and sexual practices exist (Ridge et al 1999:62). For this reason Minh does not like to go out in commercial venues: 'Judging from pictures, I think it is too provocative, too agressive. You are being noticed for what you wear or how you look and I have no need for that.'

In the scene Minh comes across sexual racism against Asian gay men. Gay men from ethnic minorities are ranked according to their attractiveness, virility and sexual prowess. As the popular Flemish gay magazine *Labels* (now called *Inch*) put it in an article on gay Asian men: 'Latinos are hot, black men virile, Moroccans horny. But Asians, they are really unlucky on all accounts' (Monami 2011:118). Certain ethnosexual stereotypes, racial fetishisms and race-based sexual rejections circulate in gay men's communities (Plummer 2007:64). Especially on dating websites – for gay and bisexual men, a very popular tool for finding partners – one can see a politics of exclusion based on race and ethnicity (Callander et al 2012:1095; Riggs 2013). As Minh explains:

> Some men just do not like Asians. When I surf on a gay dating website, some men put tactless sentences in their profile text such as: 'No Asians, please' or 'I like Asian food, but I do not sleep with them', for example. Most stereotypes I get are: Asians have a small dick, smell like restaurants, they are ugly, greasy haired, effeminate, they have no sex appeal, and they all bottom [are passive in sexual intercourse].

In the same article in *Labels*, the author (a white gay man) argued that whether one is attracted to Asians or not might be a matter of 'taste'. The article quoted one white person who dates a Chinese man as saying that what is considered 'universally beautiful' might be 'something genetic' (Monami 2011:118). Such statements overlook how what persons are considered erotically desirable is culturally and historically variable. What races/ethnicities are attractive or beautiful from a Western perspective is interwoven with ethnosexual stereotypes and prejudices that go back to the colonial period.

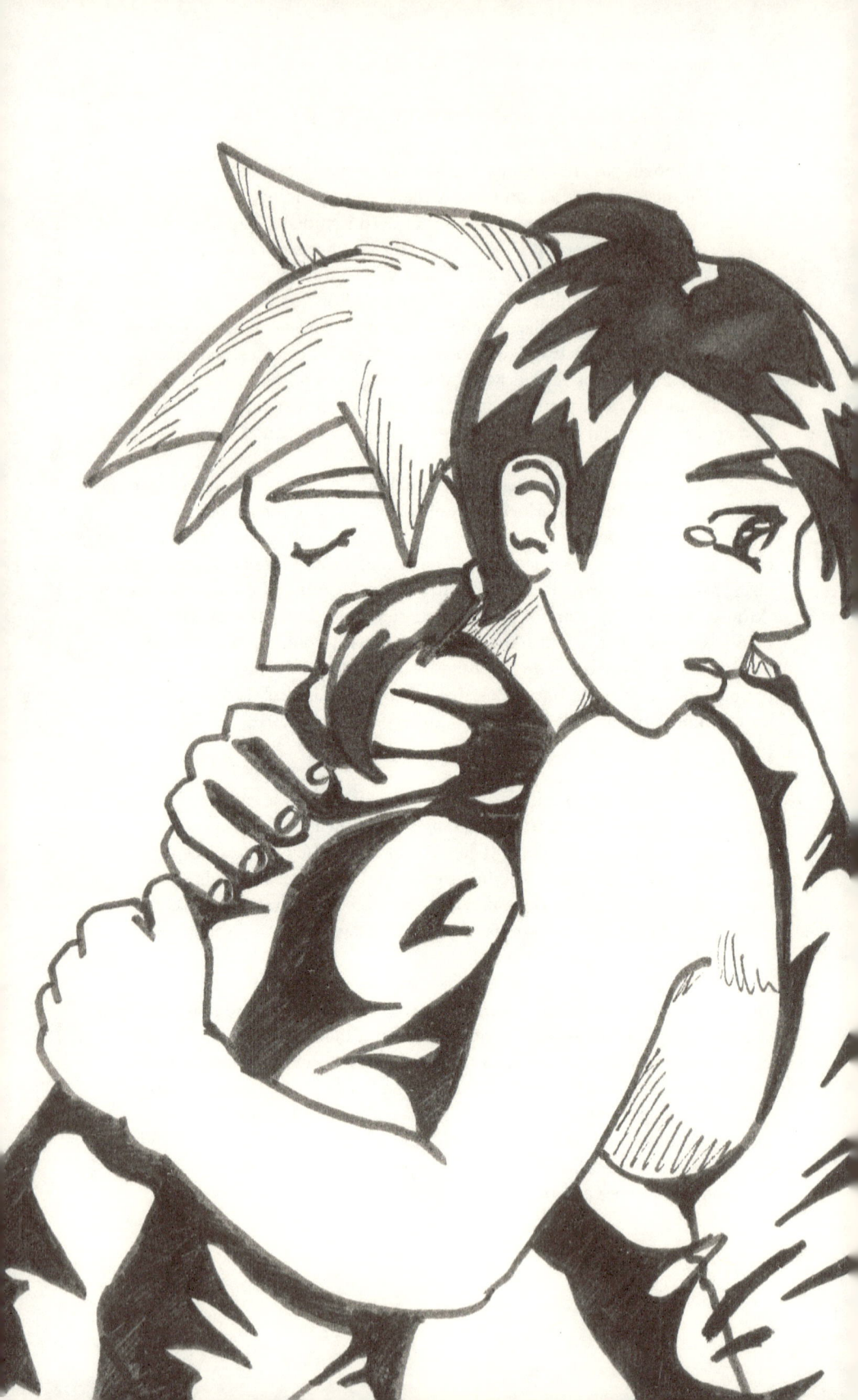

Sexual racism and discrimination of the kind Minh has experienced can crawl under one's skin. On the one hand Minh needs affection, so he will date (mostly older) men who have a thing for young Asian men. But this doesn't tend to lead to a stable relationship. Here he re-appropriates stereotypes attributed to Asian men: 'Sometimes this is just easier and less time-consuming, especially if you quickly need some attention'. On the other hand he will avoid dating Asian men himself. To learn how to deal with discrimination in the LGBT scene, he visits blogs and websites to read about the experiences of other Asian gay men:

> I never talked about these issues with anyone. My parents would feel terribly worried. My friends would not understand. I do not know many Asian gay men. I would not call this a big ordeal, but it is an annoying nuisance. Some of my friends will joke about the fact that I date elder men. They say I am 'easy' and not demanding much. It is not that I care what they say, but it does confirm how I feel they look at me.

CONCLUSION

Minh's narrative is an example of how gay men with non-European roots – in this case Asian (Vietnamese) – discover, negotiate and perform their sexuality in everyday life.

First, I highlighted two elements – surfing the web and drawing – which were important in Minh's telling of his sexual story. It was through a dialogue between both practices and engaging with the world around him that Minh gradually realised he was sexually and emotionally attracted to persons of the same gender.

Secondly, I noted how different moral frameworks and the migration background of his parents inform the particular dynamics of how Minh negotiates silence and disclosure around his sexuality.

Thirdly, in the LGBT scene, Asian gay men such as Minh often come across sexual racism and discrimination. Although he sometimes tries to turn ethnosexual stereotypes and racial fetishism to his own advantage, at other times Minh is at a loss to deal with sexual racism.

Minh's story is one of those narratives that I keep going back to and as time passes, my own reading of his story changes. While the existing literature on same-sex sexualities and ethnic minorities in Europe is slowly growing, it often focuses on the experiences of LGBTQ Muslims (although for exceptions see Haritaworn 2008). Narratives such as Minh's warrant further research, as they raise important questions – not just on an academic level, but also in terms of policies and activism: how to deal with racial and ethnic diversity and racism/discrimination within the LGBT 'community'? How to take on homo/biphobia and homo/binegativity within ethnic minorities? And what is the role of the anthropologist in all this?

NOTES

This chapter is a translation and revision of a previously published article (Peumans 2011a) and book chapter (2011b). The author is funded by the Research Foundation Flanders (FWO-Vlaanderen, project number 1126711N).

REFERENCES

Alexander, Jonathan
　　2004 In their own words: LGBT youth writing the world wide web. GLAAD Centre for the Study of Media and Society.

Buckland, Fiona
　　2002 Impossible Dance: Club Culture and Queer World-Making. Middle town, CT: Wesleyan University Press.

Callander, Denton, Martin Holt, and Christy E. Newman
　　2012 Just a preference: racialised language in the sex-seeking profiles of gay and bisexual men. Culture, Health & Sexuality 14(9):1049-1063.

Eurostat
　　2013 Migration and migrant population statistics. *In* Statistics Explained. Brussels: European Commission.

Goffman, Erving
　　1963 Stigma: notes on the management of spoiled identity. Upper Saddle River: Prentice Hall.

Gross, Doug
　　2013 UK Wants to Restrict Access to Online Porn: CNN.

Haritaworn, Jin
　　2008 Hybrid Border-Crossers? Towards a Radical Socialisation of 'Mixed Race'. Journal of Ethnic and Migration Studies 35(1):115-132.

Hillier, Lynne, and Lyn Harrison
　　2007 Building Realities Less Limited Than Their Own: Young People Practising Same-Sex Attraction on the Internet. Sexualities 10(1):82-100.

Kunstman, Adi
　　2004 Cyberethnography as home-work. http://www.anthropologymatters.com/index.php?journal=anth_matters&page=article&op=view&path%5B%5D=97.

Pang, Ching Lin
　　1999 Why are the Chinese invisible and/or unproblematic? Exploring some viable explanations. Ethnologia 9(11):105-120.

Peumans, Wim
　　2012 To the Land of Milk and Honey - Migration as a Stigma Man agement Strategy. Studi Emigrazione/Migration Studies 187:541-559.

　　2011a 'Nee, ik denk echt wel dat ik het ben': Homoseksualiteit bij Jongeren uit Etnische Minderheden. WelWijs 22(4).

2011b Seks en Stigma over Grenzen Heen - Homoseksuele en Les
bische Migranten in Vlaanderen en Brussel. Leuven: Acco.

Plummer, Kenneth
1995 Telling Sexual Stories: Power, Change and Social Worlds. Lon
don: Routledge.

Ridge, Damien, Amos Hee, and Victor Minichiello
1999 "Asian" Men on the Scene. Journal of Homosexuality
36(3-4):43-68.

Riggs, Damien
2013 Anti-Asian Sentiment Amongst a Sample of White Australian
Men on Gaydar. Sex Roles 68(11-12):768-778.

Valentine, Gill, and Tracey Skelton
2003 Finding oneself, losing oneself: the lesbian and gay 'scene' as a
paradoxical space. International Journal of Urban and Regional
Research 27(4):849-866.

Wekker, Gloria
2009 Van Homo Nostalgie en betere Tijden. Multiculturaliteit en
postkolonialiteit. In George Mosse Lecture. Amsterdam: Univer
sity of Amsterdam.

Woodland, Randall
2000 Queer spaces, modem boys and pagan statues. Gay/lesbian
identity and the construction of cyberspace. In The cybercul-
tures reader. B.M. Kennedy and D.J. Bell, eds. Pp. 416-431.
London: Routledge.

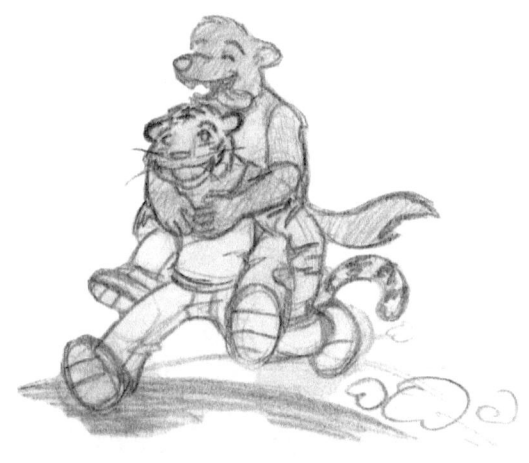

MANY WAYS OF LEAVING

Christina Lovin

There are many ways
of leaving. Part by part:

head first, like the hound
circling too far afield
to hear the call
and cry of downing dusk,
of chase's end,
but ring of eye and brush
of feathered tail entreating
until the trail is lost and
so is home;

or blindly, as the heart
when surgeons grope in cavities
for tendril vein and shard
and clot, but with feeling
sheathed against the stain
and blood-borne ill,
the wound is closed
around the unseen
fatal cut;

or yet, the body leads—
emerging like the moth
from stifling chrysalis,
bent and bruised
but poised
for certain flight
toward some brilliant death;

or leaving simply
for the sake of leaving:
the maverick craving
wild grass more than hay
or grain; the pigeon, homing
back once more,
passes on, then up
into the loss of open sky—
not from, but to

like me to me,
from you.

Francis Kruk

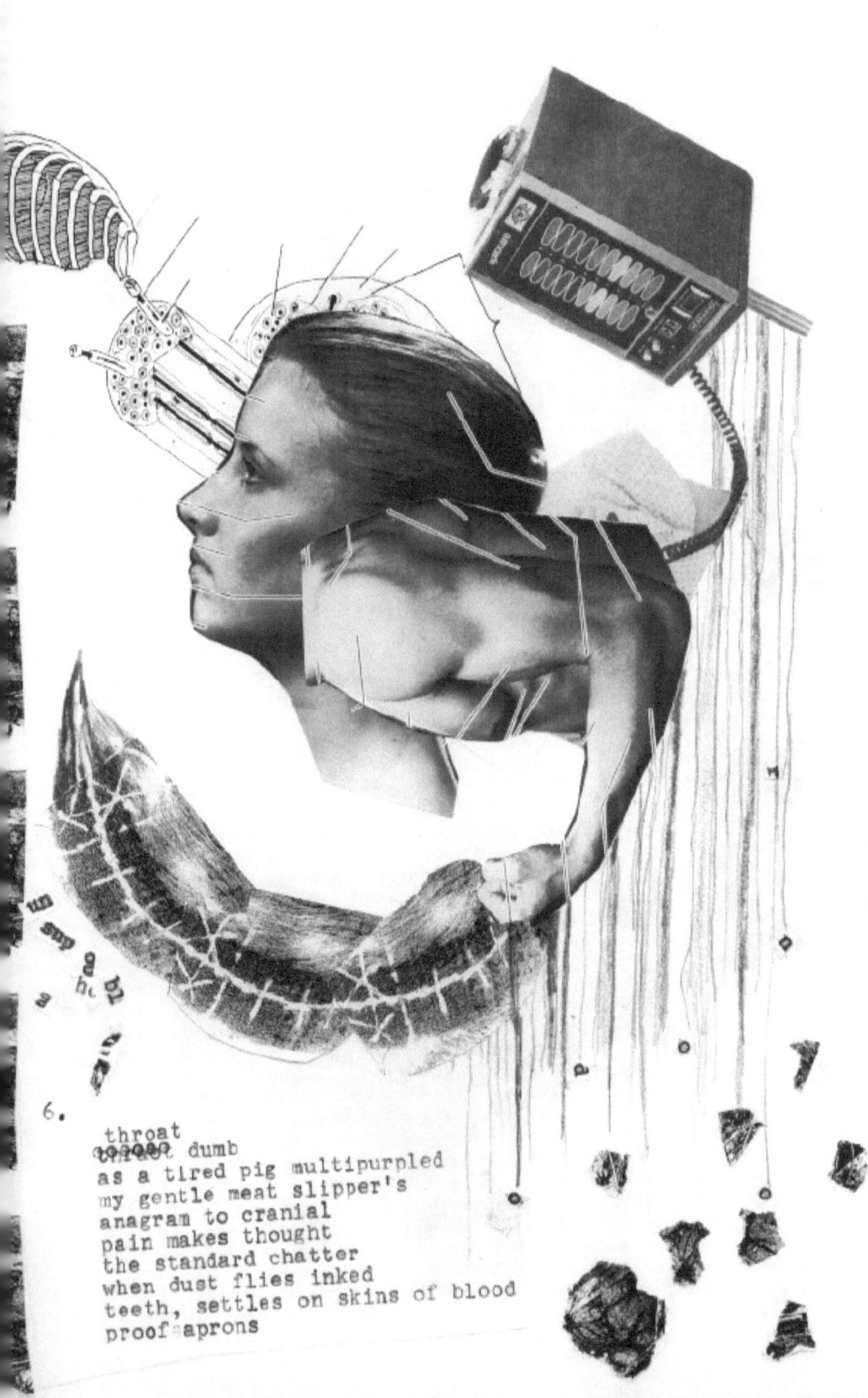

6.

throat
~~tongue~~ dumb
as a tired pig multipurpled
my gentle meat slipper's
anagram to cranial
pain makes thought
the standard chatter
when dust flies inked
teeth, settles on skins of blood
proof aprons

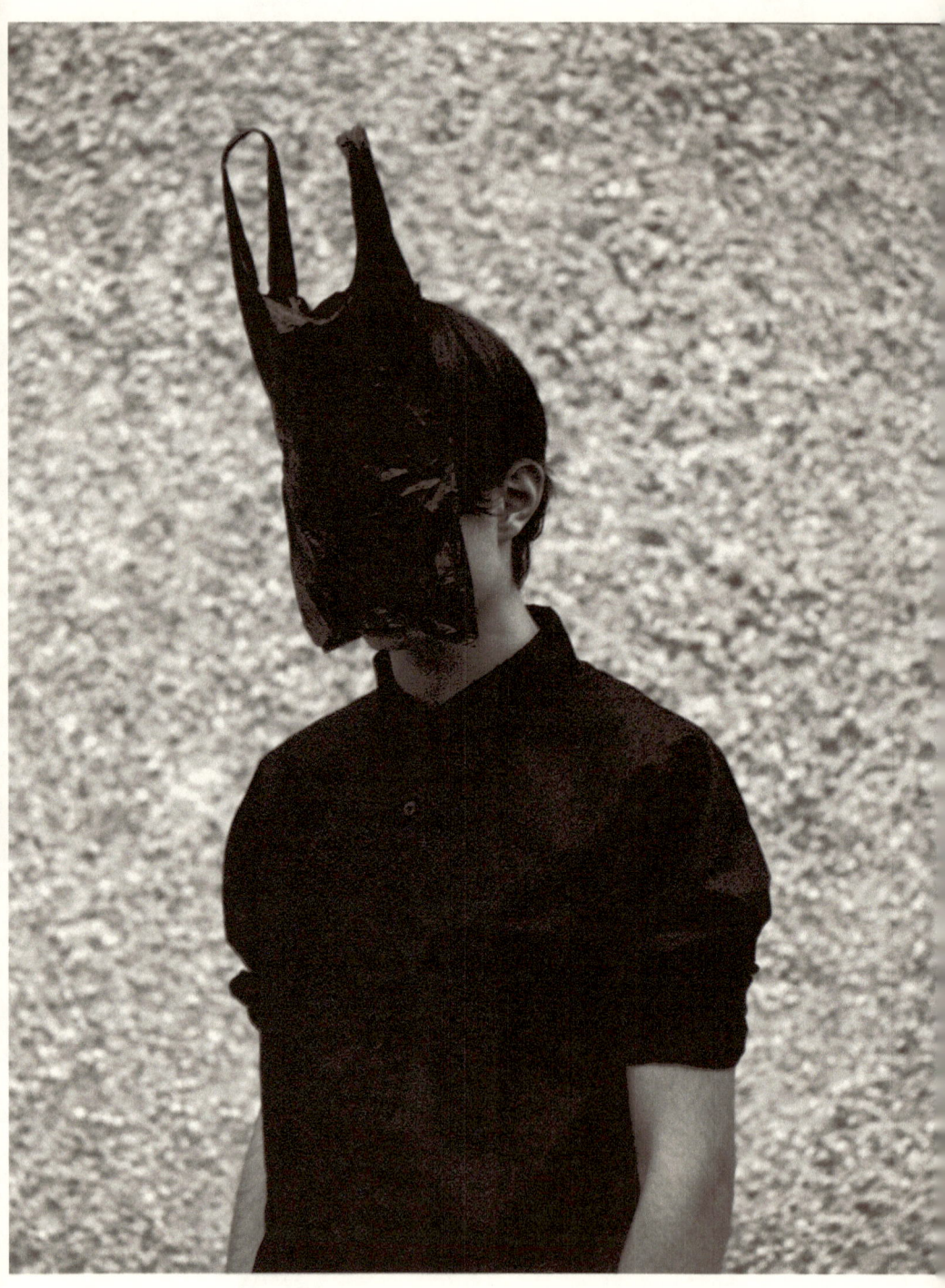

DAMN ROMANCE

photography...robert glowacki
fashion editor...christos kyriakides
make up artist...ken nakano
model...ash at storm models
all clothes...damn romance

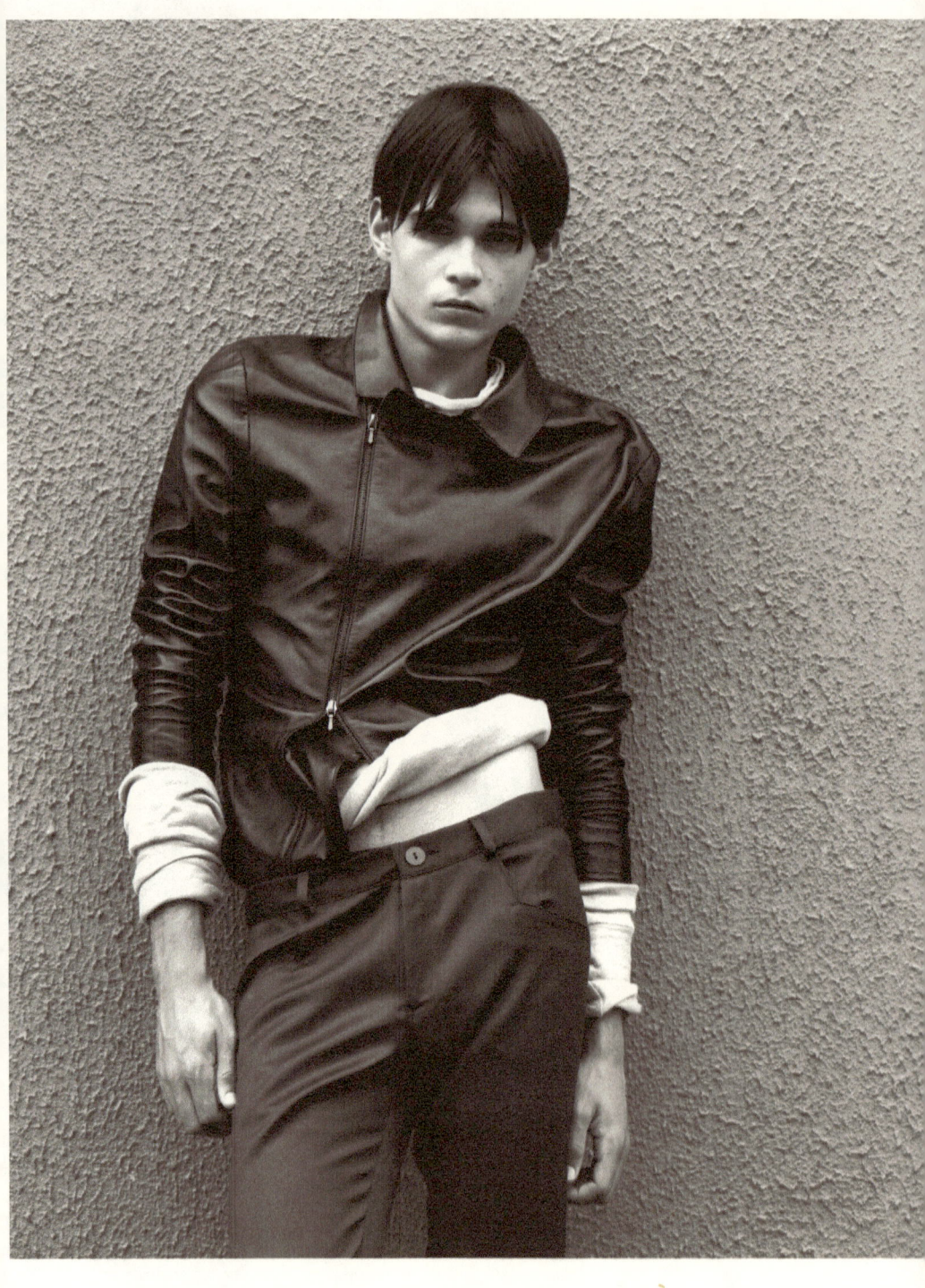

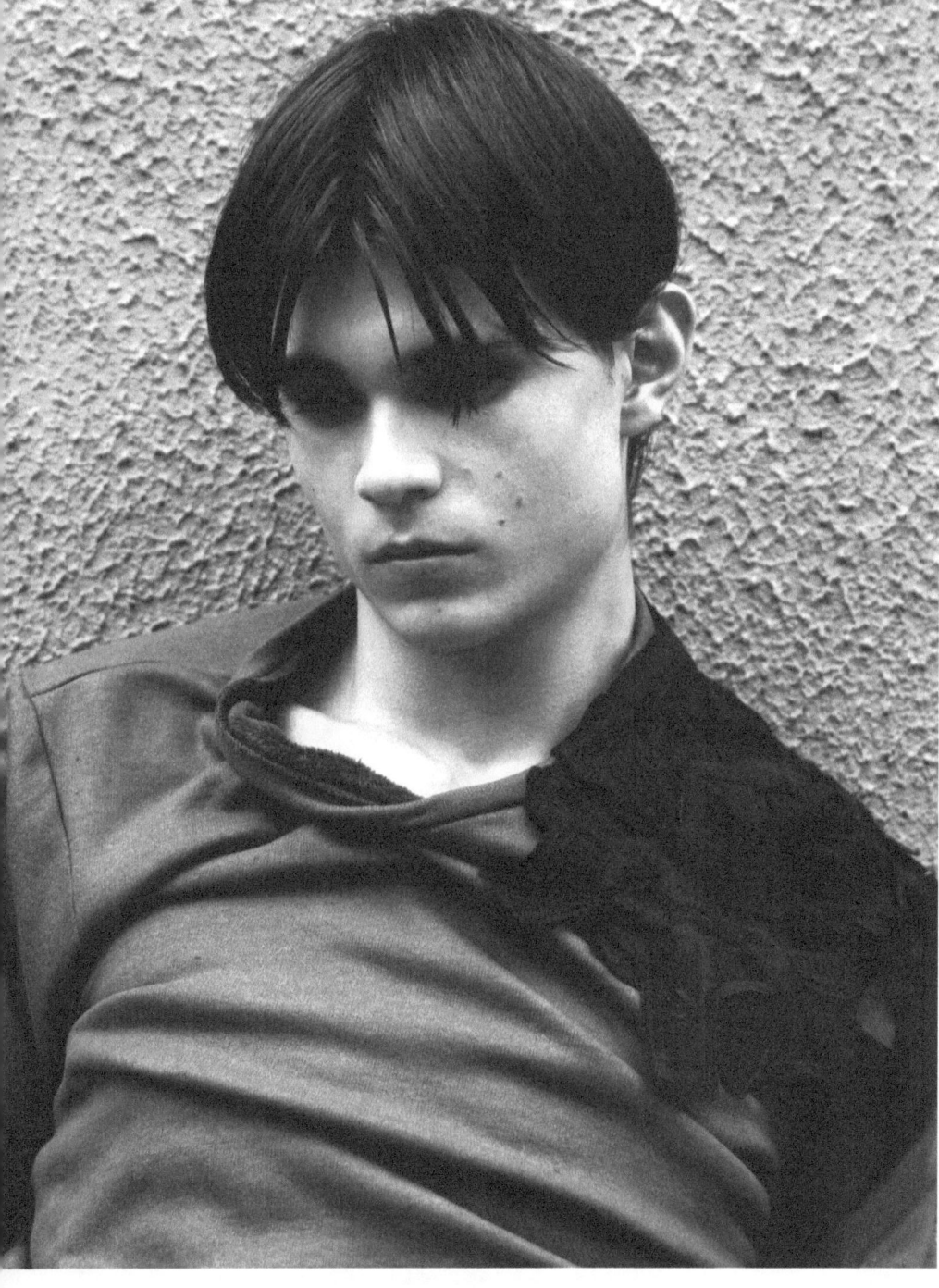

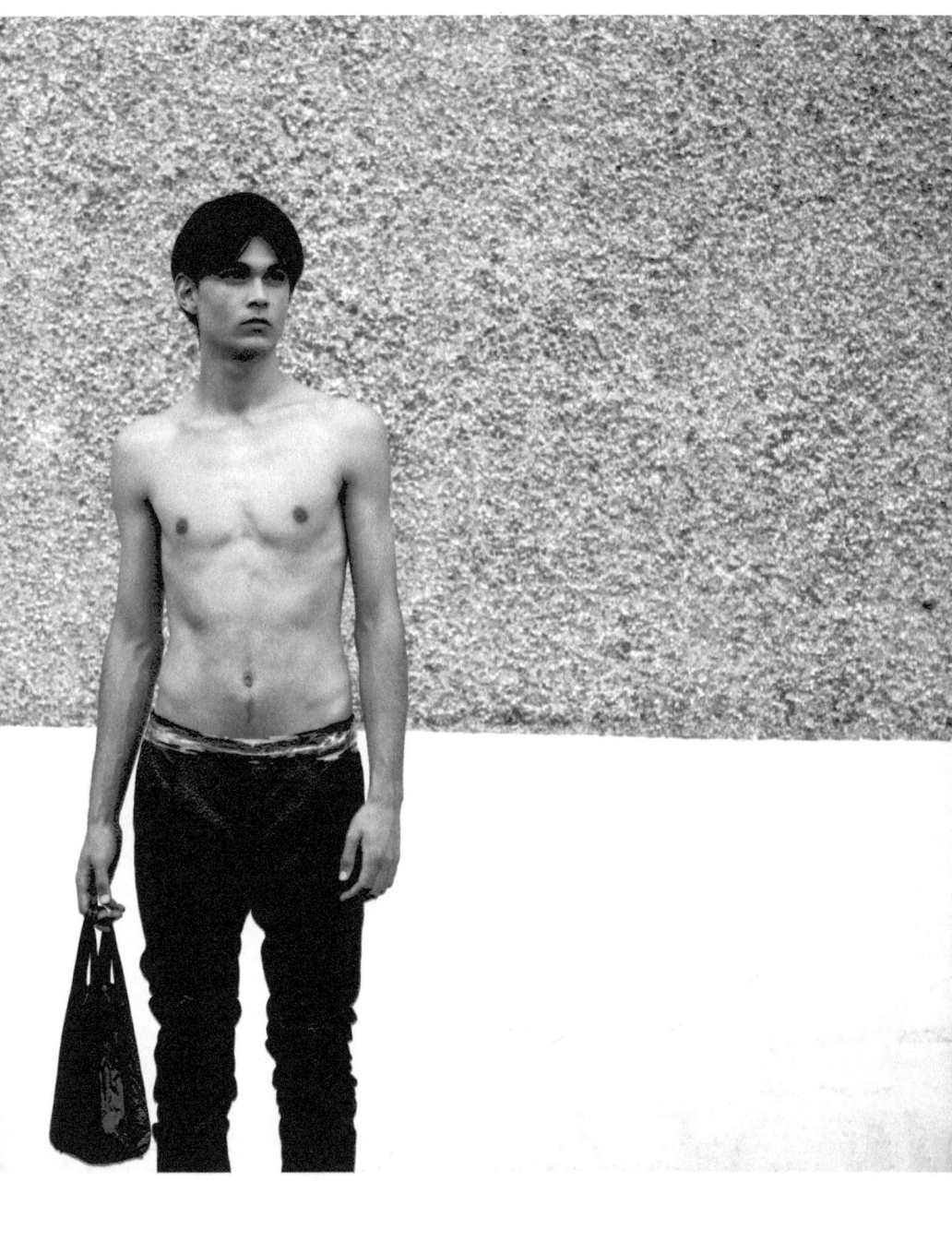

SEVEN DRAWN DAYS

Phil Sawdon

Today

This is a type of a room, a space for graphite the like not known anywhere else that I know of, except with the nurse and legless soldier in the cellar of Gallery #1 in *The Fictional Museum of Drawing* kept there to review argument among the shepherds, that is to say, to adjust shallow spats with drawing.

Here they summon a master and forty-two academicians (at least one with her left-hand cut off) that have the power to set out the bounds of the works on grounds, the terms are these; they are empowered to set off the dusts (so they call them) of grounds in a pipe and a flat, that is to say, ninety two miles long (crow flies) in the first, and fourteen square (swims over the one and scales the other) in the last; when any that has found a line in another's ground, except orchards and gardens; they may appoint the passage.

The limit also scribes conventions to the field, and limits their proceedings on the works grounds; also they are our peers of all their miniatures, as well as out, and, in another word, keep the concord among them; which, by the way, may be called the most ineffective of all the phenomena, for they are strange, turbulent, quarrelsome in disposition, and inflexible in subterraneous relationships.

Day 1

It is evident that as conjecture marks the northern frontier or bounds of the drifting drawing south, so there can be no distinction east through Westway, both break up, fragments The Other and do not stop at their frame.

Each beginning and ending their line by being confronted by the marks and forced back on themselves, 'they' are split, rising in oppositions, tensions, confusions, elisions and anon whilst nibbling Aether.

'They' require a further compass and maps secrete.

Each green pencil is a cylinder of light labelled with a series number to indicate the différance hidden within. Pencil 010 is intact and pencils 020 to 040 are for subject fields. The maps secrete are vellum.

No noise when opened and durable once marked.

In the night the autosarcophagic donkey that ate his pencil passed scumbling and stumping, meanwhile the factory was closed.

Day 2

In our way we past an ancient 'calligram', large, but not yet mature, of the Duck-Rabbit, a noted and inextricable weaving of representation and game.

Hence we kept the thought on our left-hand, but kept our distance, the drawings being out; for the text is a frightful creature when the pen loads the syntax looking for grammar; I say we keep our distance, and content ourselves with hearing the roaring of its waters, 'till we came to the frame or boundary, a little ragged but noted edge, where there is a chalybeate spring, to which the colic, the melancholy and the vapours go in the season to loosen the clammy humours, as also a cold bath.

There are likewise hot springs which run waste into the ditches and brooks, and are taken no notice of, being remote among the borders, and out of the way.

Each sign gesturing the lean fat, the fat lean and goodness gracious the flat worms in the gut.

Further we found the ink in wells, as custom bids us entitle them, full of iron gall, and the waters good, and carnal, however wretched the subject, so I resolved to break until I came to the south and make shift.

Day 3

I think, foolishly that I am come to an awful circumstance, where strange long stories of curiosities as they are so-called, are drawn before us; and that we arrogantly censure so many travelling concepts who have written as if we were all fools, so I give you two lines, by which to see some wonder.

A cave, the wonder is;
Lead sheep are useful.

Which by the same hand are thus?

A cave, the wonder is;
Lead sheep are useful.

You shall soon find all that is about it and what it is about this that is all about.

Day 4

Upon the very edge, is, as above, a marking sequence, where there are several flaccid silhouettes, lately one of these being outlined by a stone wall by which lampblack, glue and water is brought to rise to a due height, is made into a horse trough with a Museum built over it, and room within each Gallery to walk round the newly made black liquid, and so by steps go down gradually into the India ink bathtub.

Once submerged two things do not enthral; namely, a base, stony, mountainous way, and no natural gift when you are within: the intention is to endow a souvenir of quality, or such that would pause at it; but it is not as yet so far: The milk is ink, or rather blood, is very pleasant, very sanative, especially for dust pains and welts.

Day 5

For some miles, we draw the baths so to be able to pass over by the mouths and entrances of the lead-mines, where there are melting-houses for the preparing of the oars, and casting into pigs.

We gorged on a pottage of cheese and meal sweetened with honey and wine whilst our host attended to her loom and I looked for moly.

On the other, or east side, stands a high work, which rises from the very bottom; I say, it rises perpendicular as a wall, my face bare and smooth like one plain stone, to such a prodigious height, it is surprising.

At the beginning of it on this side it is not quite so much although a fee is assumed.

Birds, a Monkey House and various wolves attract in this the Lover's Walks, our eldest of the five works.

The monkey (Monsieur Lièvre on his way from the Rue Morgue) is in its tree (we noted le singe est sur la branche and that le branche is horse chestnut), Monsieur Lièvre draws with an impotent (impuissant) pencil whilst at the foot of The Cascades we attempt *The Flight* on a donkey (Gabriel Chêne) that ate the pencil.

The horse chestnuts devoured three or four at a time giving relief to Gabriel's chest complaint in particular his cough and worm diseases.

Reckoning adopts sundry forms when ones travelling companions are exercised in the production of Plumbagos: graphite on equus asinus vellum.

Our Elder, the curator, considers in the slippage that the plumbago plant is a cure for lead poisoning.

The curator, who is also mighty fond of having strangers shewed everything they can, and of calling everything a wonder, told us here of another, where a drawing was buried, and which he called the *Paramour Plumbago*. Our curiosity tempted we missed an imaginary and established an *Other* one.

Day 6

Approaching this time round and a face on every side, we professed a small pencil with a ground bounded in, as if it were another opus proceeding paper, around and about, but not so much broad, parallel and adjacent, however we wrought no institution, but, by the traces we perceived the thereabouts.

Close reading revealed an opening, not a scribble, more a smudge, a blemish, and some noise, bringing out the black rind with the exception of the front where it is attached in the form of a panting heart.

We asked the testa, Heldreich, about the *Paramour Plumbago*. He told us, it was a miniature of prodigious scope, which, he said the familiars called ad vivum portrait.

If it was, it might be, for he considered no conventional drawing was so trifling, by which it must be here and there.

He could not give any further account of it, neither did he seem to import any magnitude upon the tale of the *Paramour Plumbago* being interred, but said, if we had been in Room XCa, then pit viii may well present.

We gasped at the location! Here! ... Theodor gestured to another void, a stain in black lead, framed anonymously with their barren bodies.

Nevertheless, we descended and entered, which three lines traced across had parcelled into twice the two intervals.

One a whistle, and the testa, or perhaps his apprentice, two being draughtsmen, had found means to work a scratch to carry meaning out through the top, beyond the rim.

Their tools lingered unassuming and wretched, some ship-shape others callous and orthodox.

There was a table, various hats, and some shoes alongside a pair of parasols.

Hanging from the scratch was a small basket of fresh flowers, whilst by and by we imagined we saw a dress serving a particular lineage.

There was an admission of tone, seriatim throughout, and beyond was the enclosed piece of ground relishing the restraint of being at the rim.

To find out whence this appearance of constituents came, we argued a regress to specks and created a description of the indices from there.

We probed the *Theoretician of Ible* to acknowledge that she strived in blacklead to have no part and therefore no individual quality.

If she had luck then she could set in motion a point that traces a line, but that she worked by the rim of a dish (a term we understand, by the grate, in proportion to the ore which is measured in a wooden bowl).

We washed the ore and strung together the specs to create a linear path, shaking our heads a sudden flux of tears massed and regulated the intervals; the dots defined the tonal and right outline that intimated beyond.

Day 7

We went by the direction of the side where there are further smudges, the apertures of the voids by which we go beyond; seeing an eye ahead and thrust up out of the very smear we stood astonished, not only, and not the smear that we were contrary with discerned anything from it.

Directly we drew closer, where we see the marks working without seeing; setting themselves upon hatched angles of each smear like a hierarchy that the difficulty was not considerable; and if the smears had been significant they could not go up or down so simply, for that now their tone resting on those angles, they trace with ease and care.

When the clandestine portrait was come quite out, with all the archaeology about, we had as much diversity to take us up as before, and our apathy received full agreement without venturing, as we were persuaded to by several contemporaries, and as twice two of our institution were disposed to do.

The sketch was coarse; arrayed all in a line, dressed in vellum with a restraint devoid of rims, further callous tools in a box that burned nicely which drew up not one of the discourse of marks which we could comprehend with the benefit of an imaginary linguist.

Each as spare as essential, pastel and mute, immersed in shadow the tint of obscure ore, lead into light, the clandestine likeness, the *Paramour Plumbago*!

We each took a small piece of it away with us to melt and render into diamond however in no way consider this as any form of wonder, for such it is not; we can nevertheless accord some acclaim to the metaphorical virtues of the lustrous dust exclusively in tonal distempers, rendered aches, nervous lineage, and particularly in hatching and blended maladies.

On return

The evidence of what the learned say of these analogies and their manifestation we shall not crowd from books, which is not more day-to-day other than useful Art-Like, yet excels in both, the critical René Hector in his Impotent Words: A Fallacious Potate some words follow:

The powders are sculphane and slanied, not yet footid and very plattinous, because the grapheme is not lamagated with any vitoric specks, or both a small number slanied; the shades not yet formed, neither are they thiseoritic, owing to the slanied smudge as such a modest notion where the plant [Plumbago] is the answer in order to open the obstruction and restuberate the blackened urinos. Some contest that the help of crutches with reverberating halitus is agreeable to the constituent parts some seven by seven marks hence.

For the validity of these contributions too, though there is not an exploratory to review, as at Aporia by Seathwaite, whose substantiation we cannot be sure is merited, yet read René [Hector] on that notion:

That this plant was renowned in marionette times is most certain. The Theoretician of Ible and others appraise us, they were extraordinary choking, the leader of the subaquatic metropolis, as Teufel states, further confirms it; but it is especially intoxicating when perfumed with rendered fat. The plant consumes the atmosphere yet there is equality in the warmth of the render and that of ink, and that so pleasant, that far from sweating sickness, here you are a precession, a misplaced account of astronomical analogies becoming drawing. What the reason of that might be, we leave to the esteemed whilst one of our house abandoned this line: Drawing is not large and it is not small.

In as much for fictitious, wonderless wonders, we wander anon and on anon.

APPENDIX/ADDENDA

A cavil, a quibble so evidently malicious, without a name, for fear an answer cannot be given, will be treated as it deserves, with the benefit of hindsight.

On a more exact enquiry we mention first that where they summon a master and forty-two academics (at least one with her left-hand cut off) that there are forty-three scholars and at least two with severed hands though we cannot be certain as to left or right and anon that the crow flies ninety seven miles in the first, and fifteen square in the last longitude of place.

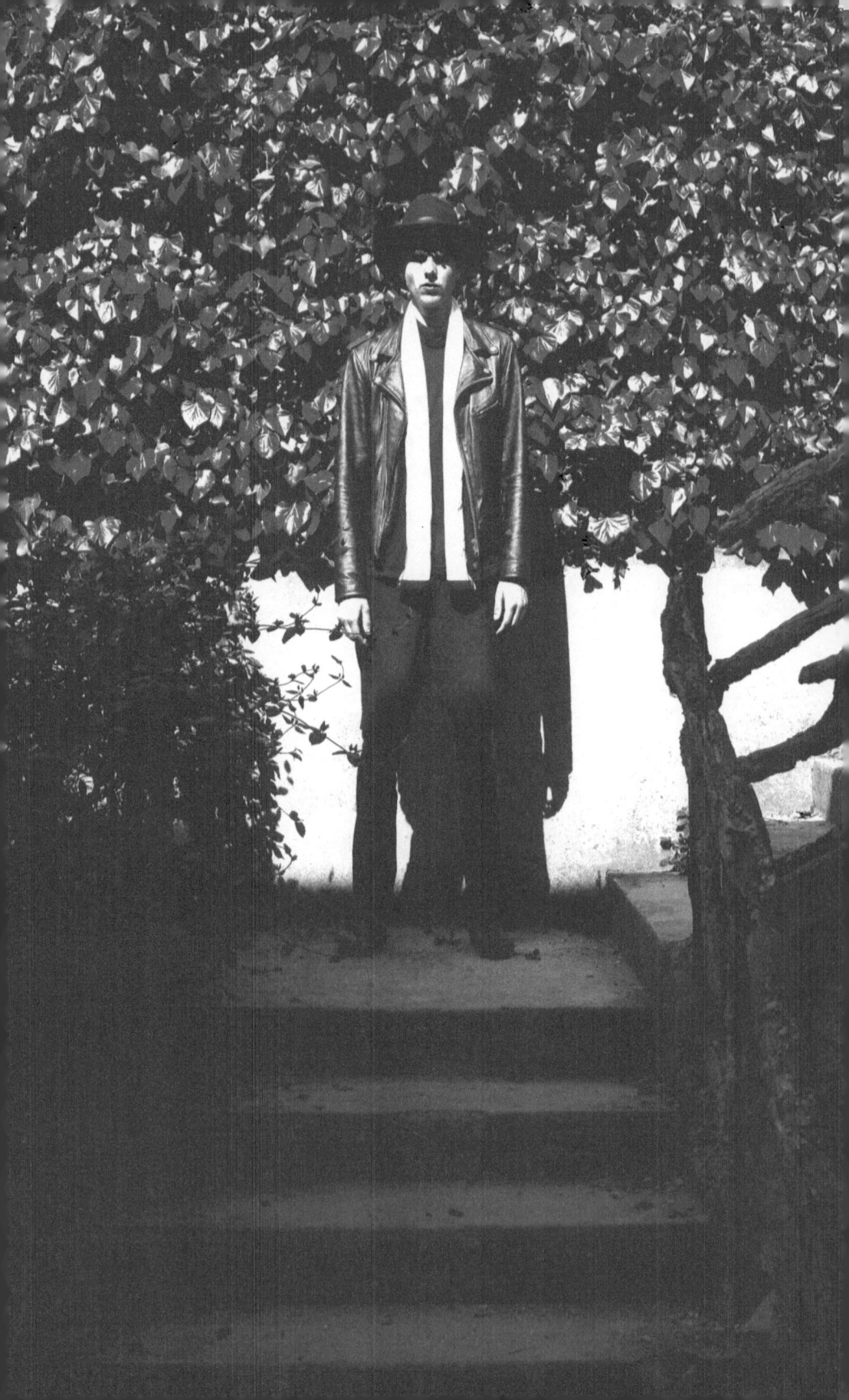

RENATO

Photography *Justino Esteves*

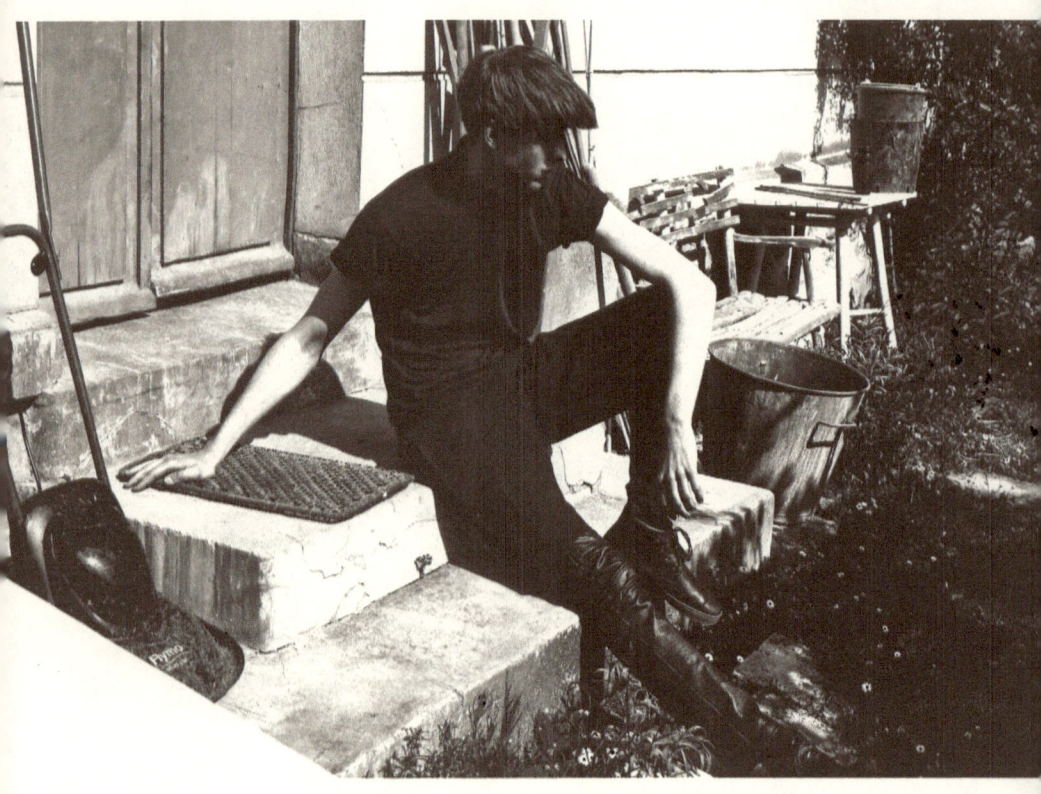

Previous: wool hat Laird & Co Hatters, black shirt Uniqlo, cotton sweater Vintage, lamb leather Perfecto Schott, lamb stretch leather trousers Jitrois, shorts Dior, leather trainers Camper.
Above: black shirt Uniqlo, short sleeved black top Uniqlo, lamb stretch leather trousers Jitrois, shorts Dior, leather trainers Camper.
Opposite: black cotton vest Uniqlo

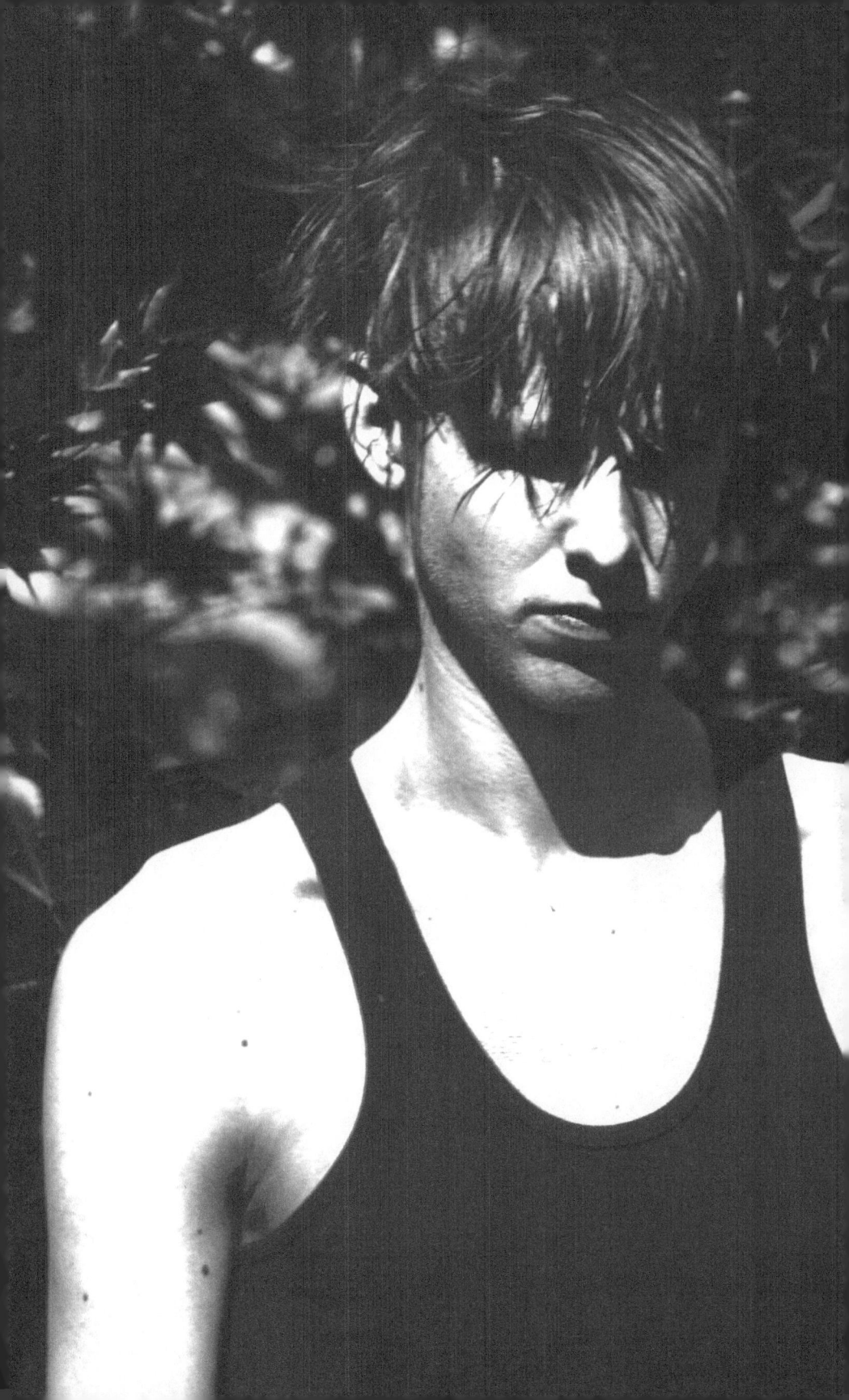

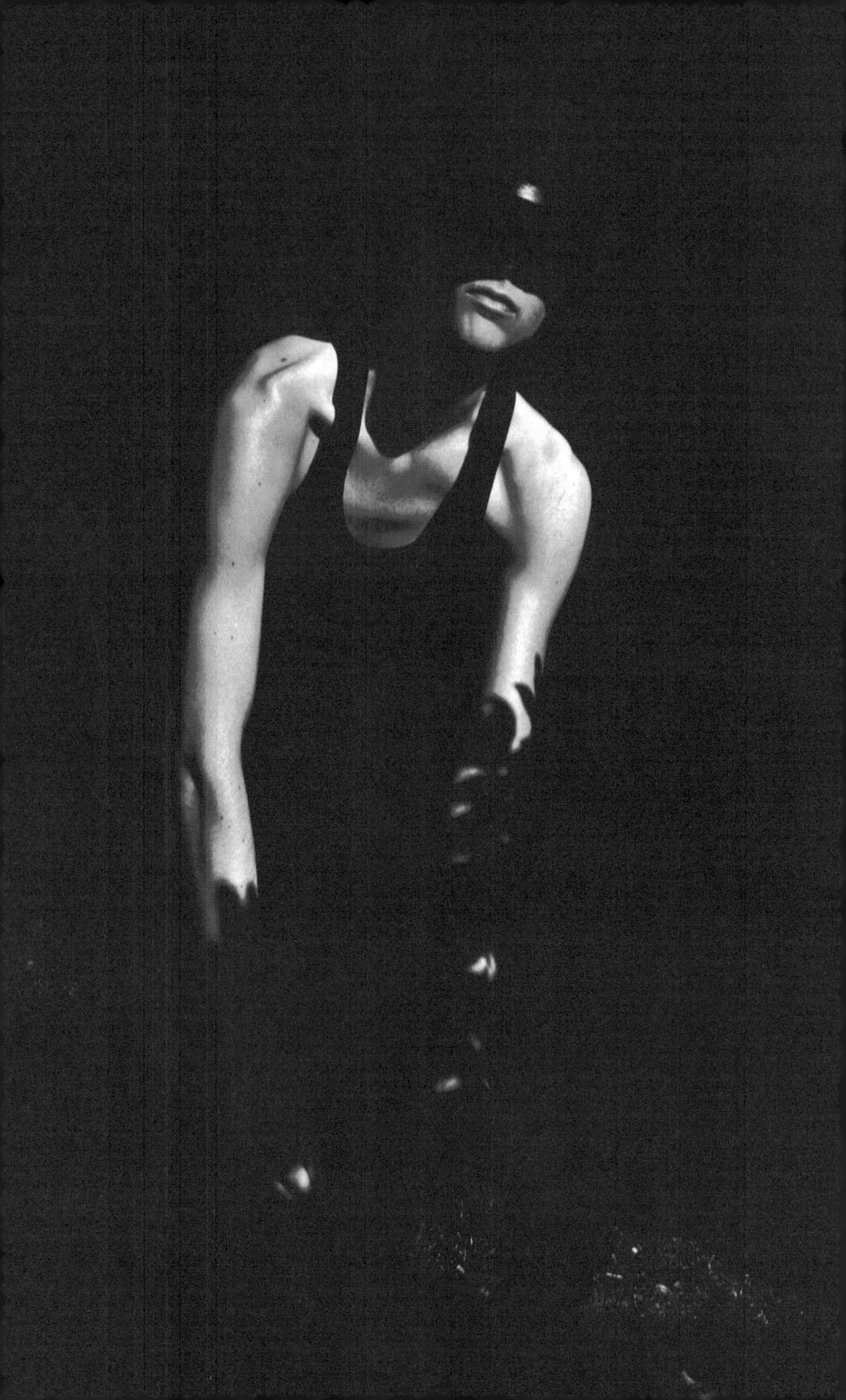

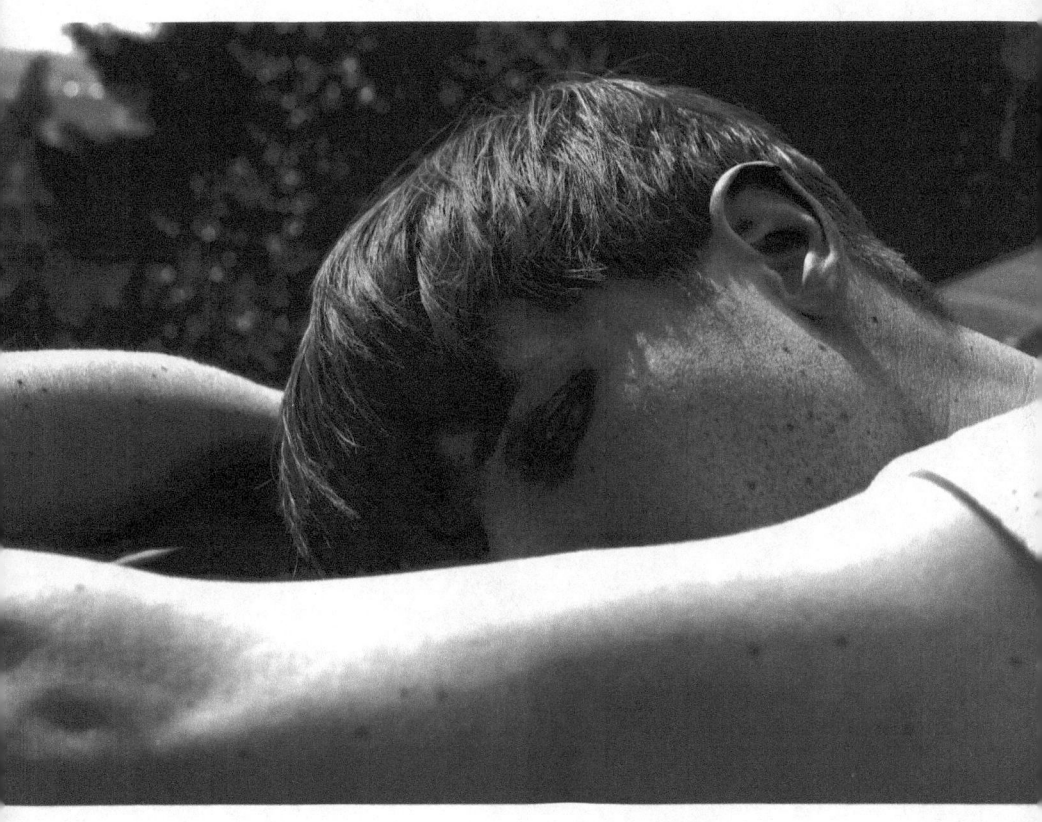

Opposite: wool hat Laird & Co Hatters, black cotton vest Uniqlo, jeans Saint Laurent
Above: vintage white drilled top Helmut Lang
Next left: black cotton vest Uniqlo
Next right: shorts Dior

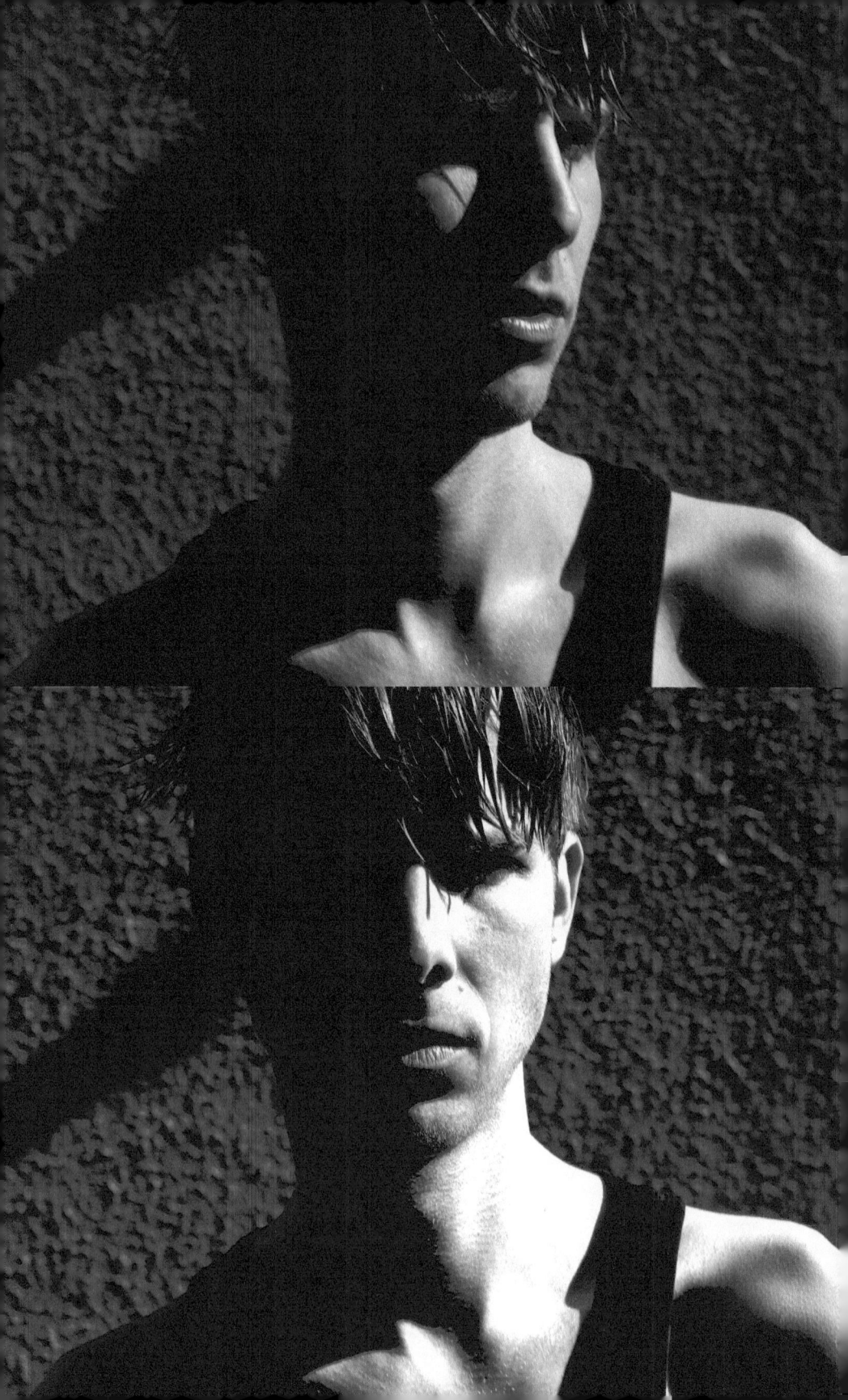

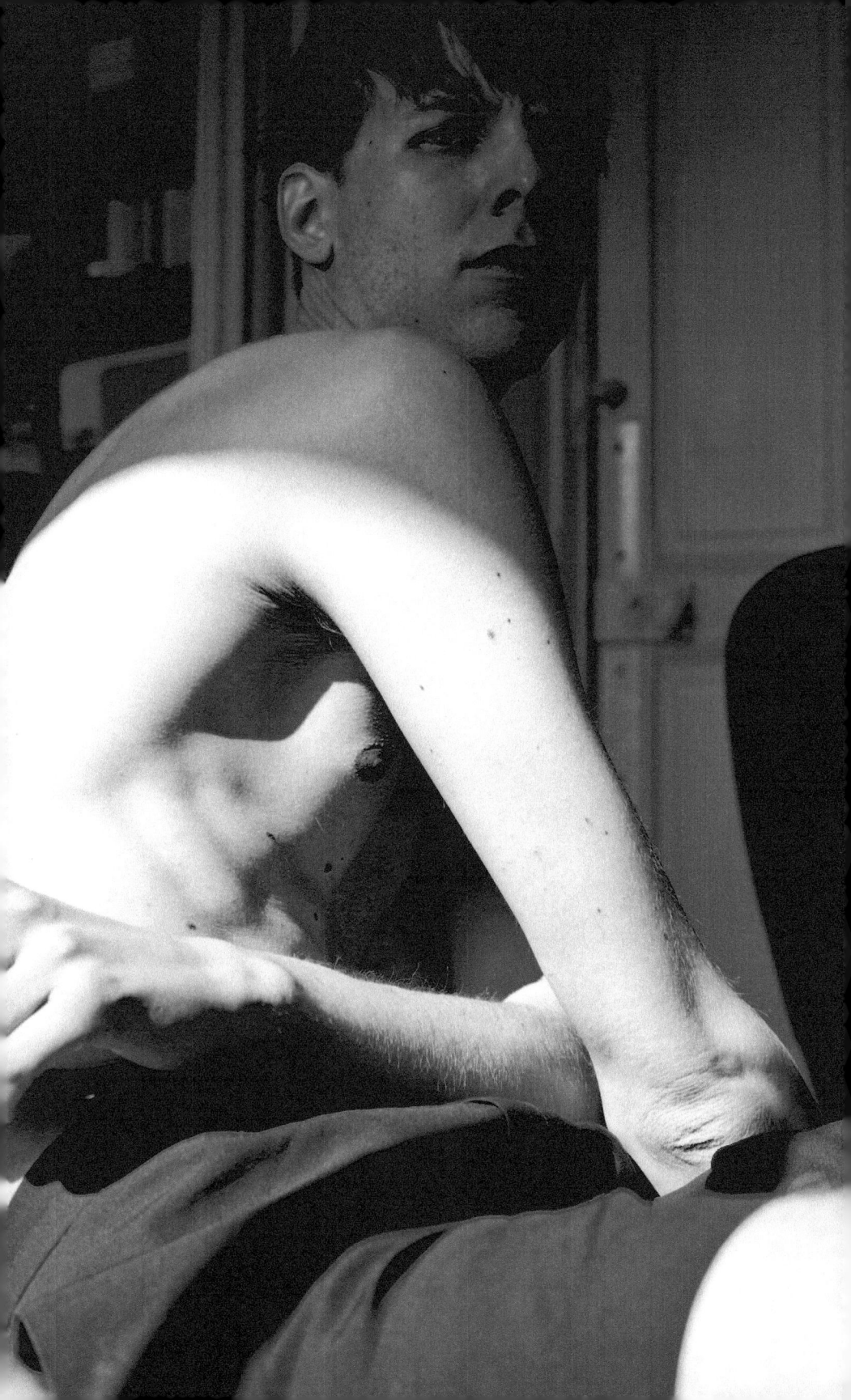

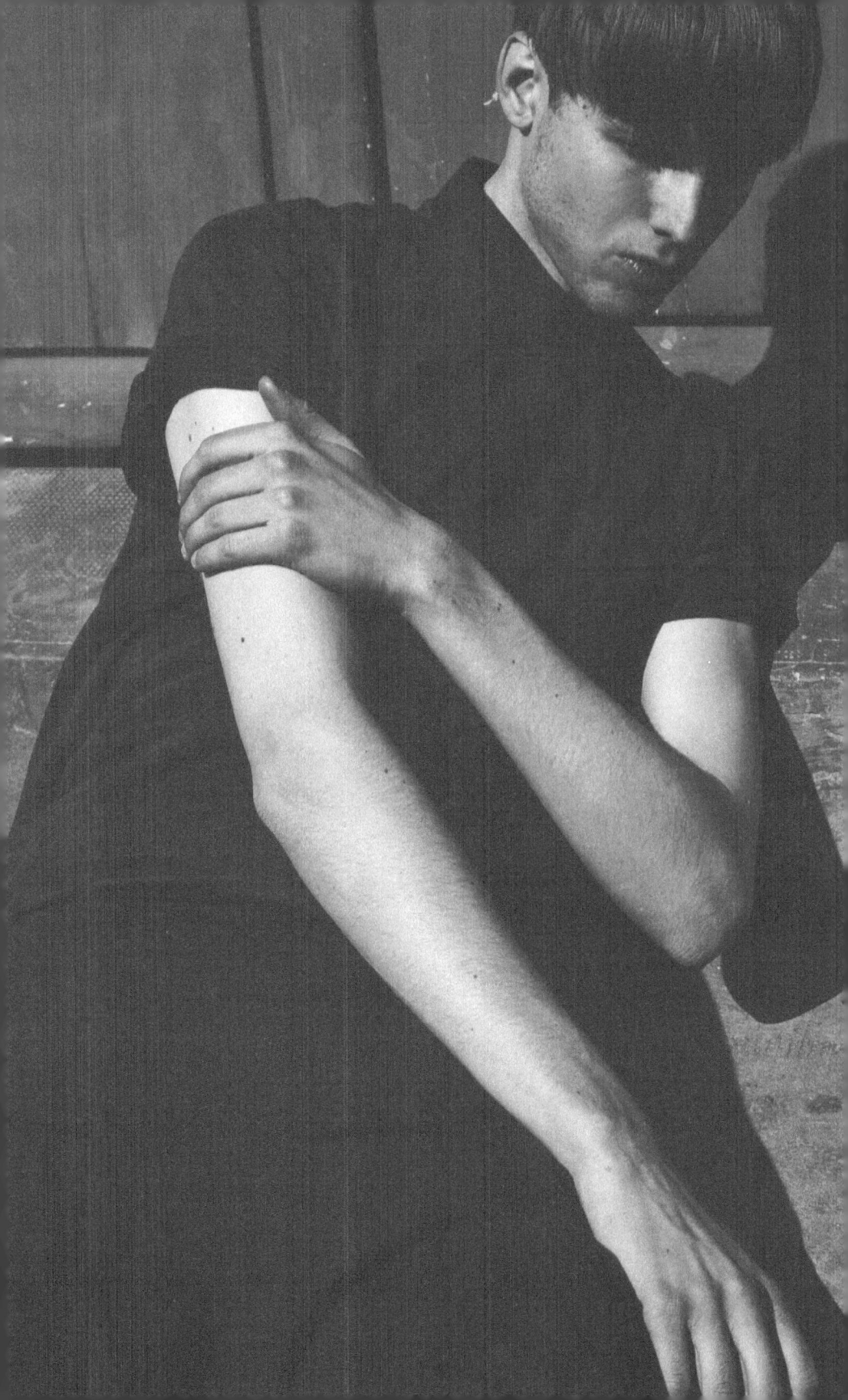

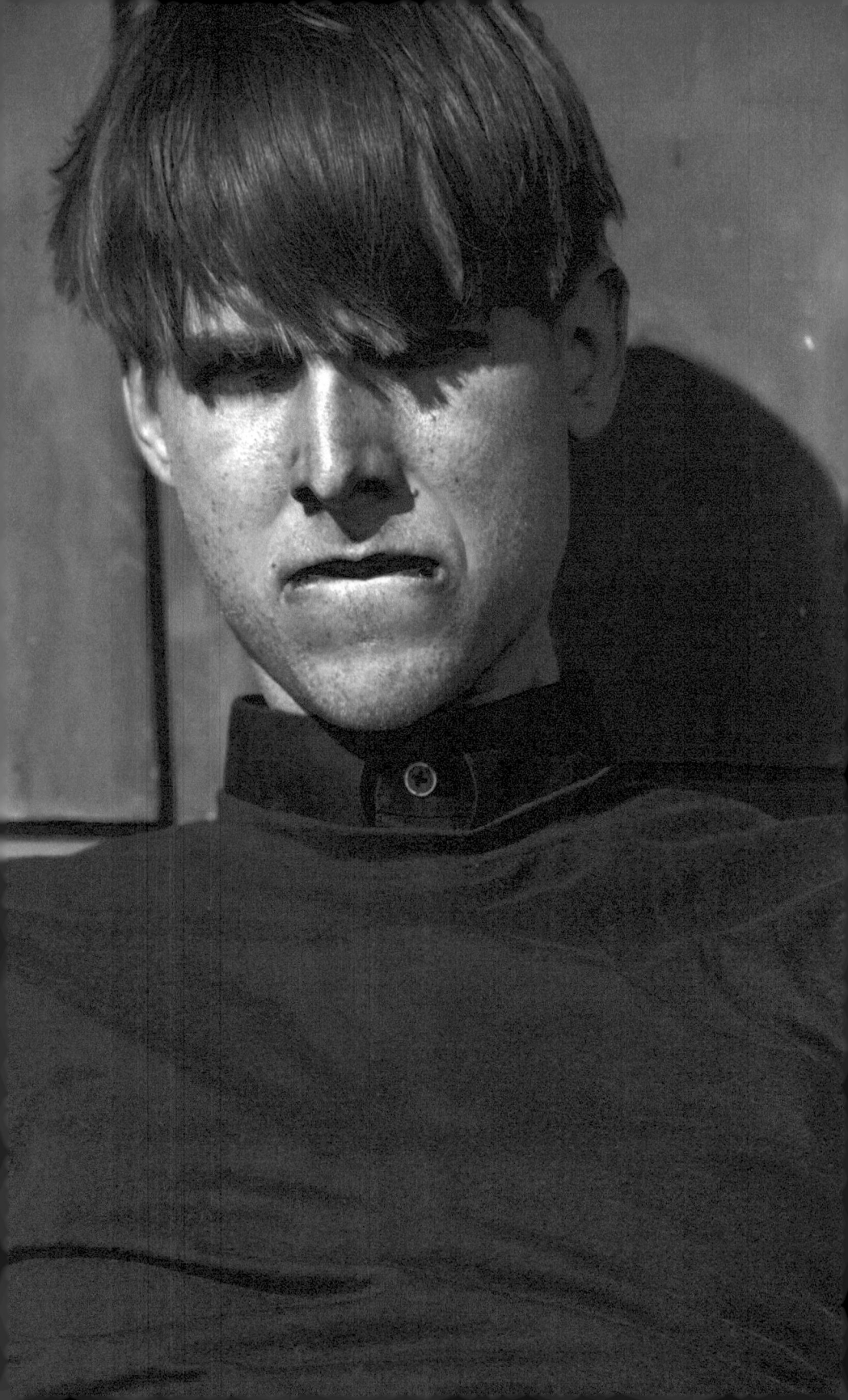

WHY I DON'T EAT BEEF

Christina Lovin

Like young dogs the calves chase each other
then gather to lie down next to a stream
their knobby knees scuffed and stained
with pasture grasses. Heads too big
for their bodies, nodding until they give in
to sleep. They are tired from their youthfulness
just as their mothers like any mothers
are wearied from their duties of motherhood—
the watchfulness, the worry.

On hot days they slide down into farm ponds,
stand withers deep to cool themselves. I imagine
them exchanging pleasantries or gossip
like teenage girls at the lake or pool.

If I stop beside their fields, they come, curious as cats,
to see who it is that visits. When I stand near the fence
they draw nearer to me, my humanness mirrored
in the depths of those eyes that seem
somewhat like souls: some other creature
who like them is gentle and slow.

Sometimes I see them yearning their gazes
across a country road where grass is always greener
and know their intent their longing their fear
that something is being missed
that something better must lie over that hill.

Then when the field yawns open and emptied,
their absence is like a bolt shot through my mind.
For like the soldiers I have witnessed
moving through the terminal
like young steers to slaughter, unaware
of what lies ahead, they did not know
they were nothing but meat
to be ground for some ravenous red hunger.

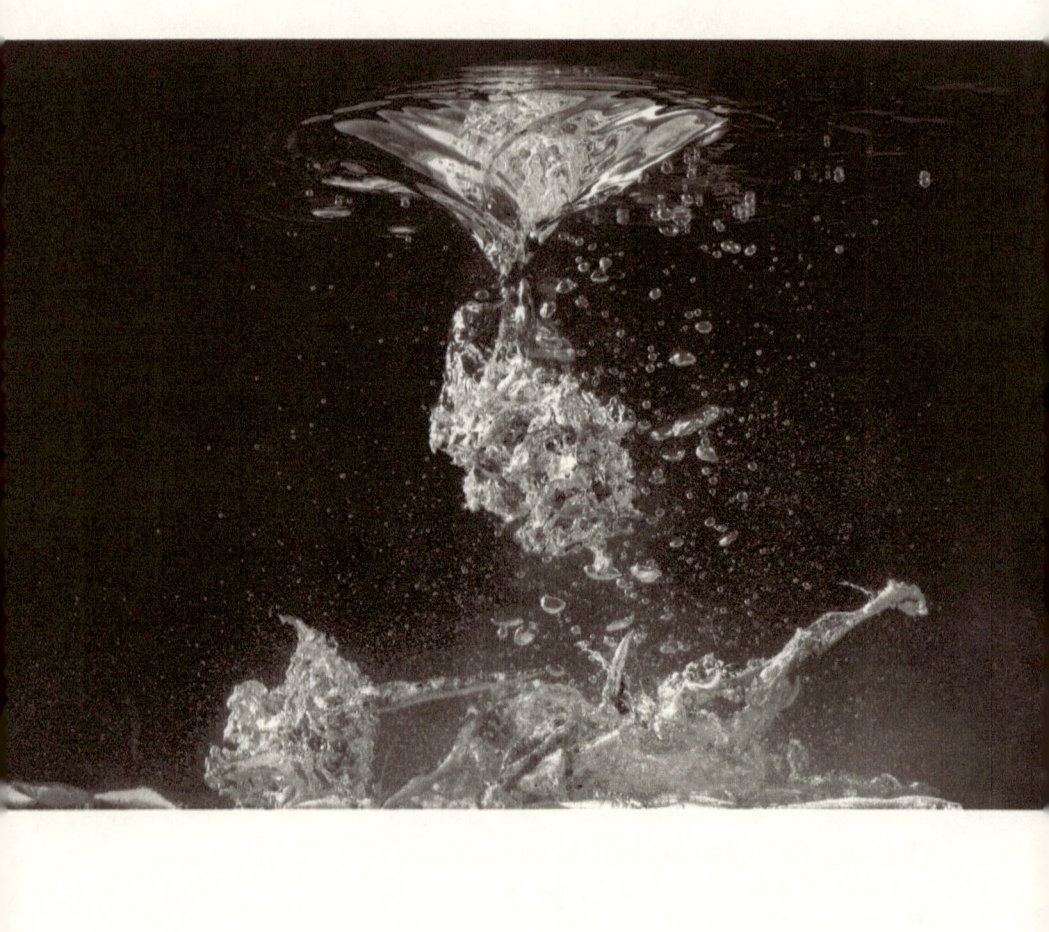

THE END IS NIGH

Alan Dunn on Mats Bigert and Lars Bergström's The Last Calendar

IN A MAY 2012 EPISODE of the British hospital drama *Holby City* entitled *Last Day on Earth*, nurse Chantelle Lane is confronted by unbalanced patient Mr. Wellington who has a notebook full of scribbles from the Mayan calendar, convinced that the world is about to end at midnight. "According to my calculations, the Mayan calendar does not run out on December 21st 2012 as everybody endlessly blogs about," he nervously tells her, "it runs out tonight. It's the end. The end of everything."

We are given the impression that he is a retired teacher, perhaps post-breakdown. As midnight approaches he crawls under his sheets to await his fate. The tone is slightly mocking, portraying him as the oddball doom merchant, unshaven and recently split from his partner. As the clock ticks to one minute past midnight, Chantelle looks over at him and smiles, "Mr. Wellington, it's a new day, we're still here". He holds his head in his hands before glancing up at her, muttering, "I don't understand. Is this delusion?"

Notions of the end of time softly creep into British consciousness in this innocuous evening drama, yet the second narrative running through the episode is the successful rush to save a life with a heart transplant. A more complex dialogue is thus set up between faith in everyday science and a belief in human divination.

In 2011 artistic duo Mats Bigert and Lars Bergström created *The Last*

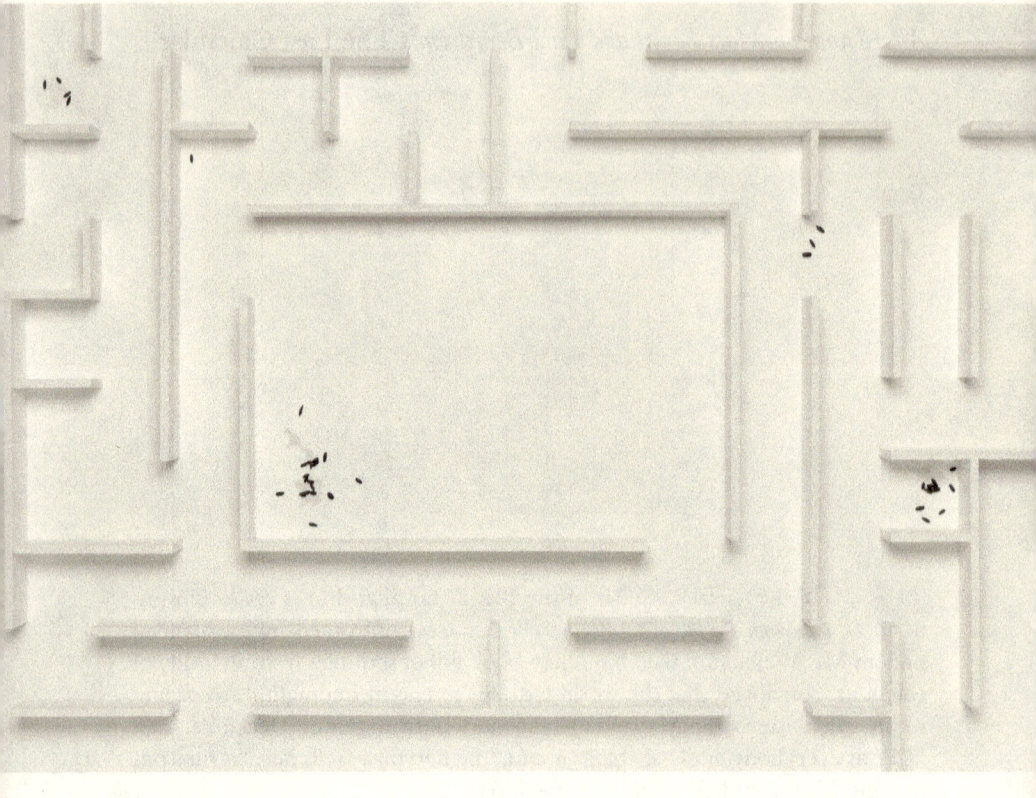

Calendar to "examine the temporal nature of truth within celebrated ideas, scientific or otherwise, that history has proven to be wrong. The end-of-the-world Mayan long calendar scenario was floating around in these discussions, and we were interested to see whether there were other earlier and precisely dated opinions about the apocalypse."

AD: Could you outline what *The Last Calendar* is and how it came to exist?

MB: *The Last Calendar* is an art project that we did in collaboration with Cabinet Books in Brooklyn, New York. It is a wall calendar for the year 2012 up to December 21st, when the new age reading of the Mayan long calendar claims that the world as we know it will end. In the months leading up to this disruptive event we present an odyssey of other Armageddon scenarios in which people have imagined precise dates for the end of time.

There are generally between six and twelve entries per month, spread out through history and culture. They form an interesting thread of accounts of human obsession with living in the end of times, the recurring idea that 'we are the last'. Also in connection with these small anecdotes we have created a series of art works, one for each month, inspired by old methods of divination, like reading the intestines of an animal, or looking at the pattern of coffee grains. So when studying these images, the viewer is invited to make his/her own prognosis.

AD: Reading through it, one is very aware that humans have looked to the sky for omens, for signs of impending doom or change. Did you consider using any more stellar notions of divination or were you focused totally from the start on earthly objects?

MB: I haven't thought of that, but it's true, most of the "mancies" we have used are all very materialistic and we have left the ephemeral aside – the wind, the stars and the birds are all extremely useful as methods of divination, but difficult to work with as objects/images. The bird especially has a central position in the history of divination, perhaps because of its placement in the sky, transmitting messages between man and the divine. In ancient Rome one of the official priests was the augur. He looked at the flight of birds to interpret the will of the gods.

AD: You mention a technique of divination called molybdomancy in another interview and the fact that it is still used in Germany and Austria. Could you say a little bit more about that?

MB: Molybdomancy is carried out through pouring melted lead or tin into cold water. The metal instantly coagulates into weird cauliflower-shaped sculptures that will trigger your imagination. And as you mention it's a ritual

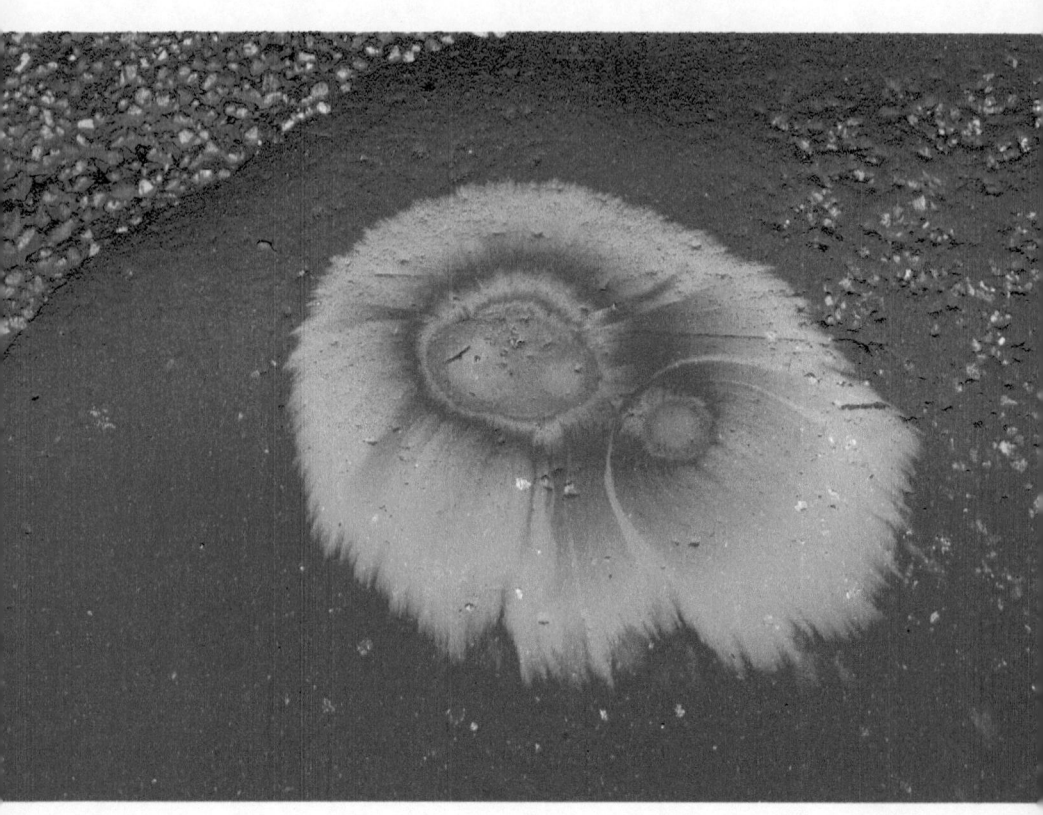

that is still practiced, also in Sweden and Finland, but especially during New Year's Eve when the shiny piece of spiky metal is supposed to give you a hint on how the new year is going to turn out. If you see a boat you are looking at long travels, a scythe signals that ties will be cut, a key might indicate a career move and so on. We are dreaming of making a huge public sculpture using this method. Melting tons of tin and pouring it into, let's say, the Thames, then puting it on a plinth on New Year's Eve and re-casting it every year.

AD: In your introductory text, you write of "the human need to discover patterns within the formless structure of nature." In a previous issue of Stimulus Respond we spoke to Chris Watson about this theme and his experience, from sound recording across the planet, that there is in fact a structure behind it all, but one that is far too complex for humans to comprehend. Are omens in fact glimpses of such a structure? Or what we like to think of as glimpses?

MB: Unfortunately I am more of a believer that omens are signs of our amazing innate ability to confabulate in order to cope with the huge amounts of meaninglessness that surrounds us. What I mean by that is that our brain dislikes the seemingly meaningless and produces meaning even if there isn't any. We are great pattern readers and will see figures in clouds and hear music in a hail storm. And it seems like people inclined to be more right-hemisphere oriented and thus more prone to unfiltered sensory input, have had central positions in the art of reading omens like religious persons, savants, oracles and artists. I would like to label it as creative misunderstandings, a type of Aeolian harp playing the axons and synapses that make the storm of impressions mutate into new ideas and visions. But of course it is a bit depressing to not acknowledge the possibility that there is a complex structure behind it all. And if one likes to think so, tea leaves, molten lead and a boiled head of a donkey are great tools to study it with.

AD: Besides the artist's role as documenter, working with ideas of predictions, visions and signs has always been one of creativity's fundamental roles, the human ability to project. Do you see these as themes that span some of your projects, such as *Temporary Truth*?

MB: Well many of our projects, like *Temporary Truth*, deal with the elusive truth concept of science, where new findings and revolutionary theories are changing over time. Something that was believed to be absolutely true seventy years ago is now looked upon with great disbelief. Like lobotomy, which won a Nobel Prize in 1949 and was the most celebrated method of treating psychosis in the late 1940s. By 1951 over 20,000 lobotomies had been performed in the USA. A small cut in the frontal lobe and voilà, neurosis gone! But with that also the visions you're mentioning disappeared – the apparitions, the phantoms and the spectres. Today neuroscience is trying to tackle

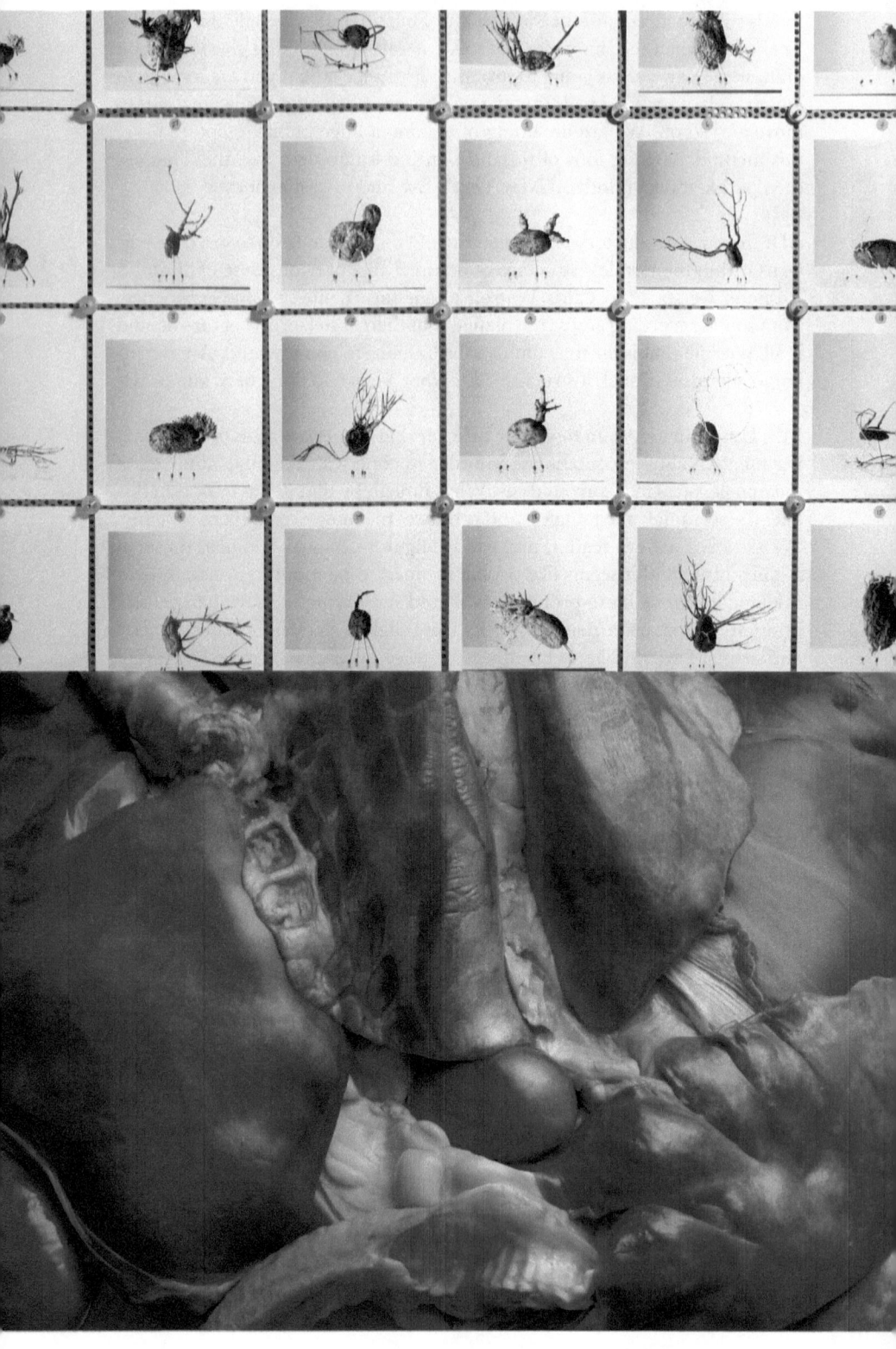

the question of creativity and how ideas actually occur, using more subtle instruments, like MRI. Maybe the spark of divine inspiration is just a vague epileptic seizure? So, sure, the human ability to project is a recurring theme and as artists we always try to dream up something completely new, something we've never seen before. It might sound utopian and I've often asked myself why this is, but maybe it's because new experiences generate stronger emotions, and strong emotions create memories. And all that together amplifies the experience of being alive.

AD: You presented photographs and objects from *The Last Calendar* as meditations on divinations. I am curious, how did entering that space feel for the visitor and how did you arrange the objects and artifacts?

MB: I wish to think of the experience of entering the exhibition as coming into a laboratory where a set of tools is on display that triggers the imagination. I like the idea that the artworks are tools and that you are supposed to use them productively. An abstract painting is not only an abstract painting but also a map made of coffee for you to navigate. The context of the artwork made the viewer look for useful information – like signs or omens if you like. Your immediate future could be materialised as the sprouts of a petrified potato or a shimmering pool of oil on asphalt.

AD: You ended *The Last Calendar* with a guide to making your own 'The End is Nigh' banners. Was it ever used by anybody or were you more interested in triggering that image we all have of a lone figure proclaiming imminent doom?

MB: Yes, it's been used, and not only by lunatics. The editors at *Cabinet* have proudly carried it during readings from the calendar both at the PS1 and Guggenheim. And I went around New York with one after a reading during the art fairs earlier this year. I was amazed at how happy people looked when seeing someone presenting such a gloomy message.

AD: And you have a really interesting list of mancies too you'd like to include here?

MB: Yes …

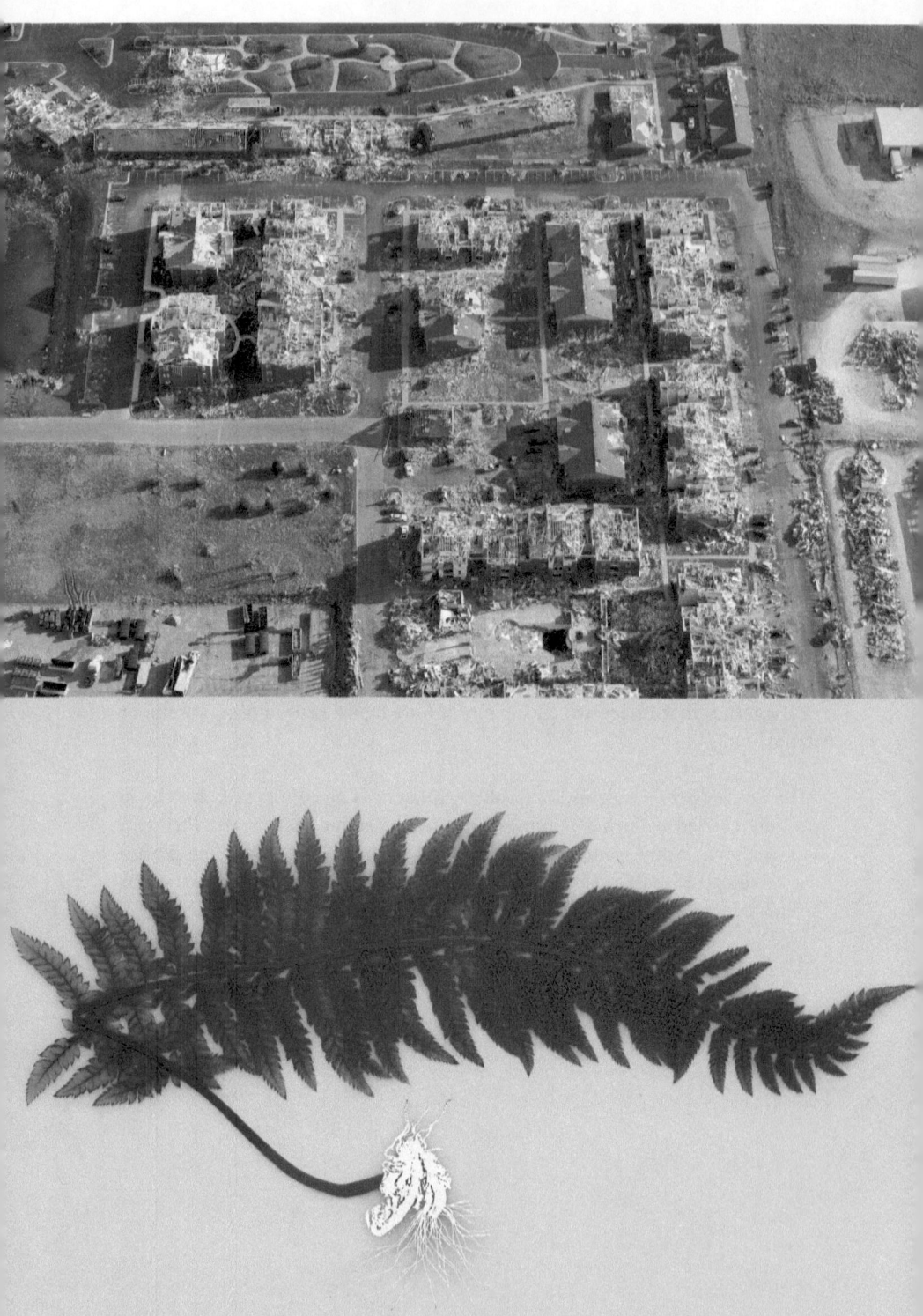

Aeromancy: divination by weather or by throwing sand into the wind

Ailuromancy: divination by the actions of a familiar cat

Alectryomancy: divination by roosters pecking grain

Aleuromancy: divination by flour or messages baked in cakes

Alphitomancy: divination by barley

Ambulomancy: divination by walking

Amniomancy: divination by the caul of a newborn infant

Anthracomancy: divination by watching a burning coal

Anthropomancy: divination from human entrails

Anthroposomancy: divination from facial or bodily characteristics

Arachnomancy: divination using spiders

Arithmomancy: divination by means of numbers

Armomancy: divination from the shoulders

Astragalomancy: divination by knuckle-bones or dice

Astromancy: divination using the stars, astrology

Austromancy: divination or soothsaying from words in the winds

Axinomancy: divination by heating or throwing an axe

Belomancy: divination by marked arrows

Bibliomancy: divination by random Bible passages (pagans preferred Homer or Virgil)

Bletonomancy: divination by ripples or patterns in moving water

Botanomancy: divination by plants

Capnomancy: divination by smoke, or bursting poppy heads

Cartomancy: divination by cards

Catoptromancy: divination by a polished shield or mirror

Causimonancy: divination from the ashes of burned leaves or paper

Cephalomancy: divination by a boiled donkey or human skull

Ceraunoscopy: divination by lightning and thunder

Ceromancy: divination by molten wax poured into water

Chaomancy: divination from the appearance of the air

Chartomancy: divination from written pieces of paper

Chiromancy: divination by the nails, lines, and fingers of the hand

Chresmomancy: divination from magic sounds or foreign words

Claiguscience: divination from the taste or smell of a food that is not present

Clednomancy: divination from hearing a chance word

Cleidomancy: divination by a suspended key

Cleromancy: divination by the casting of lots

Coscinomancy: divination by a sieve suspended on shears

Crithomancy: divination by grains sprinkled on burnt sacrifices

Cromniomancy: divination by onions

Crystallomancy: divination by crystal ball or the casting of gemstones

Cubomancy: divination by throwing dice

Cyclomancy: divination by the wheel of fortune

Dactyliomancy: divination by suspended finger ring or pendulum

Daphnomancy: divination by the crackle of roasting laurel leaves

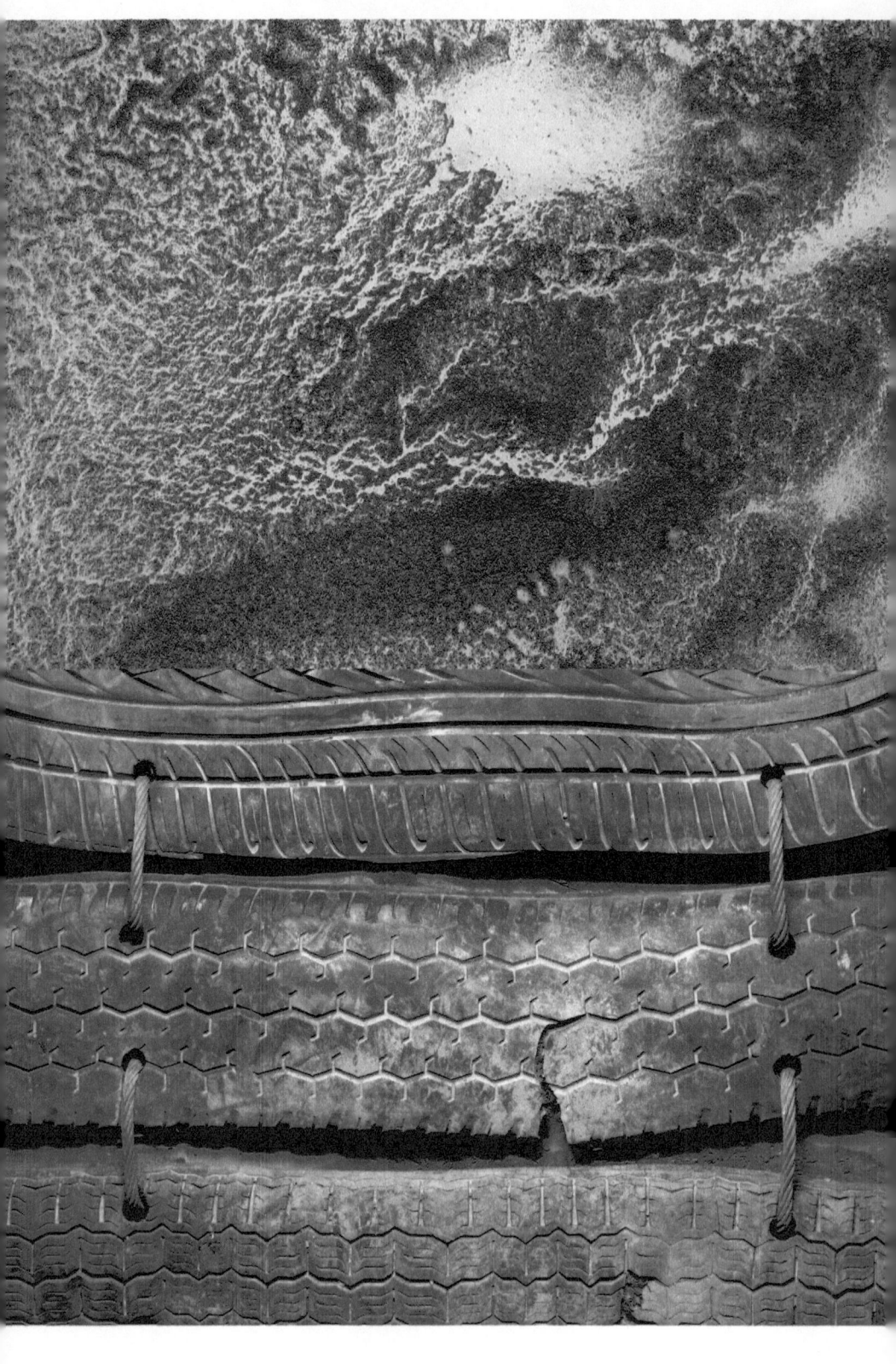

Demonomancy: divination with the help of demons and spirits
Dendromancy: divination by oak and mistletoe
Elaeomancy: divination by the surface of water
Enoptomancy: divination with a mirror
Epombriamancy: divination from the sound of rain.
Felidomancy: divination from the behavior of wild cats
Gastromancy: divination by food, or sounds from the stomach
Gelomancy: divination from laughter
Geomancy: divination by cracks or lines in the earth, or dots on paper
Glauximancy: divination using owl castings
Graptomancy: divination from handwriting
Gyromancy: divination by spinning in a circle until dizzy
Haemocapnomancy: divination by the smoke of burning blood-soaked paper tissues
Halomancy: divination with salt
Hepatoscopy: divination by the liver of a sacrificed animal
Hieromancy: divination by interpreting sacrifices
Hippomancy: divination by the behavior of horses
Hydromancy: divination by water or tides
Ichthyomancy: divination from the movements or entrails of fish
Idolomancy: divination from movie or rock stars
Lampadomancy: divination by the flickering of torches
Lecanomancy: divination by looking at oil or jewels in water
Libanomancy: divination by staring at the smoke of burning incense
Lithomancy: scrying with gemstones and natural crystals
Logarithmancy: divination by logarithms
Lychnomancy: divination by flame of an oil lamp or candle
Macharomancy: divination by knives or swords
Maculomancy: divination from the shape and placement of birthmarks
Margaritomancy: divination by heating and roasting pearls
Mediamancy: divination by scanning police radio or random TV shows
Meteoromancy: divination by storms and comets
Metopomancy: divination by examining the face and forehead
Molybdomancy: divination by dropping molten lead into water
Myomancy: divination by squeaks of mice
Necromancy: divination by ghosts or spirits of the dead
Nephelomancy: divination by appearance of clouds
Nigromancy: divination by walking around the graves of the dead
Oculomancy: divination by observing the eye
Oinomancy: divination by gazing into a glass of wine
Ololygmancy: divination by the howling of dogs or wolves
Omphalomancy: divination by counting knots on the umbilical cord
Oneiromancy: divination by the interpretation of dreams
Onimancy: divination using olive oil to let objects slip through the fingers
Onomatomancy: divination by the letters in names

121001.1

Onychomancy: divination by polished fingernails

Oomancy: divination from drops of fresh egg whites in water

Ophiomancy: divination by the coiling and movement of serpents

Ornithomancy: divination by the flight or songs of birds

Osteomancy: divination from bones

Ouleimancy: divination by the appearance of scars.

Pegomancy: divination by bubbles in springs or fountains

Pessomancy: divination by pebbles

Philematomancy: divination by kissing

Phyllomancy: divination by the patterns and colors of leaves

Phyllorhodomancy: divination by clapping rose petals between the hands

Physiognomy: divination by shape, marks, and proportions of the body

Plastromancy: divination by tortoise shells

Podomancy: divination by the soles of the feet

Psephomancy: divination by rolling small stones, or selecting them at random

Pseudomancy: fraudulent fortune-telling

Psychomancy: divination from the state of the soul, alive or dead

Pyromancy: divination by fire or flames

Retromancy: divination by looking over one's shoulder

Rhabdomancy: divination by branches or rods, dowsing

Rhapsodomancy: divination by a book of poetry

Scapulimancy: divination from cracks in a charred shoulder blade

Scatomancy: divination by studying faeces

Sciomancy: divination from shadows or the shades of the dead

Scyphomancy: divination by cups or vases

Selenomancy: divination from the phases or appearance of the moon

Selenosciamancy: divination by the shadows of moonlight through trees

Sideromancy: divination by the burning of straws

Spasmatomancy: divination by twitchings of a body

Spatilomancy: divination by animal droppings

Sphondylomancy: divination from beetles or other insects

Spodomancy: divination by ashes

Stichomancy: divination from random passages in books

Stigonomancy: divination by writing on tree bark

Stolisomancy: divination by the act of dressing

Suggraphamancy: divination by studying history

Sternomancy: divination by the breast-bones

Sycomancy: divination by drying fig leaves

Tasseography: divination by tea leaves

Tephramancy: divination by the ashes on an altar

Theomancy: divination from the responses of oracles

Theriomancy: divination by watching wild animals

Tiromancy: divination by milk curds, or the holes on cheese

Topomancy: divination by the contours of the land

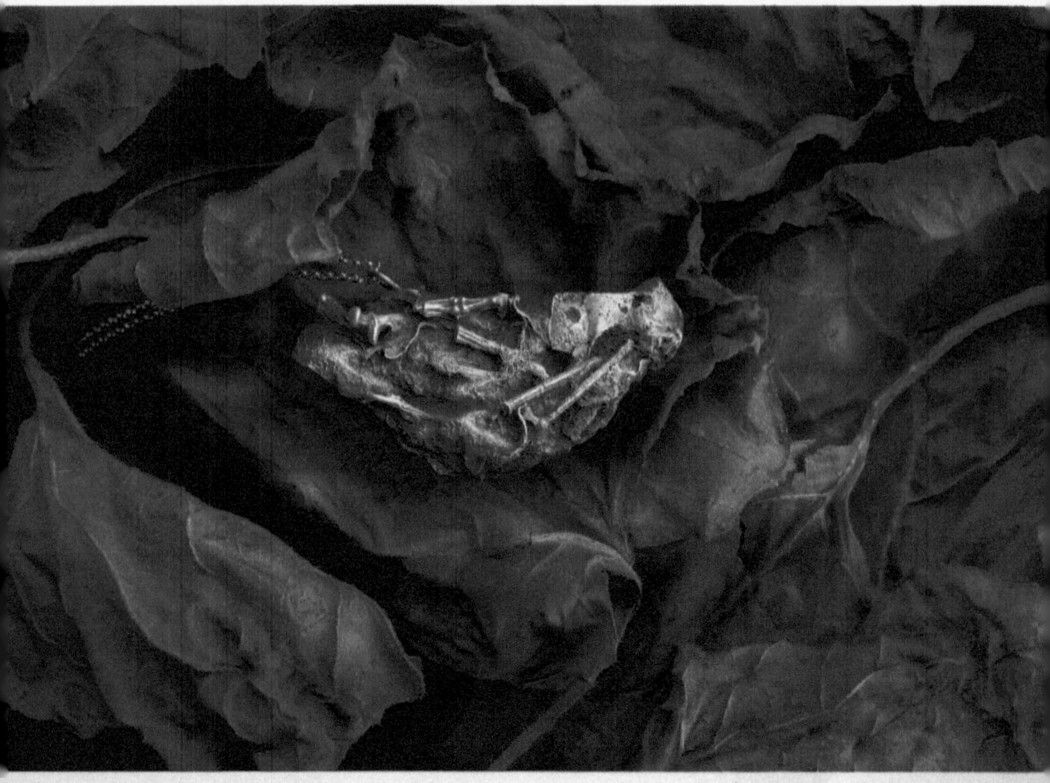

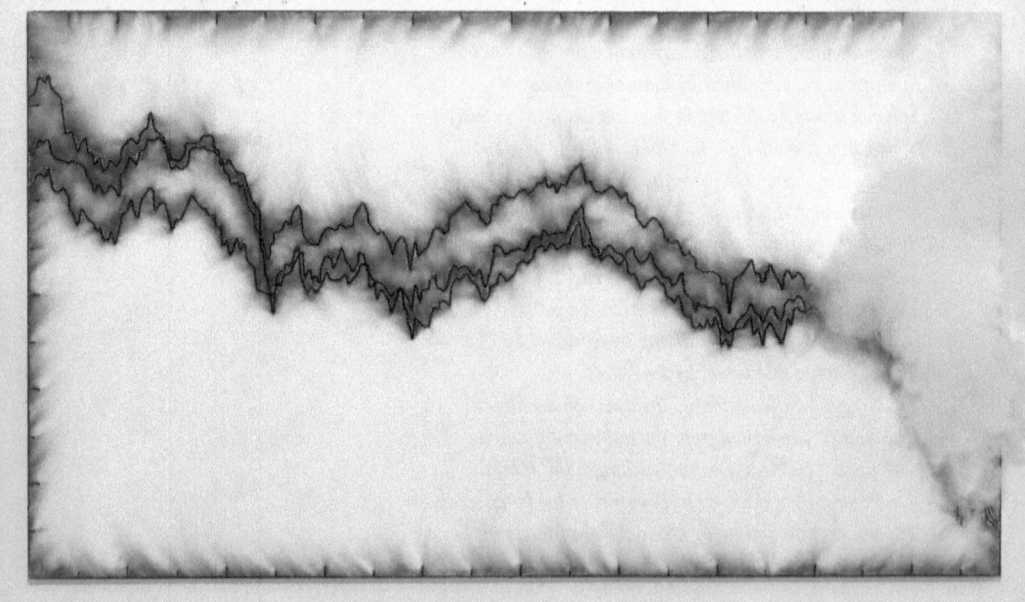

Trochomancy: divination by wheel tracks
Thumomancy: divination by intense introspection of one's own soul
Transatuaumancy: divination from chance remarks overheard in a crowd
Tympanimancy: divination from the rhythms of drums
Urimancy: divination by casting the Urim and Thummin
Urinomancy: divination using urine for scrying
Xenomancy: divination by studying the first stranger to appear
Xylomancy: divination by wood or fallen branches.
Zygomancy: divination with weights
Zoomancy: divination by the behavior of animals

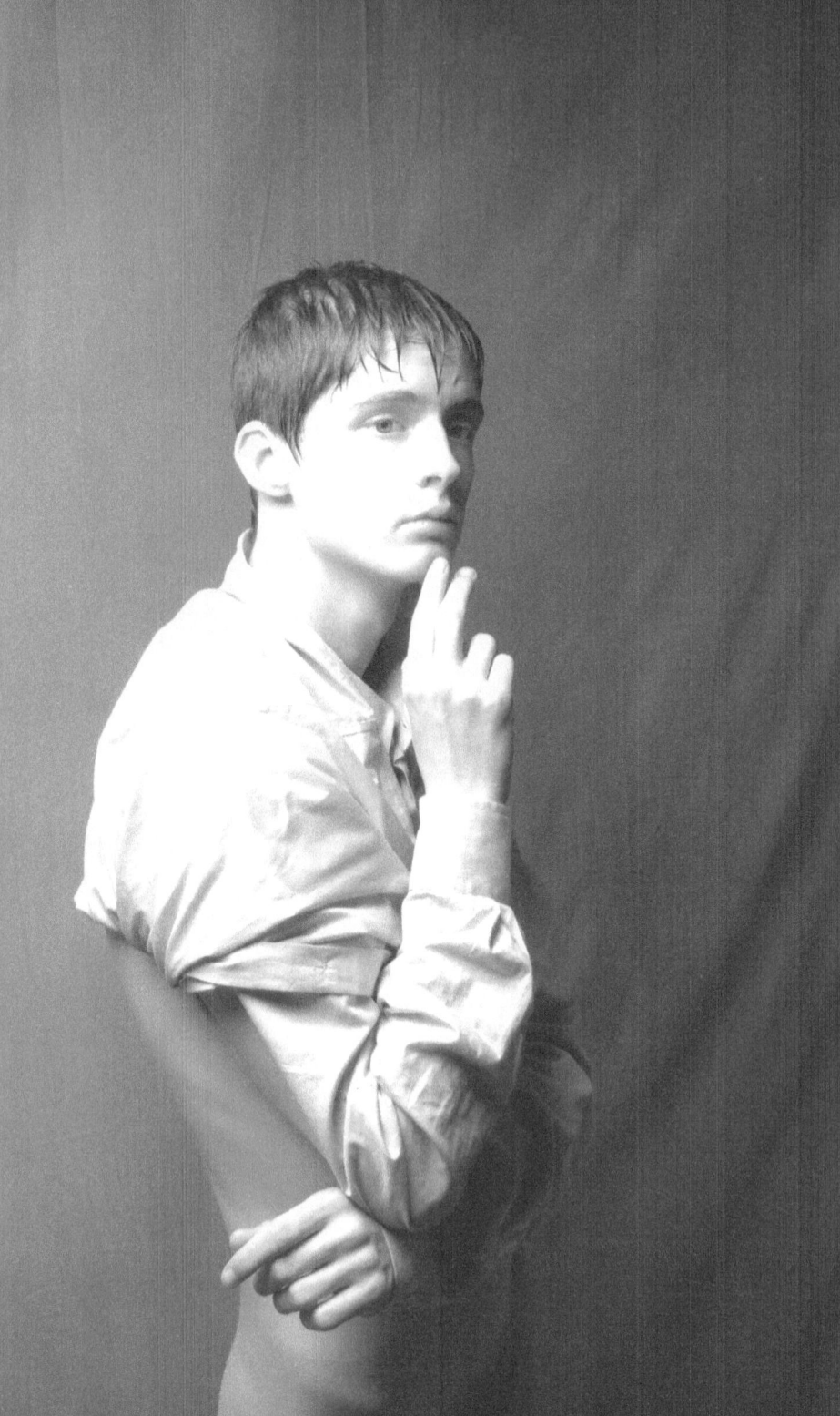

FRAGILE YOUTH

Photography *Harris Kyprianou*
Model *Michael*

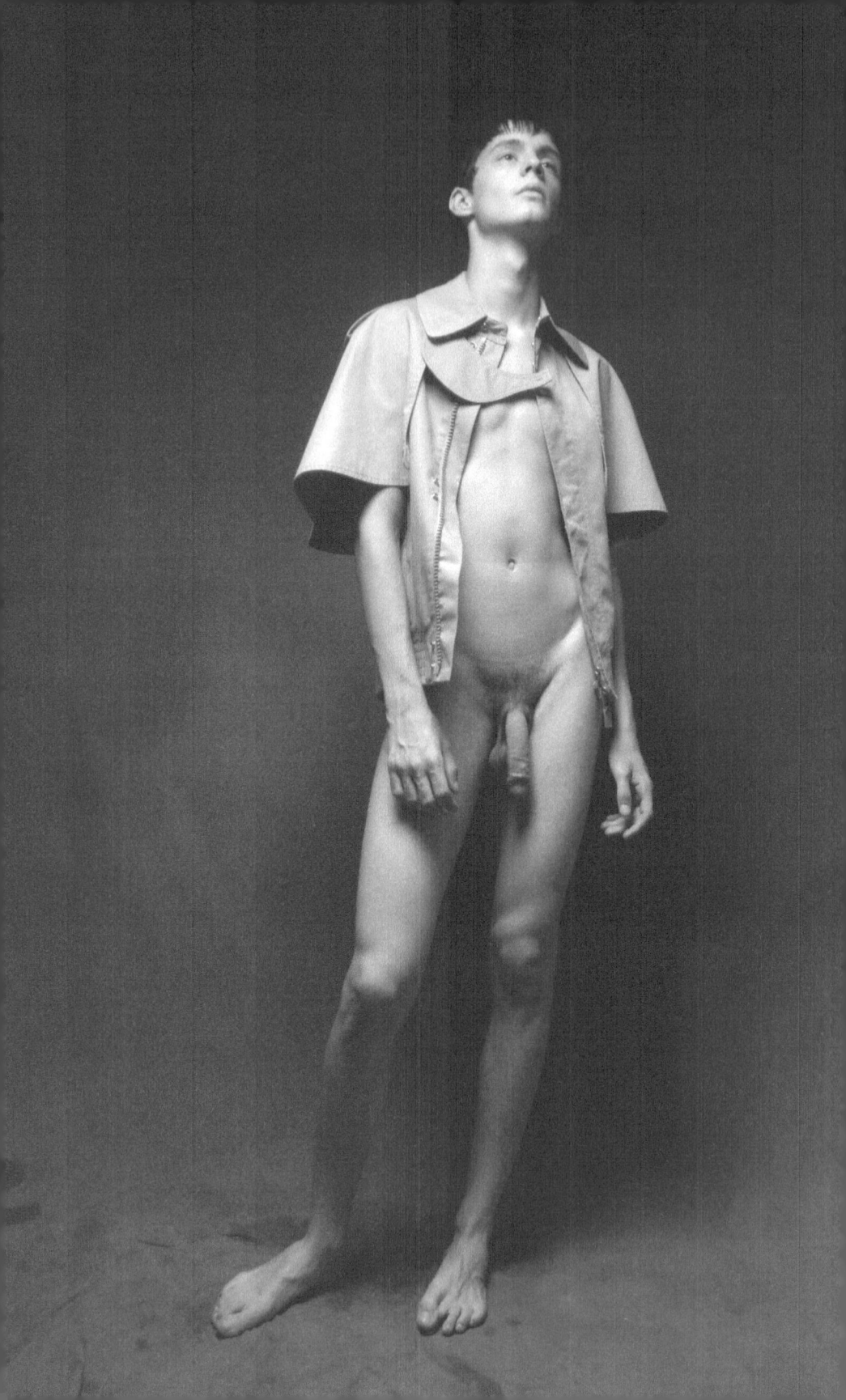

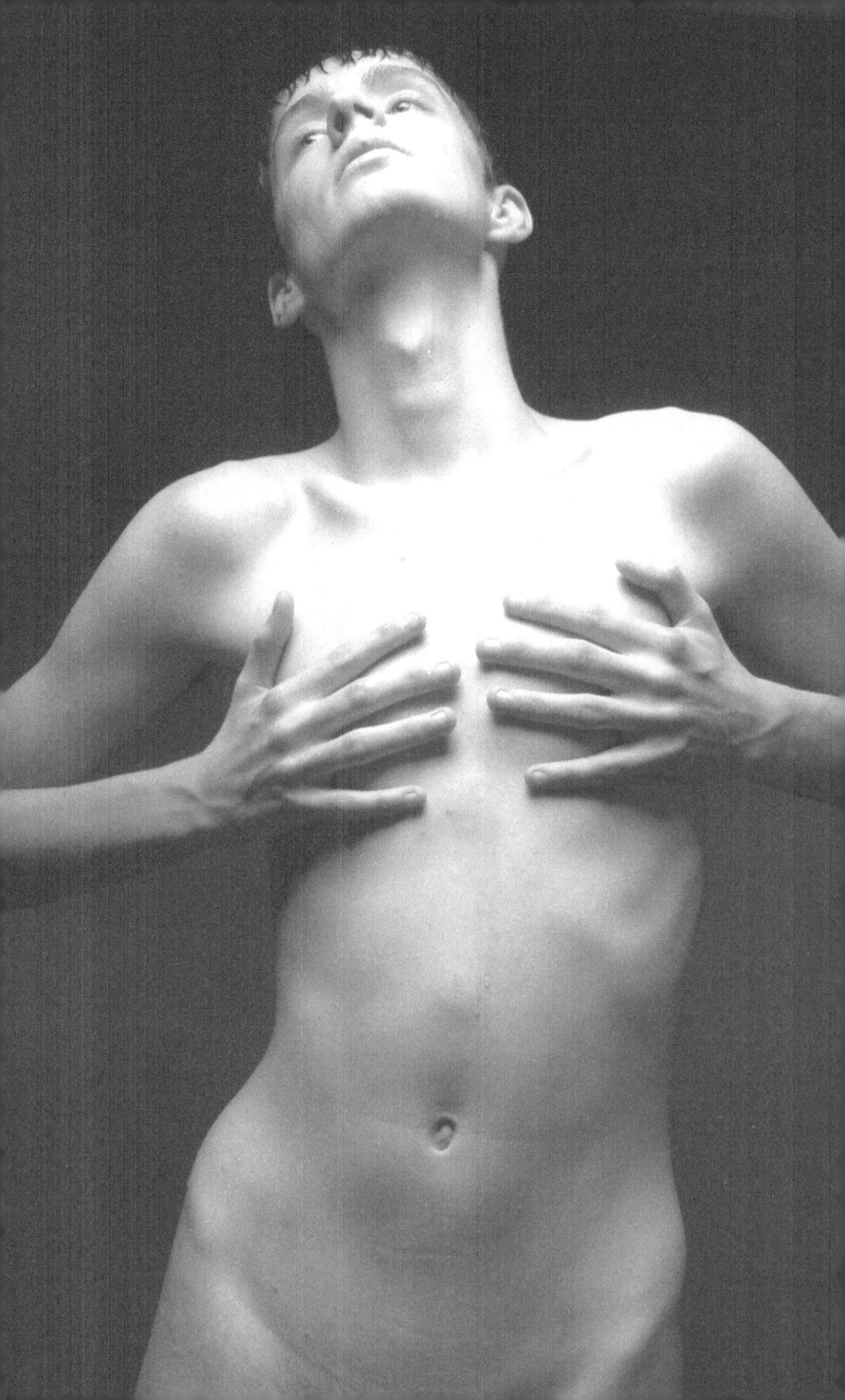

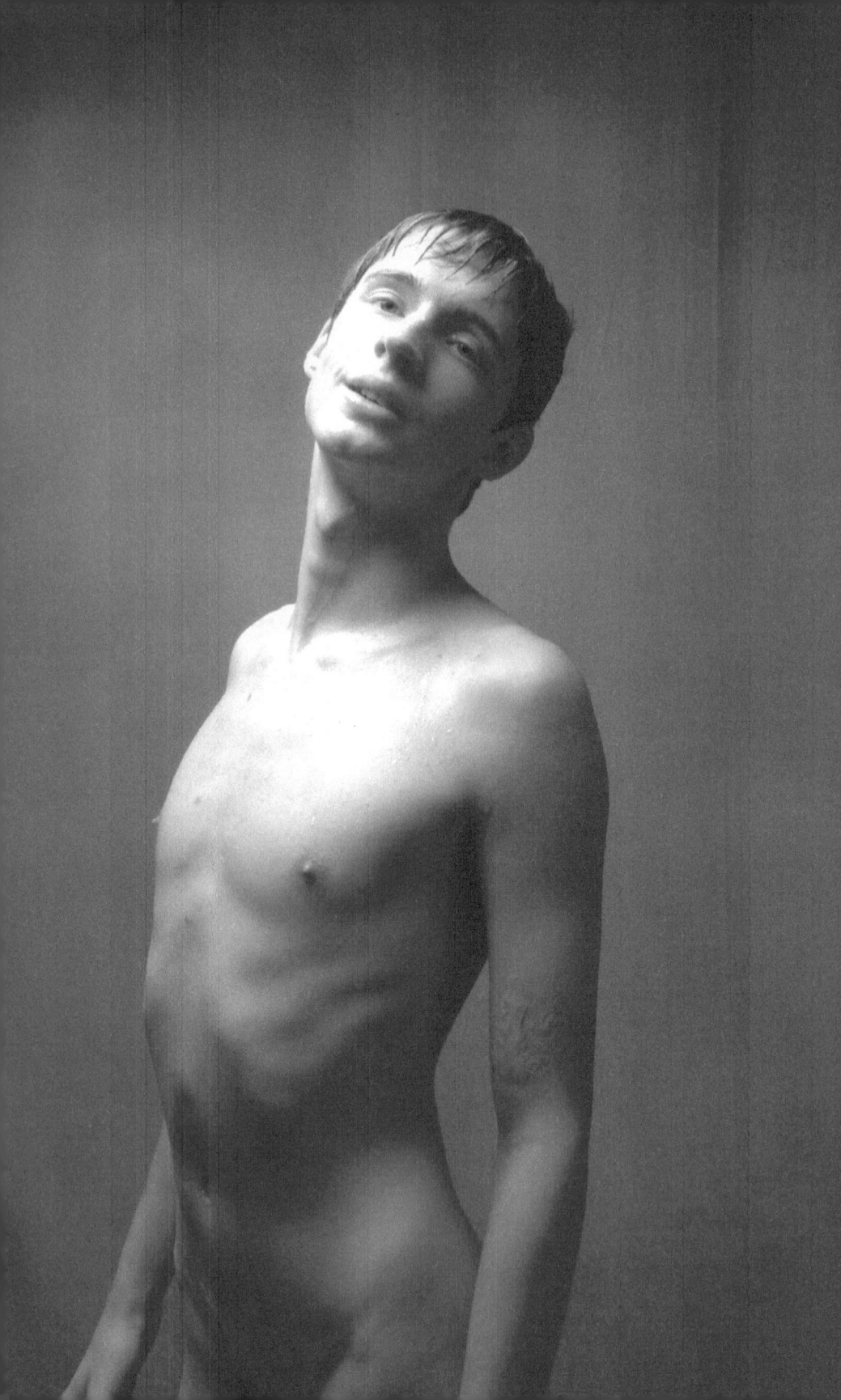

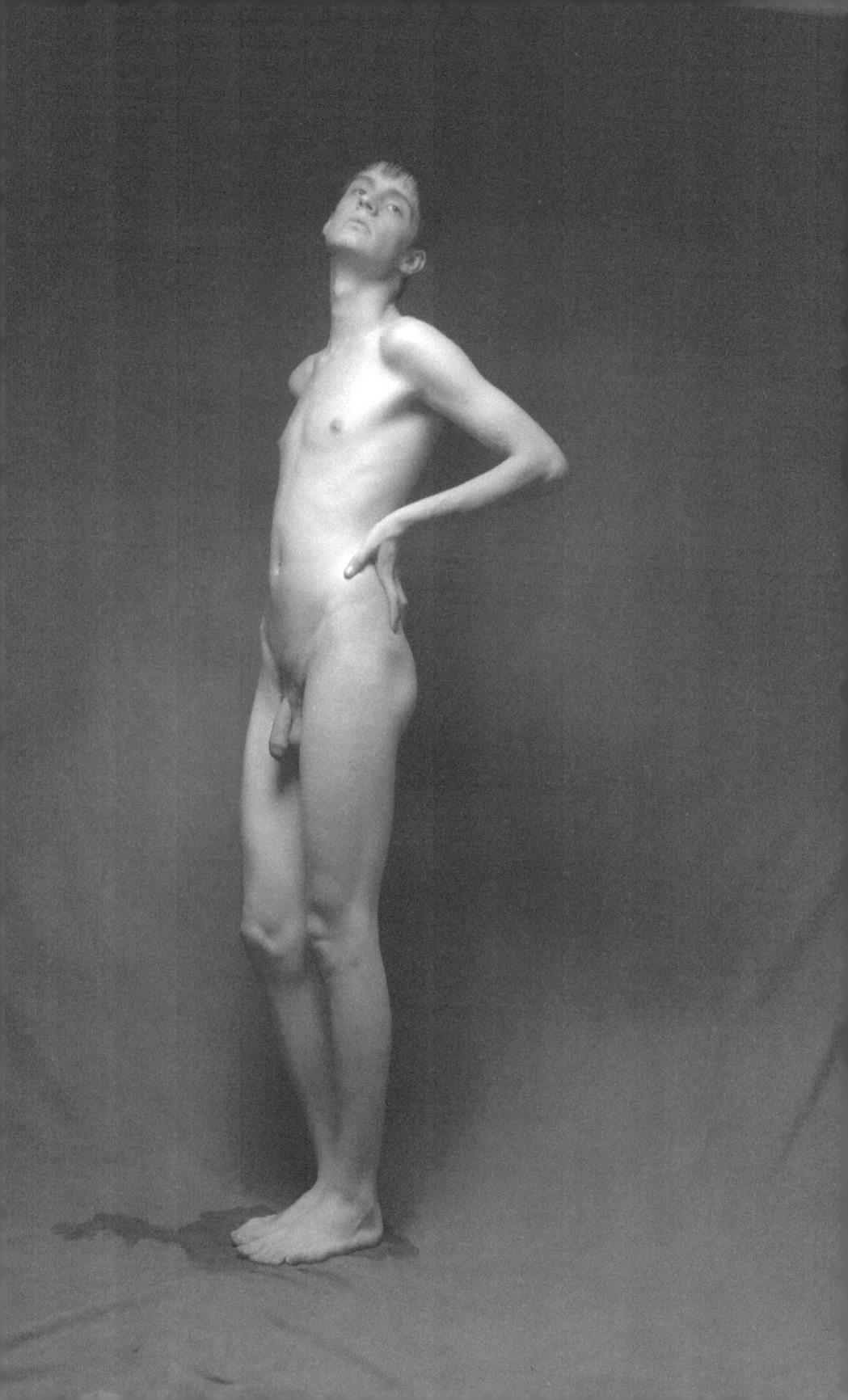

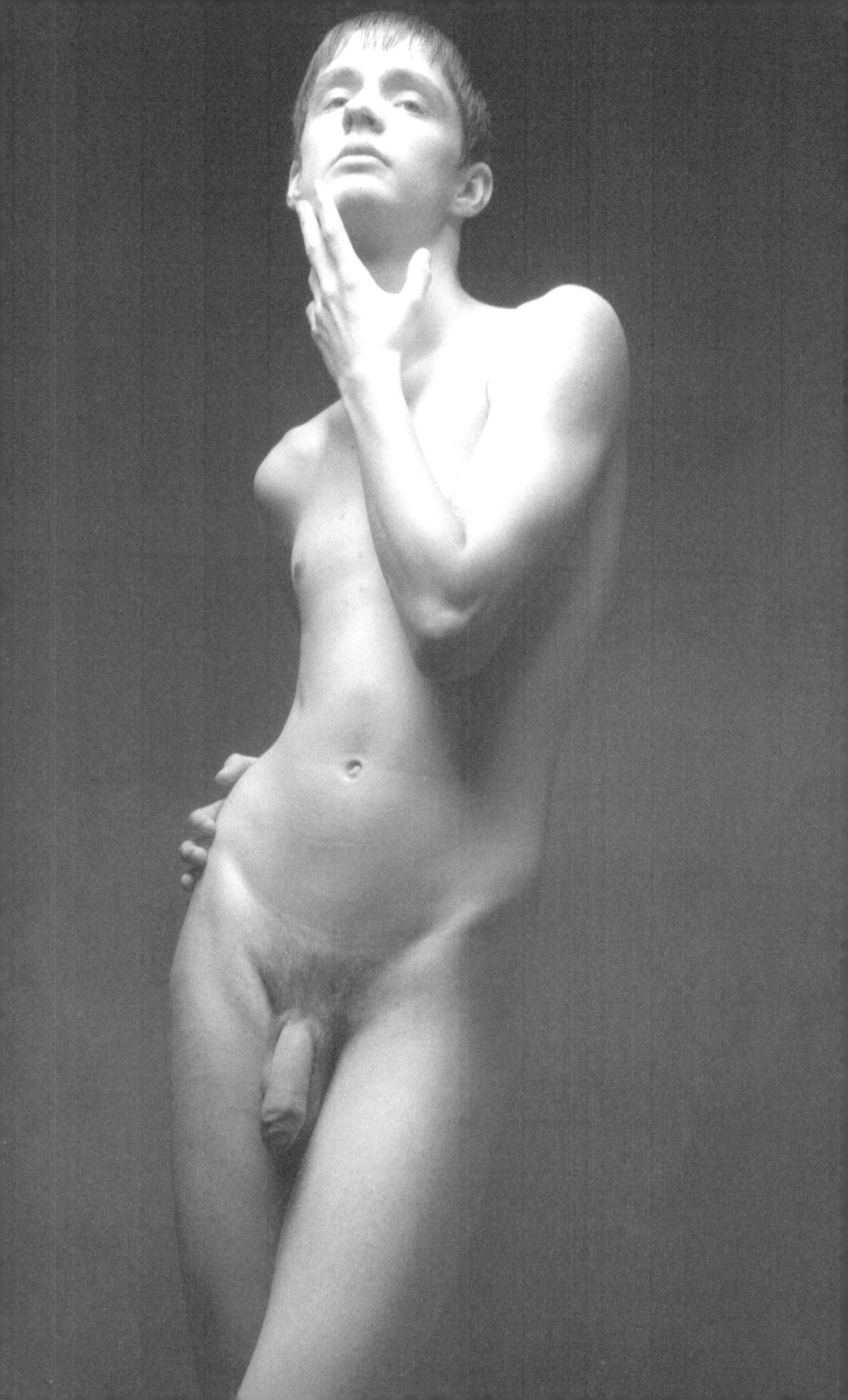

Metaphors for various species of flowers, taken from Sylvia Plath's Ariel *(1965, London: Faber and Faber) and arranged alphabetically*

VEHICLES

Yannis Tsitsovits

a dozen red lead sinkers round my neck,
black eyes and leaves like bored hearts,
cold folds of ego
hanging its hanging garden in the air,
its blond colonnades,
late mouths crying open,
little hell flames

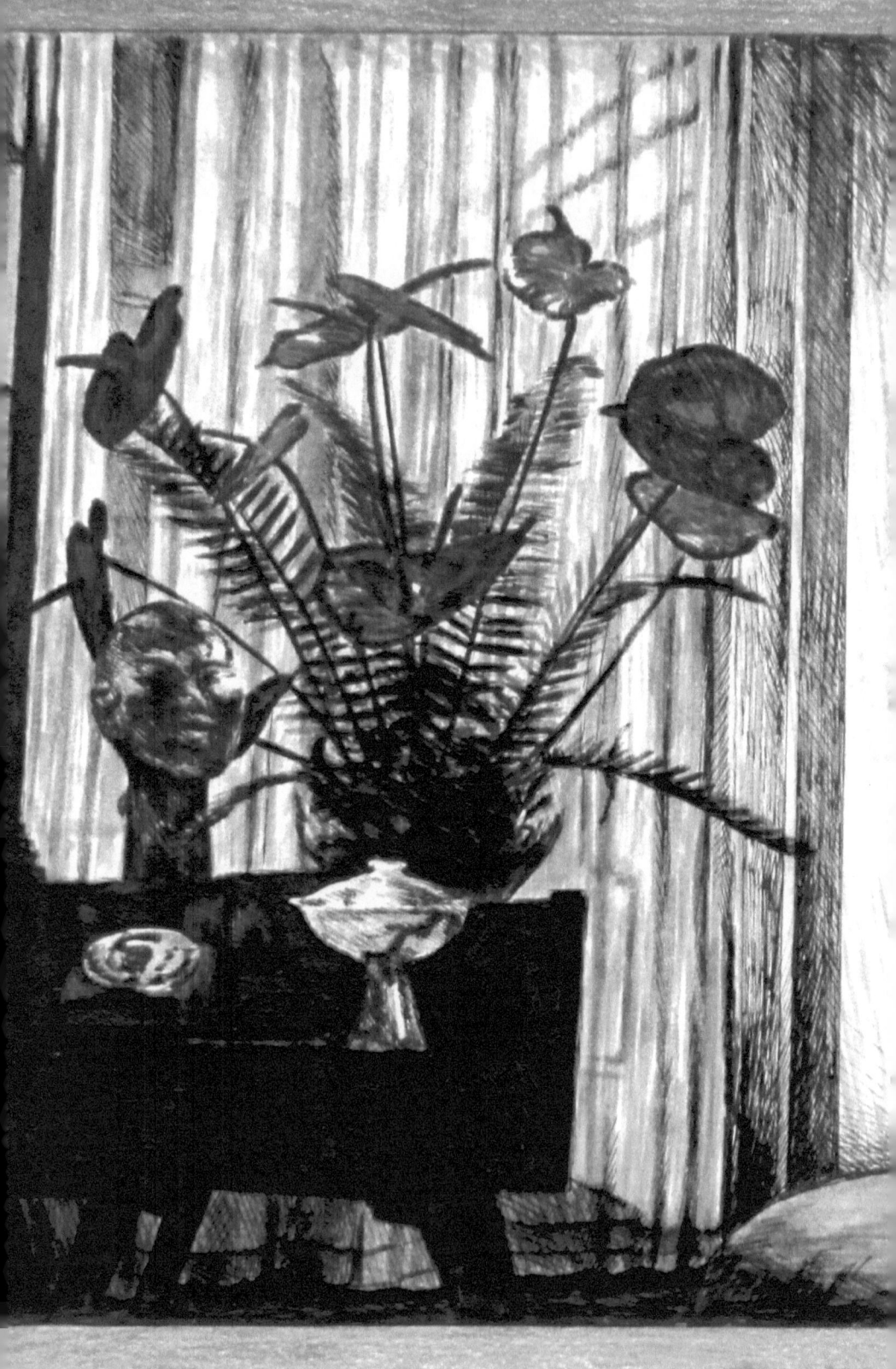

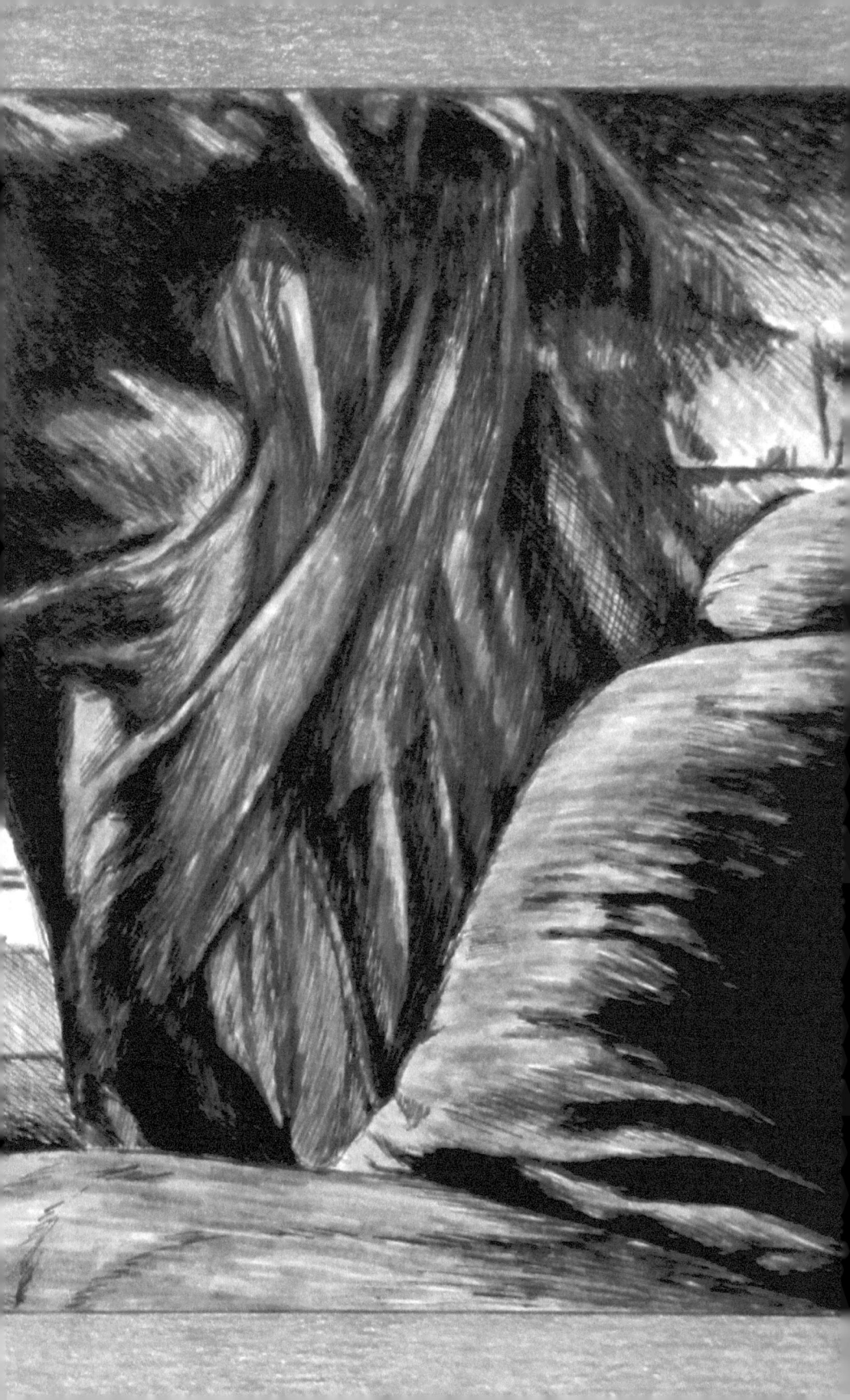

www.ingramcontent.com/pod-product-compliance
Lightning Source LLC
Chambersburg PA
CBHW020902180526
45163CB00007B/2601